Praise for

The 6Rs of
Bullying Prevention

"This book provides real results for bullying prevention, awareness, and education and will make a difference not only in the lives of children, but in our communities. Dr. Borba's expertise in bullying is second to no one: she is a leader in her field and this book will change lives."

—Sue Scheff, Internet safety expert and author

"Dr. Borba compiles and succinctly summarizes the weight of available evidence about what works to prevent bullying at school. Building safe and bully-free schools is not easy and there are no shortcuts. It takes coordination and collaboration by all concerned community stakeholders. This book offers a potent and pragmatic road-map to help schools achieve that goal."

—Justin W. Patchin, Ph.D., codirector, Cyberbullying Research Center

"Dr. Michele Borba's contributions to the field are always practical, relatable, and powerful. Her newest book is no exception and provides a valuable step-by-step guide to help school communities reduce peer harassment and hate from the inside out through policy and programming."

—Dr. Sameer Hinduja, codirector of Cyberbullying Research Center and professor of Criminology and Criminal Justice, Florida Atlantic University

"An important addition to any educator's toolbox for breaking the cycle of bullying violence and creating a more deeply caring school environment."

—Barbara Coloroso, educator and author of *The Bully, the Bullied, and the Not-So-Innocent Bystander*

The 6Rs
of Bullying
Prevention

**Best Proven Practices
to Combat Cruelty
and Build Respect**

Michele Borba, Ed.D.

free spirit
PUBLISHING®

Library of Congress Cataloging-in-Publication Data

Names: Borba, Michele, author.

Title: The 6Rs of bullying prevention : best proven practices to combat cruelty and build respect / Michele Borba.

Description: Minneapolis, MN : Free Spirit Publishing, [2016] | Includes bibliographical references and index.

Identifiers: LCCN 2016011723| ISBN 9781631980206 (paperback) | ISBN 1631980203 (paperback) | ISBN 9781631981036 (web pdf) | ISBN 9781631981043 (epub)

Subjects: LCSH: Bullying in schools—Prevention. | Bullying—Prevention. | BISAC: EDUCATION / Leadership. | EDUCATION / Classroom Management.

Classification: LCC LB3013.3 .B67 2016 | DDC 371.5/8—dc23

LC record available at https://lccn.loc.gov/2016011723

Cover and interior design by Colleen Rollins
Edited by Meg Bratsch

10 9 8 7 6 5 4 3 2 1
Printed in the United States of America

Free Spirit Publishing Inc.
6325 Sandburg Road, Suite 100
Minneapolis, MN 55427-3674
(612) 338-2068
help4kids@freespirit.com
www.freespirit.com

Dedication

This book is dedicated to the unsung heroes of the world: educators. Your compassion, competence, and commitment to children are the best hope for bullying prevention and producing a generation of empathetic, caring, and courageous upstanders.

Acknowledgments

No book is ever written alone. Countless people were instrumental in helping me develop these ideas, and I express my heartfelt appreciation:

To the extraordinary teachers, counselors, and administrators who allowed me the privilege of conducting research, trainings, and student focus groups at their schools to analyze the effectiveness of the 6Rs.

To the hundreds of educators who invited me to share and implement the 6Rs in schools around the world: United States, Canada, Colombia, Mexico, Egypt, the Philippines, England, Germany, China, and the U.S. garrisons in Europe and the Asian Pacific. In working with you, I learned that bullying has no borders; our children are suffering in every region of the world. Your example also showed that bullying prevention is indeed possible. This book would not have come to fruition without your practical wisdom on how best to implement these practices.

To the parents from whom I have been privileged to learn during the past three decades—those who attended my workshops and also those who shared personal stories about their children who have endured horrific harm from bullying. Thank you for your guidance and your honesty.

To the numerous people whose work has contributed enormously to my thinking about the development of bullying prevention, including Dan Olweus, Thomas Lickona, Nancy Eisenberg, Dorothy Espelege, Susan Swearer, Rachel Sim, Wendy Craig, Debra Pepler, Justin Patchin, Sameer Hinduja, Barbara Coloroso, Trudy Ludwig, and Ken Rigby. I only hope I accurately interpreted your work and gave it the credit it deserves.

To my agent, Joelle Delbourgo, for believing in this project and in me as a writer. Every writer should have this woman in her corner.

To Judy Galbraith, whose vision and integrity in leading Free Spirit Publishing has inspired me from the moment we met over thirty years ago. Thank you for the honor of allowing me to write for you.

To Meg Bratsch, editor extraordinaire, it has been a delight from your first phone call. Your insight, guidance, patience, and competence blew life into these pages. Words can never be enough to express my gratitude for having you as my editor.

To my growing, fabulous family for giving me so much moral support over the years of developing, researching, and writing this book, and recognizing its importance for children. As always, I could never have done this without the support of my husband, best friend, and rock of my life, Craig.

And to all the children around the world I interviewed. Your insights and ideas about how to stop bullying were always on the mark. In fact, the best ideas in these pages came from you. We would all do well to listen to you more.

Contents

Part III: The 6Rs of Bullying Prevention— Rules, Recognize, Report, Respond, Refuse, Replace

List of Figures

List of Reproducible Forms

Customizable digital versions of all reproducible forms can be downloaded at **freespirit.com/6rs-forms**. Use password **4respect**.

Introduction

"Sticks and stones may break my bones, but names will never hurt me" is a myth that needs to be dispelled. Bullying means that a child is intentionally causing another child pain. That pain may be inflicted emotionally, verbally, physically, or electronically, and it is *always* harmful. Whether a child is bullying others, witnessing bullying, or the target of bullying, the behavior wreaks havoc on children's emotional, moral, and cognitive development; demolishes feelings of safety; and, if not stopped, can shatter young lives. In fact, bullying is viewed as one of the most serious public health problems in the United States and Canadian school systems.

The effects of peer cruelty are far-reaching and can cause immense stress, anxiety, health problems, depression, and humiliation that may result in serious mental health issues for children. Bullying also induces fear and insecurity, which impacts students' concentration, academic achievement, and learning performance. This is the reason why educators need to make an earnest effort to prevent bullying on school campuses, and it's why I wrote this book.

I've spent nearly three decades studying youth violence and bullying and working with hundreds of educators, counselors, and law enforcement officials around the world. I know the horrors of school shootings and I've held the hands of too many parents whose children have ended their lives because of peer cruelty. I've also spoken to countless kids who have witnessed or been involved in bullying at their schools for years and feel powerless to stop it. We need to put an end to childhood aggression, and this book provides a concrete plan to do so. Bullying is learned, and it can be unlearned. Caring, committed educators using research-based strategies can turn this terrible trend around, and I will show you how.

"I used to tell the teachers I was bullied but I stopped because they never did anything. I don't think they believed me . . . but maybe they didn't care." —Kara, age 11*

"I was bullied for three years. The school librarian finally realized I was hurting and let me stay in the library at recess. If it wasn't for her, I don't know what I would have done." —Jamil, age 10

The Facts About Bullying

"Bullying is unwanted, aggressive behavior among school-age children that involves a real or perceived power imbalance. The behavior is repeated or has the potential to be repeated over time." —*StopBullying.gov*

Bullying has no boundaries and impacts all geographical regions. Though it is more prevalent in the middle school years, it affects all school-age students of both sexes. Here is a sample of the latest data about school bullying from StopBullying.gov and other sources that reveal the urgent need for educators to find solutions:

- Bullying happens every 7 minutes in every kind of school: private and public; rural, urban, and suburban[1]

- Over 70 percent of students say they have seen bullying in their schools[2]

- Nearly 50 percent of students report being bullied at least once during the past month[2]

- More than 40 percent of students say they are *frequently* involved in bullying (two or more times in the past month)[3]

- Approximately 30 percent of students in grades 4 through 12 report bullying others[3]

- More than 70 percent of school staff has seen bullying; over 40 percent witness bullying once a week or more[3]

- Only 20 to 30 percent of students who are bullied notify adults[4]

---

* *Note:* The student quotes throughout this book are ones I've personally gathered in my trainings; all names have been changed to protect the individuals' privacy.

1. National Education Association, October 2011.
2. Espelage et al., 2003.
3. Bradshaw et al., 2007.
4. Ttofi et al., 2011.

Bullying Prevention in Schools Today

"Children and youth who are bullied are more likely to be depressed, lonely, and anxious; have low self-esteem; feel unwell; and think about suicide." —Dr. Susan Limber, bullying expert

"Students who watch as their peers endure the verbal or physical abuses of another student could become as psychologically distressed, if not more so, by the events than the victims themselves." —American Psychological Association

"School bullying is the single most enduring and underrated issue in U.S. schools." —The National School Safety Center

Long ago bullying behavior was considered almost a child's rite of passage and largely ignored. After all, many thought: "Kids will be kids." Some even believed that "bullying will toughen up kids, it builds character." Then a deadly chain of incidents on school campuses made us rethink everything. Most infamous was the shooting at Columbine High School in Littleton, Colorado, on April 20, 1999. Two teens brought guns to school, killing thirteen people and wounding more than twenty others. During the years that followed, dozens more school shootings transpired. A 2002 report by the United States Secret Service, who studied thirty-seven school shootings on American campuses, confirmed that bullying is a key factor in many shootings. Their report stated:[5]

> Almost three-quarters of the attackers felt persecuted, bullied, threatened, attacked, or injured by others prior to the incident. In several cases, individual attackers had experienced bullying and harassment that was long-standing and severe. In some of these cases the experience of being bullied seemed to have a significant impact on the attacker and appeared to have been a factor in his decision to mount an attack at the school. In one case, the attacker's schoolmates described the attacker as "the kid everyone teased."

In addition to homicidal violence, bullying victimization has also been shown to inspire youth suicide. There is even a disturbing term for those who take their own young lives due to bullying: *bullycide*. The list of these victims is long and growing: Tyler Clementi, Ryan Patrick Halligan, Megan Meier, and

---

5. Vossekull et al., 2002.

Phoebe Prince, among dozens of others—and those are just the ones whose names made news headlines. Who knows how many more there have been.

> "School got to be unbearable. All I could think about was what the boys might do to me at recess. My grades went down, and all I wanted to do was get home safely. Being bullied puts your whole body in nonstop 'fear factor' mode." —Jacob, age 12

Another dynamic adds to our concern that bullying needs to be taken far more seriously: the electronic age ushered in a new form of peer torment called *cyberbullying,* in which young people use devices such as cell phones, tablets, computers, and digital cameras to bully others. A large global survey scanning eleven countries and almost 5,000 children revealed that one in five teens is cyberbullied. Roughly 85 percent of the time the bullied child knows the child doing the cyberbullying, and that means the child may have to endure seeing his tormenter at school. Though the majority of cyberbullying attacks occur off school grounds, they cause severe distress among students. Forty-one percent of teens said cyberbullying made them feel depressed; one-fifth felt suicidal.[6]

> More than half of teens think cyberbullying is worse than face-to-face bullying and 43 percent believe it is a bigger problem for young people than drug abuse.[6]

The impact of bullying on our children's mental health has led to heightened demand among educators for answers. Today, school bullying is finally receiving the attention it deserves from educators, governing bodies, law enforcement officials, and medical professionals, as well as parents. In recent years, the White House held a special conference on bullying, while state and provincial governments began passing mandates for school districts to implement anti-bullying practices. At this writing, fifty states, several Canadian provinces, and a few other countries have passed anti-bullying legislation, and a lucrative cottage industry of products for schools to use to combat bullying has flooded the market. Schools across the United States, Canada, and other countries have implemented hundreds of these "bullying prevention programs"; unfortunately, current studies show that at best only a quarter of them will actually reduce bullying behaviors.[6] The problem is that the majority of these programs are not research-based so there simply hasn't been solid research in the field. That is, until a few large studies on bullying were published—some of which I've already cited here—and for the first time pointed to hope: educators *can* make a difference and bullying *can* be

---

6. Vodafone, 2015.

reduced. But there is a caveat: only certain procedures and approaches work to reduce aggression. One mistake educators make in trying to stop bullying is failing to base their efforts on proven evidence and faithfully apply those findings. While our aim may be to stop bullying, our approach is too often not scientific, systemic, or sustained, and so our results are mediocre at best.

What Works and Does *Not* Work to Reduce Bullying

Bullying is learned behavior and can be unlearned, but solutions to peer cruelty are not simple. All those eye-catching posters and buttons, T-shirt contests, song competitions, one-day trainings, packaged worksheets, or "stamp-out bullying campaigns"—while they may mean well—are not effective solutions. Bullying prevention is not a one-size-fits-all approach that uses the same strategy for the targets, bystanders, and students who bully. After all, each bullying incident differs in motivation, type, and dynamics, just as each student's learning needs differ.

> Educators *can* make a difference and bullying *can* be reduced. But there is a caveat: only certain procedures and approaches work to reduce aggression.

The best way to reduce bullying is with the ongoing, homegrown, data-driven efforts of a committed, informed school community trained in anti-bullying. The approaches that are most promising tackle bullying dynamics from many angles and involve all stakeholders—students, parents, administrators, teachers, and *all* school staff, including bus drivers, custodians, cafeteria workers, yard supervisors, counselors, psychologists, secretaries, school nurses, librarians, volunteers, coaches, and crossing guards. The foundation is always based on building a culture of respect and changing destructive attitudes and behaviors by replacing them with healthier habits and views. Applying the right classroom management and discipline policies is also crucial: zero tolerance and expulsion have proven to be ineffective and can backfire.

Ultimately, what works to reduce bullying is *not* implementing a specific program but consistently using a few key evidence-based bullying prevention principles, policies, and practices. Those proven elements form the basis for this book.

Proven Strategies That Decrease Bullying

Researchers Maria Ttofi and David Farrington conducted a meta-analysis of fifty-nine evaluations of bullying interventions such as the KiVa Anti-Bullying Program, the Olweus Bullying Prevention Program, and Second Step to identify the features that had the greatest impact on decreasing bullying behaviors. They found that the most important components were:[7]

- parent training

- improved playground supervision

- appropriate disciplinary methods

- student-run school assemblies that raised awareness of the problem

- classroom rules against bullying

- classroom management techniques for dealing with bullying

- tapping the power of peers to combat bullying.

All of these proven strategies are described throughout this book.

How This Book Is Unique

"My seventh-grade teacher figured out that my grades were so bad because I was being bullied. I couldn't think. She told the other teachers to watch out for me and not to let the kid near me. I survived the terror because of her." —Will, age 12

No single program (not PBIS, not Olweus, not Second Step, not Responsive Classroom) provides a one-stop shop for preventing bullying and improving school climate. All programs have blind spots, biases, and flaws. *The 6Rs of Bullying Prevention* is not a program; it is a process to reduce peer cruelty with an "inside-out" approach that relies on those who have the best pulse on the issue: the actual stakeholders. This book will strengthen any program you already have in place by drawing on the best elements from all evidence-based programs and helping you integrate those elements into your own program so your program is rooted in research, culturally specific, and addresses your unique learning environment and students' particular needs. And if you don't

7. Farrington and Ttofi, 2009.

have a program already in place, I'll share which ones are proven to be most effective.

I'll also share new research, best practices, social-emotional learning (SEL) skills, and character habits that are most likely to reduce the cycle of youth cruelty and create a safe and respectful school community. By far the best result of any of these efforts is when your students perceive their school as a caring place they want to be part of.

The strategies in this book are designed to be incorporated school- or district-wide. Each activity can also be adapted for individual classroom use, but research is clear: the most favorable outcome of bullying reduction involves a three-tiered approach: school-wide, classroom-wide, and addressing individual students. This book is based on a systemic, sustained approach that involves *all* school staff: classified and certificated personnel as well as students, parents, and the community. Each person offers a different set of eyes and ears to identify why and where bullying may be happening as well as solutions to solve it. When adults exert a joint effort to make all students feel respected and welcomed at school, wonderful transformations take place.

THE INSIDE-OUT APPROACH TO THE BULLYING PROBLEM

"Creativity is a lot like looking at the world through a kaleidoscope. You look at a set of elements, the same ones everyone else sees, but then reassemble those floating bits and pieces into an enticing new possibility."
—Rosabeth Moss Kanter, *The Change Masters*

Rosabeth Moss Kanter, a Harvard Business School professor, is the author of the best-selling book *The Change Masters*. She is also a famous business innovator who has worked with dozens of Fortune 500 companies. Though her book focuses on corporate leadership, the basic principles also can apply to schools. Too often, Kanter tells companies, we make a major mistake of looking to the outside for sources of innovation and change. A more effective approach, she states, is to look within. Kanter calls her approach *kaleidoscopic thinking*.

To understand the concept, recall a time in your childhood when you looked inside a kaleidoscope. Each time you twirled the cylinder, colorful new patterns formed. In fact, you could literally spend hours turning the dial to create beautiful new patterns, but not once did you stop to put in new pieces. Instead, you re-created new schemes and structures by using what was already inside. That is precisely what kaleidoscopic thinking entails. Kanter urges leaders to look at what they already have in place in their organization and restructure from the inside out, and that is the method you'll use in this book.

The 6Rs of Bullying Prevention is a radical new approach to reducing bullying: I am not advocating one particular program to purchase or strategy to adhere to, but instead will guide you to use the kaleidoscopic thinking model to develop the most effective organic prevention approach. Instead of bringing in new pieces from the outside, I'll guide you to restructure your key elements for change, which are the critical parts of any organization: your programs, practices, policies, principles, and people. Not only will rethinking and restructuring those elements save enormous expenses and time, but what you create will be homegrown. Your bullying prevention efforts will be more likely to succeed because the approach is customized to fit *your* students' needs; match *your* culture, demographics, and beliefs; and apply to *your* evidence.

THE GOALS OF THIS BOOK

This book aims to help you develop an approach to bullying prevention that not only reduces aggressive behaviors but also teaches students proactive skills and cultivates a respectful school climate. Here are the core goals of this approach:

- Ensure that your entire school community supports a comprehensive, systemic bullying prevention effort and train them so that everyone is on the "same page."

- Create a safe, caring school culture based on respectful relationships and social responsibility as the foundations for bullying prevention.

- Engage *all* stakeholders—staff, students, parents, and community—in bullying prevention efforts.

- Implement bullying prevention practices that are evidence-based and address your school culture as well as your students' unique needs.

- Use a three-tiered systemic approach that addresses bullying prevention school-wide, classroom-wide, and with individual students.

- Replace aggression and bullying behaviors with prosocial behaviors by teaching SEL skills.

- Use a systemic and sustained implementation process based on your evidence and needs to create real and lasting change.

About This Book

The 6Rs of Bullying Prevention is a comprehensive guide to bullying prevention that offers the most effective proven strategies to stop bullying and create safe, caring school climates. It provides detailed guidelines for strategy implementation, data collection, team management, student and parent involvement, skill building, and assessment—everything your school needs to reduce peer cruelty and teach all students proactive, healthy behaviors to replace inappropriate ones. The practices, policies, and procedures herein are culled from a review of hundreds of studies on bullying as well as my thirty-year career working in violence prevention in schools around the world.

I wrote this book with a broad audience in mind—namely, any member of a school community who is or wishes to be involved in bullying prevention. But I expect the book to be of particular interest and usefulness to administrators, principals, assistant principals, behavior program coordinators, bullying prevention teams, and teacher leaders, as well as individual teachers and counselors who are especially committed to reducing peer cruelty. While the strategies here work best when implemented school-wide, they can also be modified for use in classrooms, clusters of classrooms, grade levels, or youth programs. Unlike some highly structured programs that require a "top-down" approach to implementation, the strategies in this book are flexible and can be tailored to meet the needs of many different audiences—from a school principal looking to engage her staff in optimizing existing anti-bullying efforts; to a behavior specialist who is part of his school's bullying prevention team and wants to share the latest research and best practices; to a math teacher who is looking to form a book study with fellow teachers and model some of these practices, and perhaps even convince other teachers, staff, and school administration to join in (a "bottom-up" approach). However this book is used, the goal in each case is the same: employ evidence-based practices with as many stakeholders as possible to address all facets of bullying: from creating rules for behavior to replacing aggression with acceptable skills.

"It is easier to build strong children than to repair broken men."
—Frederick Douglass

A Note About Terms Used in This Book

No *victims* or *bullies*. I've deliberately refrained from using the label *bully* or *victim* in this book, and I strongly urge you and your colleagues to do so as well. Labels can become self-perpetuating, so children might grow to see themselves as *bullies* or *victims*. Terms also typecast kids, affect their self-esteem, limit their potential, and impede their willingness to change. What's more, roles often shift: a child who bullies at recess may be the bullied child on the bus or the witness after school. For all of these reasons, educators need to do away with these labels. Good alternatives to use include *bullying student*, *child engaged in bullying-like behaviors*, *target*, or *bullied child*.

Also, throughout this book, I use the term *parents* to denote a student's primary caregiver(s) or legal guardian(s), while realizing many children have a single parent and/or may not use the term parent.

THREE PARTS OF *THE 6RS OF BULLYING PREVENTION*

The book is set up in three distinct parts and each is crucial to bullying prevention.

Part I: Establishing the Foundation of Bullying Prevention— Respectful Relationships and a Positive School Climate

The first part of the book addresses how to create a positive school climate and nurture beneficial relationships among students and between students and school staff. You'll learn why creating such a climate is crucial to preventing bullying and will find dozens of positivity-building practices, including:

- Building caring connections and a more inclusive environment

- Helping students be more kind and respectful with peers

- Creating positivity practices for playgrounds, cafeterias, and student clubs

- Empowering students to shift their school norms from cruel to kind

- Restoring student relationships to reduce bullying

- Conducting class meetings and developing a code of ethics

- Teaching SEL skills to help students get along

- Learning problem-solving and conflict-resolution strategies to reduce friction

Part II: Getting Started to Make Real and Lasting Change

The second part of the book addresses how to get started implementing bullying prevention efforts at your school site, in your classroom, and with your students. You'll learn how to form and implement student bullying surveys and focus groups and how to use the resulting data to select the best programs and practices to reduce bullying in your school. You'll also learn how to create and sustain a bullying prevention team to support your efforts (if you don't already have a team in place).

Part III: The 6Rs of Bullying Prevention

The third part of the book presents the 6Rs of preventing bullying: *Rules, Recognize, Report, Respond, Refuse,* and *Replace.* Together they offer a blueprint to implementing the best research, policies, and practices for effective prevention. Each of the six chapters is instrumental in creating what all students deserve: a safe and caring learning environment that breeds acceptance and respect. Implementing each "R" as a whole school and community will optimize success.

For more than three decades I've researched how to stop the cycle of violence in schools, which led me to develop the 6Rs. I've shared this model with hundreds of educators worldwide, including in the United States, Canada, Germany, South Korea, Colombia, Mexico, the Philippines, New Zealand, Egypt, and on U.S. Army bases. I continue to help educators implement the 6Rs in their classrooms, schools, and districts, and even in whole counties. Each chapter described here provides specific, no-cost ways to apply the Rs to your setting.

R1: Rules—Establish an Anti-Bullying Policy and Expectations for Respect. Here you'll learn how to create and disseminate an anti-bullying policy that fits your school values, focuses on prevention, features strong parental involvement, builds a respectful climate, and gets *everyone* onboard.

R2: Recognize—Teach Stakeholders How to Recognize Bullying. This chapter addresses the importance of all stakeholders understanding what bullying is, recognizing indicators, and receiving ongoing training so they can intervene appropriately and consistently. Then, it shows you how to achieve those goals.

R3: Report—Create Procedures to Report Bullying. The third R shows you how reports about bullying incidents from staff, students, and parents provide crucial evidence of bullying frequency, locales, and participants, and boosts student security. It offers efficient, easy, and effective options for stake-holders to report incidents and for staff to analyze the reports.

R4: Respond—Teach Witnesses How to Respond to Bullying. In a caring climate where staff, students, and parents are united, kids are more likely to take responsibility for reducing bullying. This chapter shows you how to mobilize your students' compassion and teach specific skills so they can safely step in to help stop bullying incidents, become upstanders, and change your school norms so "it's cool to be kind."

R5: Refuse—Help Targets Refuse Provocation and Cope with Victimization. Ongoing training is essential to help everyone in a school community identify and support targets and potential targets of bullying. In addition, this section offers strategies for targets to reduce future victimization and learn coping strategies.

R6: Replace—Help Students Replace Aggression with Acceptable Skills. The goal of this chapter is to help students displaying bullying behaviors adopt prosocial habits and beliefs. It offers proven skills to replace aggression with socially acceptable behaviors.

Consider the 6Rs as your major decision-making rubric to help you select the best prevention and intervention strategies and the most effective anti-bullying techniques for your students. In addition, you'll find the following repeating features throughout the book:

- **Social-Emotional Learning (SEL) Skill Boxes.** These include crucial skills related to each section's topic with suggestions for how to teach the skills to students to nurture their social and emotional learning, prevent bullying, and cultivate kindness.

- **Brave Staff Chat Boxes.** These are ideas for courageous conversations to have among your staff—in weekly meetings, professional learning communities, or informal groups—to help them reflect on their own habits and performance related to crucial bullying topics. It is not always easy for a staff to admit that the school may not have the best bullying prevention policies or even could be contributing to the problem. That's why these chats are often necessary to create needed change.

- **Tip Boxes for Administrators, Counselors, and Teachers.** These offer simple, actionable bullying prevention strategies and tips specifically designed for each of these core audiences.

- **Ways Educators Are Empowering Students.** These provide dozens of examples of ways educators are empowering students to make a difference in reducing bullying in their schools.

- **Ways to Involve Parents.** These important sidebars present ideas for how to create stronger home-school partnerships so your bullying prevention results are more effective.

- **Further Resources.** Whenever you would like more information, turn to the Resources section on pages 243–256. This section lists books for teachers, staff, parents, and students to enhance your efforts to make your school cruelty-free.

Finally, the book includes a digital download that contains customizable PDFs of all the reproducible forms in this book for your personal use and sharing and a PDF presentation for use in professional development. See page x for downloading instructions.

"'Bullying is never okay. Period.' If the whole school just used that one rule my life would be so much easier and I could breathe! When you're bullied, the air gets sucked out of you." —Henry, age 10

How to Use This Book

This book is designed for use in a variety of ways so it is relevant to your needs. Effective bullying efforts involve implementing the combined elements of Parts I, II, and III, so your aim is for prevention *and* intervention, but use your judgment as to which sections are most relevant to your immediate concerns. Delve in anywhere you want to begin. For example:

- Consider reviewing your survey data (see Part II) to assess what your stakeholders feel is most pressing and then honing in on the sections of the book that address the areas of concern.

- Some readers may already have a safe and caring school initiative and/or a bullying prevention team in place, so feel free to skim one or both of the first two parts and go straight to learning about specific interventions for students in Part III.

- You may come to this book with a particular concern about bullying, for instance: a student who is a target, a child who is chronically bullying, or helping your students who witness bullying have the courage to step in. Dig deeper into those particular chapters.

The bottom line is to make this book work for you and your needs.

In Closing

KEY BULLYING PREVENTION POINTS IN THIS BOOK

- Bullying affects *all* kids, including the children bullying, the targets, and the witnesses.
- Effective bullying prevention is a process, not a program.
- The best bullying prevention approach is research-based, systemic, sustained, and homegrown.
- Bullying is learned and can be unlearned, but solutions are never quick fixes.
- Bullying prevention doesn't have a "cookie cutter" approach: the specific needs of each student involved in the bullying dynamic need to be identified and the appropriate intervention applied.
- Tackling bullying involves all stakeholders—administrators, teachers, *all* staff, students, parents, and community members—committed to creating a culture of respect.
- Change happens when stakeholders exert a joint effort to increase the positive tone of the school and make all students feel welcome and respected.
- Bullying prevention is not a poster campaign or a school assembly. It's an ongoing process that aims to change a culture of cruelty to one of kindness.
- The true indication of success is positive and lasting change in student behavior and attitude.

"It takes a whole village to raise a child." —African Proverb

Over the past three-plus decades, I've worked in too many communities torn apart by youth aggression or racked with grief when one of their own ended her or his life due to bullying. I still carry a photo of a sixth-grade boy who hanged himself when he could no longer endure the endless brutality of two peers. The boy's father handed me the photo after I had given a speech on bullying in Canada, and asked me to make a promise. "Please," he said. "Don't stop. Keep training adults about bullying. It would have saved my son. Hopefully it will save other children, too." Writing this book is one way I've kept my promise to that grieving father. I won't stop, and I hope you're with me.

The good news is that while bullying is learned, so too are peace, respect, and compassion. Working together in a committed, sustained effort as a staff and applying proven practices to reduce bullying and create caring communities is the way forward. Our students deserve school experiences that provide them with the opportunity to grow into adults who are kind and respectful of others and who work to resolve their differences peacefully.

We have work to do and not a minute to waste. Let's get started!

I'd love to hear how this book has helped your bullying prevention efforts. If you have stories or questions for me, or if you would like me to speak to your staff or parents about *The 6Rs of Bullying Prevention,* you can reach me through my publisher at help4kids@freespirit.com or visit my website micheleborba.com. Follow me on Twitter @micheleborba.

All the best!
Michele Borba

Part I

Establishing the Foundation of Bullying Prevention

Respectful Relationships and a Positive School Climate

In Part I, you will learn:

- four ways to build respectful staff-student relationships and why they are key to a positive school climate

- strategies to build positivity and inclusiveness in classrooms, in cafeterias, and on playgrounds

- how to remedy bullying "hot spots" in your school

- eight ways to help students gain a sense of belonging, resist cliques, and make new friends

- six ways to stomp out put-downs and boost kindness

- classroom practices that encourage student cooperation

- effective methods for problem solving and conflict resolution

- how to empower students to shift their school norms from cruel to kind

The first part of effective bullying prevention is creating a safe and positive learning community to support *all* students' cognitive, social, moral, and emotional development. Doing so will not only prevent bullying and other forms of aggression, but, according to research by the National School Climate Center, it will also increase student achievement, enhance school connectedness, and reduce potential drop-out rates—all because you're developing an environment where students want to "drop in" not "drop out."[1] Creating a caring climate requires schools to build respectful relationships among staff and students and a culture where students can relate to and appreciate one another.

Research shows that *respectful relationships* among students and teachers are key elements of a positive school climate.[2] Indeed, improving relationships can be effective in reducing bullying and antisocial behavior—especially if that approach is comprehensive and involves *all* school stakeholders. Bullying breeds in climates where there are negative relationships between teachers and students and destructive behaviors are left to flourish.

Included here are ideas, skills, and best practices to teach prosocial behaviors and nurture caring climates that you can implement at your school, in your classroom, and with individual students. All of these elements will serve as a foundation for the chapters to follow.

1. Cohen and Freiberg, 2013.
2. Wang et al., 2013.

Brave Staff Chat: What Behaviors Are We Modeling for Our Students?

To create a positive school climate, all adults need to promote and model attitudes and behaviors such as caring, empathy, and respectful interactions. What behaviors are most of your staff modeling for students? If you were to ask students, would they give the same response? How can you better model respect and caring for your students?

Practices That Build Caring Connections and an Inclusive Environment

"Once the staff began to build one-to-one relationships with students, some of the most hardcore bullying students began to change their ways. I guess they just needed to know that someone cared!" —teacher, Los Angeles School District

Ultimately, bullying prevention practices are only as effective as the people who deliver them. Thus, school staff members play a pivotal role in creating the type of environment to help students feel safe and respected. This section offers ways to build caring connections with and among students and develop positivity and inclusiveness in all areas of school life: to create, in the words of the theme song to the television show *Cheers*, a place where everybody knows your name, and they're always glad you came.

The Four Factors of Strong Staff-Student Relationships

- Adults connect with students and create the trust that helps students come forward if they are bullied.
- Adults create a safe and welcoming environment that promotes inclusion, respect, and acceptance.
- Adults model respectful, empathetic behaviors and reinforce those behavior expectations in students.
- Adults take bullying seriously and monitor inappropriate behaviors. This helps students take bullying seriously and shows them that the staff cares.

WAYS TO BUILD RESPECTFUL STAFF-STUDENT RELATIONSHIPS

Here are several no-cost practices to nurture caring, respectful relationships between staff and students.

Adopt a student. Staff volunteers are each assigned one student who needs special attention, such as a bullied child or a child who bullies. The adopter's job is to support that student in any way possible, such as reinforcing new prosocial skills, monitoring aggressive behaviors, or just taking the time to say "hello." This extra TLC can have a miraculous impact on the student's behavior, simply because someone cares.

Instate a teacher advisor-advisee program (or "TAP"). The TAP program was initiated at Jefferson Davis Junior High School in Duval County, Florida. Students with academic or behavior problems were "tapped" into the program and assigned a special teacher advisor. Each advisor oversees no more than six advisees and contacts each student an average of nine times per quarter. The advisors also contact the students' families twice per quarter to encourage parents to participate in school activities, discuss academic progress, and counsel students on personal and academic problems, including bullying incidents. Whether the contact is for two or thirty minutes, the at-risk students appreciate the personal attention and their grades and behavior improve while aggression declines.

Use "guardian angels" (or caring mentors). At Desert Middle School in Desert Hot Springs, California, "guardian angels" are caring adults who volunteer to work with at-risk students, targeted kids, or those who bully. The staff creates a list of these students, and volunteers each choose one or more students to connect with. The adult may send notes of encouragement and spend a few minutes (or more) with the students during the school day to reinforce new skills and create respectful relationships.

Form "family" groups. Staff members as well as community members volunteer to lead group of students once a week through the year in teaching the bullying prevention strategies and SEL skills in this book. A certificated teacher, counselor, or other bullying prevention team member plans activities that reinforce the school's bullying prevention efforts. Students' names are randomly selected from the school computer and paired with a staff or community volunteer. Groups generally consist of ten to twelve students representing various grade levels. Since there will be more groups than classrooms, other meeting places need to be considered, such as the principal's or secretary's office, faculty lounge, nurse's room, cafeteria, or library. Each group (called a "family") meets with the same adult (or "family head") in the same location throughout the year. Many schools are so committed to the approach that they elect to keep students in their same "family" each year. For some students, these group meetings may well be the only time they get to feel a real sense of family.

Tip for **TEACHERS**

University of British Columbia researchers found that children who perform small acts of kindness may help counteract bullying. One student group was asked to perform kind acts throughout the week, like sharing their lunch or giving their mom a hug if she appeared stressed. A second group of students kept track of pleasant places they visited, like the playground or a grandparent's house. At the end of the week, both groups reported a boost in happiness, but the group who performed kind acts said they wanted to work with a higher number of classmates on school activities.[3] Ask students: "How can you act kindly toward others throughout the day?" Students can also create an ongoing poster of "ways to care about friends." Most important: encourage your students to be kind!

WAYS TO CREATE A POSITIVE RECESS

Recess is often identified as the time when bullying is most frequent. Boost adult supervision in "hot spot" locations and offer more proactive play opportunities (see page 26 for more on remedying hot spots). Here are two approaches.

Playworks. In 1995, Jill Vialet got an earful from a principal in Oakland, California, who told her that recess was a hotbed for bullying and discipline. Jill founded Playworks to make recess more positive and a place where kids belong and contribute. The approach teaches elementary students how to play with each other and resolve conflict amicably using trained coaches who guide students to play hard but fair. In a randomized control trial, research

---

3. The Canadian Press, 2012.

found that schools using the Playworks program experienced less bullying and exclusionary behavior, an increased perception of safety, easier transitions to learning, better behavior, and more attention in class than schools without the program[4] (see playworks.org).

Game cans. The staff at Edmonton Elementary School in Edmonton, Canada, noticed that behavior problems and bullying were increasing at recess and many students had no awareness of how to play games (sadly, this may be a growing trend in today's play-deprived childhoods). So the staff collected game donations from local businesses and purchased large plastic garbage cans for each classroom labeled with their room number. Inside the cans they placed a number of inexpensive, easy-to-learn, and cooperative games and play materials children could use on the playground, such as jump ropes, Frisbees, rubber balls, and sidewalk chalk (for hopscotch).

> Empowering students to work together to create a caring environment is one of the most overlooked strategies in bullying prevention.

At recess, upper-grade students taught the younger students how to use the items. Game cans were rotated from class to class so that students had the opportunity to play different games. In a short time, bullying playground problems were minimized.

WAYS TO BUILD INCLUSIVENESS IN SCHOOL CAFETERIAS AND LUNCHROOMS

The school cafeteria or lunchroom can be a place of frequent bullying and peer exclusion. Here are a few ways schools are reducing bullying and making lunchtime a more inclusive experience.

Lunch bunch groups. Stout Field Elementary is an inner-city school in Indianapolis with a high population of at-risk students and an abundance of committed staff members who recognize the kids' need to connect. The teachers brainstormed groups of kids who could benefit from a more inclusive place and the list was endless: those with recently divorced parents, targets of bullying, fatherless boys, socially isolated girls, and so on. The staff grouped students according to similar issues, then volunteer staff members met once a week with a small group who became their "lunch bunch." Students shared their common problems and the staff guided the students to generate

---

4. Bleeker et al., 2012.

productive solutions, such as goal setting and problem solving. The students also formed caring relationships with an adult and made new friends.

Family-style meals. This activity helps students experience a true "family meal" and practice social skills as part of the process. Once a week, a class eats lunch in the cafeteria with their teacher or other staff member (para-professional, custodian, school nurse, secretary, and so on). Meals are served family-style, with each selection of food placed on a separate platter. Platters are passed from student to student and manners such as saying, "please pass," "thank you," and "excuse me" are practiced. It is an opportunity for students to gain a sense of group belonging and learn prosocial skills that help nurture a caring climate.

Cafeteria clubs. The student council at Black River Falls Middle School in Wisconsin has reduced cliques, intimidation, and bullying in their cafeteria by setting up randomly assigned lunch tables. The new lunchroom environment gained the principal's approval after a student survey found that the majority of students favored the new seating arrangement. The strategy reduced bullying and exclusion.[5]

Mix-it-up lunch days. In surveys, students often identify the cafeteria as the place where divisions are most clearly drawn. So the organization Teaching Tolerance launched a national campaign more than a decade ago called "Mix It Up at Lunch Day" to encourage students to identify, question, and cross social boundaries. One day of the school year, students are asked to move out of their comfort zones and connect with someone new at lunch. Many schools extend that yearly event to a monthly or weekly occurrence and are discovering that bullying is reduced as well. (See "Mix It Up at Lunch Day" at tolerance.org.)

WAYS TO ENCOURAGE STUDENT CONNECTIONS

Empowering students to work together to create a caring environment is one of the most overlooked strategies in bullying prevention. Dozens of connection possibilities exist; the key is to create opportunities where *all* students from different cliques or groups can connect, make new friends, gain a sense of belonging, and be empowered to influence their school climates.

Kid clubs. After-school activities and student clubs are rich opportunities for students to connect. Survey kids about the types of clubs they might be interested in joining. Possibilities are many and varied, including drama, math competitions, robotics, speech and debate, skateboarding, chess, music, yearbook,

5. Roou, 2004.

movie making, computer lab, study hall, sports, marching bands, character clubs, service learning groups, and bullying prevention teams. A volunteer community member or staff member leads the group of like-minded students at least once a week. (Some schools hold club meetings weekly, during the last period on Fridays.)

Student greeters. Clover Park School District in Washington recognized an untapped talent: students with strong social skills who could serve as models to other students. Every school has friendly, kind kids whose skill set can be a powerful model for peers. The staff identified these students and asked them to serve as student greeters. They wore red baseball caps so they were easily identified (other schools have made special vests). Greeters were stationed at the front door and welcomed entering students ("Hi!" "Glad you're here!" "Have a good day.") The staff reported a positive change in climate in just a short while. Students began to look forward to the greeting. And many arriving students began to return the same positive statements to the greeters. (You could also place greeters in areas identified as bullying "hot spots" to help reduce negative behavior.)

Welcome wagons. New kids can feel the pain of exclusion and are more likely to be bullied. Many schools now provide positive ways for these new students to connect. Initiate a "Welcome Wagon Committee" of students to greet newcomers, give them a school tour, and pair them with "veteran" students. Photos of new arrivals can be featured on a faculty bulletin board to alert staff members of these students. Some schools with highly mobile populations arrange "get acquainted" sessions with new students where they learn about their school, connect with others, and view bullying prevention videos so they are up-to-date on school rules and expectations.

Cross-age tutors or buddies. This approach has been effective in boosting academic achievement and creating positive student connections. Student helpers are typically two to three grade levels ahead of the peers they tutor. Not only can they tutor students on academic tasks, but they can also teach the SEL skills in this book. The experience can help build empathy in a child who bullies, especially if the tutor assumes the role of a big brother or sister to a younger child.

Peer helpers. Students are more likely to report bullying to a peer than to an adult, which is why many schools are adopting peer counseling. Peers are *not* responsible for resolving bullying incidents, but they are available to support bullied peers and help report bullying to the staff if desired. A first step is to identify students with "peer clout" by using a simple survey: "If you had a problem, name a student at this school you would turn to," or "Name a student who is easy to talk to and you can trust." Choose students who represent different groups or cliques and then train them in communication and problem-solving strategies.

Adopt-a-class. This structure involves one class "adopting" another class, usually at least two or three grades younger. Older students can help younger students with academic tasks like reading, math, or science; teach outdoor games; serve as escorts on field trips; or teach SEL and bullying prevention skills. A protective bond often forms in which the older student looks after a younger student who may be targeted by bullying.

Learning buddies. The teacher assigns each student to be the learning buddy of another student in the classroom every week or month. Students pair up with their partners a few minutes a day. The practice builds connections and enhances achievement. A few ideas for learning buddy activities:

- *Direction agreement.* Students quickly turn to their buddies and agree on the task directions before they work on the task alone.

- *Problem management.* Any time a student has a problem, she must first ask her buddy if he can solve it *before* asking the teacher.

- *Homework review.* Buddies discuss three main points from their homework assignment or from the task they just completed.

- *Affirmations.* The buddy calls or emails an absent partner to say: "We miss you," provides missed assignments, or makes a get-well card with class signatures.

Home-base teams. The learning buddy strategy can be extended to teams of four students formed by the teacher. You could also give index cards to students and instruct them to write the names of "three people you want to be on a team with." (Keep the names confidential.) The key is to discover marginalized students who are not mentioned on anyone's card and place those kids in groups with more "included" kids. Students remain in their home-base teams

Over 13,000 students in a survey by Stan Davis and Charisse Nixon of the Youth Voice Project said that the most helpful things peers can do for targeted students are to include and encourage them.[6]

for a week or more (some schools keep the same teams all quarter to build relationships) and meet for three-minute morning check-ins ("How are you today?") or end-of-day connections ("Do you have all the assignments?"). They can also practice SEL skills, character themes, and study skills. It's a great opportunity for kids to create new friends from different groups.

Remedy Bullying "Hot Spots" in Your School

Three decades ago New York City was racked with crime, and tourists and city residents alike feared walking the streets. Today crime is down and the city is safer. The approach New York used to restore order and create a safe environment is one that schools can also use. The technique is called "broken windows" and it is a simple notion: Disorderly conditions or unmonitored areas encourage further and more serious levels of disorderly behavior.[7] In other words, if criminals know that certain banks, stores, or neighborhoods are "easier" to rob because they're unmonitored, that's where they prey. And if students know that the back of the bus or certain hallway locations are untended by adults, that's where bullying is more likely to happen.

According to a survey of 25,000 U.S. secondary students, bullying was *most* likely to occur: 45 percent in a hallway or stairwell; 33 percent in a classroom; 22 percent on school grounds; 18 percent in the cafeteria.[8]

Bullying is *situational*—it does not happen everywhere. Instead, it generally happens at the same times and places in and around school sites. A key element of bullying prevention is to identify the spots and times when bullying is most frequent, and then boost adult supervision at those locations. If you are consistent with your monitoring, you should find a sharp decline in bullying behaviors at those identified locations within a short time. This section shows techniques and ways to reduce bullying in those high-frequency areas to create safer learning environments for kids. (See pages 50–53 in Part II for details on surveying students to identify your school's hot spots.)

---

6. Davis and Nixon, 2010.
7. Keizer et al., 2008.
8. U.S. Department of Justice, Bureau of Justice Statistics, School Crime Supplement (SCS) to the National Crime Victimization Survey (NCVS), 2013.

> ## Brave Staff Chat: When Was Your Last Staff Walk-Through?
>
> How often has your staff "walked your school walls"—particularly the cafeteria, playground corners, hallways, and restrooms—to assess school safety? Encourage staff members to walk through such areas and look through a new lens: "If I was a student, would I feel safe in these spots? Would I perceive our school to be safe and caring?" What can you do to increase a positive school climate in *all* areas of your school? You might also choose to take a few articulate kids with you on a walk around the school. You'll be surprised at how much information you learn if you ask the right questions. High school students in Corpus Christie, Texas, told me that security guards should board up the space under the stairwell ("Bad stuff happens down there and nobody ever checks"). Elementary kids in New York said that the back of their playground was "a really bad place for bullying because the yard duty teachers can't see it." Ask your students about safety concerns. They rarely let you down!

STRATEGIES TO REDUCE BULLYING IN SPECIFIC HOT SPOTS

There are various ways to reduce bullying in designated hot spot areas. Boosting adult presence in the spot is one of the simplest and often least-used strategies. A middle school principal in the North Penn School District shared one of the best ideas: she analyzed her student bullying surveys, identified a hallway as a top hot spot, and made a full-size cardboard cutout of herself to put in the middle of the hall. She taped a note on it that read, "We are a bully-free school. I'm watching you, and you'll never know when the real me will show up." The students loved it, and bullying in that spot was eradicated. Be creative! Here are other "hot spot" ideas passed on to me from dozens of creative educators.

School entrances. Administrators and staff can rotate meeting students in the parking lot as they arrive at school, which can send a powerful message to students (and their parents). A school in Bremerton, Washington, created a student group to be "Safe School Ambassadors" and meet peers in the morning bus lines. It set a friendly tone and reduced verbal put-downs, which had been a problem at the bus stops.

Surrounding barriers and gates. If possible, remove elements on school property that may obstruct staff's view of students. Pay attention to the far school gate entrances that are unsupervised. Lock them or assign a staff member to monitor them.

Playgrounds. Train playground supervisors in bullying prevention and have them spread apart and stand closer to hot spots, especially under playground equipment and at far corners that are more difficult to monitor. The Olweus bullying prevention program suggests that yard supervisors wear bright-colored vests to create a feeling of safety and so kids can find them easily. Designate areas of the playground as "safety zones" by putting flags or plastic cones in certain playground areas.[9] An adult is always available in the safety zone for students who feel they need protection. Just the presence of such an area can do wonders in helping students feel safer. Also, teach students cooperative skills, games, and deal breakers to use on the playground, such as "Rock, Paper, Scissors."

Halls and lockers. Students tell me the easiest way to reduce bullying in hallways and near lockers is by boosting adult visibility. Other ideas: "Tell the teachers to keep their class doors open so they can see outside." "Hang mirrors like they have in parking lots." "Put up video cameras." (The student added, "I know it's expensive but you don't have to put the film in the camera. Just make kids *think* they're being monitored.") Also, staggering class starting times, bell schedules, and recess and lunch periods can help prevent congregation in halls. Large numbers of students in limited spaces increase the potential for bullying and temper flare-ups. In areas of high density, increase the ratio of staff members to students as high as possible. Board up unused stairwells and keep hallways well-lit. Move vulnerable students' lockers closer to a teacher or keep extra textbooks in your room so students don't have to go to their lockers if they feel unsafe. Use a "foot patrol"—have students help monitor the hallways (like "traffic patrol" student monitors).

Restrooms. Many students are afraid to use school restrooms for fear of being bullied. The top cause? Restrooms are rarely monitored by staff. Set up a rotational staff monitoring system. In high-risk schools, lock your bathrooms. Students then need special keys with hall passes to use them. Some elementary schools use the "bathroom buddy" system: students use the restrooms in pairs with staff permission. Do routine checks of bathroom stalls for inappropriate language, verbal taunts, or graffiti. Some schools hold a weekend decorating party with staff, parents, and students working together to paint over inappropriate language on school property, including restrooms. A middle

---

9. Fried and Fried, 2003.

school staff said their girls' bathroom was a bullying hangout, so staff, parents, and girls wallpapered the room and hung pictures and changed the "mean girl" scene.

Cafeterias. A study of middle school bullying showed that 83 percent of the students reported seeing bullying in their lunchroom.[10] Adding structure to the cafeteria and increasing adult monitoring during the lunch period will decrease student aggression and increase pro-social interactions among students. Train your cafeteria workers in how to respond to bullying! In particular, help the staff tune in to certain students who are more likely to be targeted. A recent study published by *Pediatrics* found that roughly a third of children reported being bullied for their allergies.[11] Break up exclusion by making your cafeteria more inviting and regularly rotating seating.

> A key element of bullying prevention is to identify the spots and times when bullying is most frequent, and then boost adult supervision at those locations.

Buses. Train bus drivers in bullying prevention and alert them of students who may be targets or perpetrators of bullying. Bus drivers tell me two blind spots for them are the far back corners or directly behind the driver. The best seat is in the front of the bus on the right side. Consider putting video cameras in the front of the bus focused on students, and let students know the footage is being reviewed. Put bullying report forms on the bus and in the school so students can report incidents. Ask an older kid to watch out for a target. Assign seats on the bus. Do spot checks: a staff member can periodically ride on the bus for a certain distance. One school sets a sanction that if an investigation determines a student is bullying on the bus, his or her parent or guardian must ride the bus with the child for a specified period of time or the child loses bus privileges. Bus bullying was such a problem in one town that parents rotated volunteering to ride on the bus until the behavior was reduced.

Bus stops or walking to and from schools. An idea called "the walking school bus" originated in Australia by David Engwicht.[12] Many school districts have adopted this simple practice. A parent or other volunteer is assigned to walk a certain route to school, collect students at specified locations along the way, and drop them off on the way home. Walking together in a large, adult-supervised group has not only reduced bullying in hot-spot locations, but it also helps students learn safety skills.

10. Harris and Petrie, 2002.
11. Shemesh et al., 2013.
12. Beane, 2009: p. 116.

Tip for ADMINISTRATORS

Studies find that bullying is less likely to occur if schools increase the level of security for students through consistent adult monitoring.[13] Utilize *all* staff members to supervise key areas that surveys list as hot spots. For instance, have custodians watch back corridors, yard supervisors watch playground corners, teachers watch hallways, and bus drivers watch the back of the bus. Adult visibility in those hot spots helps students feel safe and conveys a strong message that adults care.

Encourage Students to Shift School Norms from Cruel to Kind

- *Fact:* Bullying is situational and does not happen everywhere on a school site; rather, it happens in certain areas that usually have less adult supervision.

- *Fact:* Bullying flourishes when it is supported by the school's norms.

- *Fact:* Research shows that bullying is *far* less likely to happen in classroom and school cultures with norms of caring and respect.

- *Fact:* One of the most significant ways to reduce bullying is to empower and mobilize students to create school norms where it's "cool to be *kind,* not cruel."

- *Fact:* Few schools regularly involve students in key decisions about school life.

This section shares how schools are empowering students to shift their school norms from cruel to kind and, in the process, reduce bullying and create a safer, more positive school climate.

Stop Bullying Clubs. Forming student clubs is one way that students are working together to stop bullying. Clubs can be as small as two or as large as the whole school, and meeting times can be before or after school, over lunchtime, or even on weekends. I've seen kids create posters, banners, buttons, songs, websites, and YouTube videos that feature the concept: "Let's stop bullying and be respectful." Encourage community groups (Boys and Girls Clubs, YMCA, scouts, youth ministries) to work with interested kids to extend bullying prevention efforts beyond your school walls.

---

13. Totura et al., 2009.

No Cussing Clubs. McKay Hatch, a middle school student in South Pasadena, California, was so bothered by hearing prolific bad language from peers that he founded the first No Cussing Club.* The motto is simple, "Leave People Better Than You Found Them." McKay has a "No Cussing Club Challenge," and invites kids to change the world "one word at a time." The club has over 20,000 members, including kids from the United States, Canada, Botswana, Indonesia, Mexico, India, China, New Zealand, Russia, Saudi Arabia, and South Korea. Students at Palm Desert High School in Southern California wore orange T-shirts the first week of school encouraging kids to "watch their language," other schools are putting jars around campuses for kids to drop a coin in if they cuss. (The money is then donated to local charities.) Other schools hang student-made posters in hallways bearing slogans like: "No swearing: This is a civil place." and "Watch your words: This is a place of learning!"

Compassion Clubs. Joseph Griffith at Wiesbaden High School in Germany created a Compassion Club at his school as a safe place where students can get to know one another, be free from bullying and name-calling, and experience compassion. He leads the club once a week with fellow students while a teacher serves as club advisor. The club topics may change, but the goal is always to create a caring and respectful venue for peers.

"In life we are all taught and bombarded with lessons pertaining to math, science, and literature. Kids need to also learn about compassion because without it, the future can only hold bleak possibilities." —Joe, age 14

SIX WAYS TO STOMP OUT PUT-DOWNS AND BOOST KINDNESS

Verbal abuse is cited as the most common type of bullying on school campuses. Most physical fights begin with a verbal taunt or name-calling and then escalate if not curtailed. By reducing name-calling, you reduce the likelihood of bullying. Here are a few strategies; use the ones most appropriate to your grade

* See nocussing.com.

levels. Be sure to pass along the ideas to *all* staff and parents so they also can remind students to give the ideas a try and reinforce their efforts.

1. **Set a school-wide "no put-downs" rule.** One of the first steps to reducing put-downs is to establish the norm that "our school stands for kindness." I've visited many schools and knew instantly they were curbing unkindness because reminders were posted at their front doors: "Put-downs are not permitted" and "Unkindness is not allowed."

2. **Make "no put-downs" posters.** Students at Ralph Sheppard Elementary School in Vancouver had a homework assignment: create a poster using words, symbols, or drawings showing that put-downs are not tolerated on campus. The posters were then displayed. Everywhere was the same critical message: "This Is a No Put-Downs Zone." The effect was potent!

3. **Create a "no put-downs" pledge.** Many schools and classrooms ask members to take a "no put-downs" pledge. Create the pledge by asking students for suggestions and then voting on them. The winning pledge is written on a huge banner, signed by all class or school members, and posted as a concrete reminder. Students in a primary school in Montana take an "H & H pledge": "I will say only comments that are *helpful* not *hurtful* and remind others to do the same."

4. **Hold a put-down funeral.** Chick Moorman, a national educational consultant, told me that one of the most powerful activities he ever observed was a classroom "put-down funeral." The teacher began by asking students to write as many unkind words and phrases as they could think of on slips of paper. Those were placed in a shoebox and taped shut, and the students then marched solemnly to the playground and buried the box. The symbolic gesture conveyed to the class: "Those put-downs are buried and are never to be used again." Put-down funerals can have a dramatic impact on children.

5. **Make a "turn-around" rule.** One way to help elementary kids learn to say more kind comments is by establishing a rule of "One put-down means one put-up." Whenever a student says an unkind comment, she has to turn it around and say something kind to the recipient. Suppose you hear a student say a put-down: "Kevin is stupid." Say: "That was a put-down. I need a *put-up* statement, please." The child then says a more caring statement in its place. ("Well, he's a great soccer player.") *A word of*

caution: The turnaround rule is wonderful, but it works only if it is used consistently and if children know what kind comments are. For some kids, writing the kind comment is more comfortable than saying it, and it's a first step toward becoming more caring.

6. **Use the "thumb down, thumb up" rule.** Hays Elementary School in Kansas uses a variance of the turn-around rule for younger kids. If a student hears another child say a put-down, she signifies that the comment is inappropriate by making a thumb-down gesture. The receiver acknowledges the gesture by flipping his thumb up, without saying a word.

Practices to Restore Relationships and Resolve Conflicts

At the base of bullying is a problem with relationships. If we really want to stop bullying behaviors, we need to teach students *how* to resolve conflicts and form healthy relationships so they feel safe to support one another. Here are a few evidence-based practices to build students' character, restore respectful relationships, *and* reduce future bullying incidents.

CLASS MEETINGS

When I was a teacher, I'd always start Monday mornings with a class meeting. We'd begin with a "compliment circle," where each student would say something kind to the person next to her or him, and then we'd discuss our daily agenda. The students knew my circle rules: No interrupting or put-downs, everyone's idea counts, and decisions are determined by majority rule. Meetings were also when I'd teach students SEL skills like emotional literacy, problem solving, and communication, and try to nurture a supportive class atmosphere.

> If we really want to stop bullying behaviors, we need to teach students *how* to resolve conflicts and form healthy relationships so they feel safe to support one another.

I never realized how powerful those meetings were until one day when I arrived late and saw students seated in a tight circle having a serious discussion. A girl was crying and two classmates were trying to comfort her. I snuck in to listen and learned that she was bullied by students in the classroom next door, and my kids were holding an emergency class meeting to help her. Those next few minutes proved to be one of my proudest teaching memories. I watched my students discuss a serious issue, listen to each other's views, and come up with a solution to solve their classmate's problem. I also recognized how critical it was to teach SEL skills and provide practice, so they could use those skills in real life.

Class meetings are a way for students to get together at regularly scheduled times to talk about issues in a supportive atmosphere and practice social-emotional learning. Bullying expert Dan Olweus advocates class meetings so students can combat bullying and develop positive relationships. The meeting becomes a safe venue where students become committed class members, accept differences, build a sense of fairness, and reduce peer problems. Here are the basic guidelines for class meetings:

Make it democratic. Students usually sit in a circle on the floor or in chairs so everyone can see and hear one another and feel engaged in the community. Each person's opinion is considered equal, everyone has a right to be heard, and kids can raise any concern. Encourage students to speak up, and hold your judgments. *Note:* Remind students that disclosing personal information or family matters is off-limits. If a confidential issue comes up, set up a time for the student to talk privately with you or refer the child to a guidance counselor if needed.

Determine decision-making protocol. Usually decisions are based on majority rule, though some experts feel agreement should be made by unanimous consensus. Either way you choose, make a rule that decisions made in the meeting are to be honored, at least until the following meeting where they can be changed.

Set meeting rules. Some common ones: raise your hand to speak, put your hands down when others speak, speak one at a time, respect differences, honor confidentiality, listen actively, be respectful, and use appropriate topics and language.

Hold regularly scheduled meetings. Most experts suggest meeting once a week for fifteen to twenty minutes for younger students and slightly longer for older ones. Other teachers start and end each day with a brief meeting.

Rotate meeting roles. Assigning roles that can be rotated weekly helps kids become more engaged. For example, assign a timekeeper to start and stop meetings, a parliamentarian to ensure rules are followed, a planner to post the meeting date and time, and a secretary to keep notes (which can be written on poster paper to help students track the discussion). Also, a "circle keeper" can make introductory comments, summarize ideas, and pose questions.

Create an upbeat meeting spirit. Don't hold meetings only to hash out problems. Many classes start the meeting by having members take turns complimenting each other's good deeds during the week. Keeping meetings fun and lively helps kids look forward to them.

Develop meeting routines. A talking piece (for example, a feather, rock, shell, small megaphone) is an object that allows the person holding it an opportunity to speak without interruption. Most meetings use the "circle go around" technique so only the person holding the talking piece may speak or they may choose to pass their turn and give the object to the next person. Students also develop special hand signals to signify needs like "speak up" (hands turn upward) "tell me more" (hand waves) "wind it up" (hand spins).

Use multiple topics. Meeting topics are endless: announcing class activities, settling conflicts, handling repetitive problems or inappropriate behaviors, celebrating positive events for individual class members, voicing concerns, establishing or revising class rules, and discussing bullying incidents, among others. Many teachers set aside a small box for students to suggest issues or topics they'd like to address at the next meeting.

SEL SKILL: How to Disagree Respectfully

Discord can cause friction among students and impede a positive learning environment. One way to reduce friction is by teaching students ways to disagree *respectfully*. Post suggestions, such as those listed here, on a chart and then gently encourage kids to use the phrases in class meetings, in cooperative groups, or on the playground until they can use the skill on their own.

- "I disagree . . ."
- "Here's another way to see it . . ."
- "Have you considered . . . ?"
- "Let me share my idea . . ."
- "Have you thought about . . . ?"
- "Here's why I don't agree . . ."
- "That's one way to do/say it. Here's mine . . ."
- "Here's what I think . . ."

PROBLEM SOLVING AND CONFLICT RESOLUTION

Educators have long recognized the benefits of kids learning to work together to solve their problems. After all, using problem-solving skills is one of the best ways to help kids and teens curb playground battles, deal with friendship tiffs, manage teammate squabbles, and handle the social jungle, as well as boost resilience, self-esteem, peacemaking skills, social skills, and character. New research by the American Psychological Association reveals another huge plus: Teaching problem solving may prevent bullying and reduce the odds of victimization.

Researchers analyzed 153 studies on bullying involving kids from ages three to eighteen, and they found that kids, especially boys, who have trouble solving social problems are more at risk of bullying, becoming targets of bullying, or both.[14] Children who bully or are targets of bullying often have trouble resolving problems, lack social skills, and think negative thoughts. This is why problem-solving strategies should be an integral part of every school's bullying prevention program and school climate initiative. The great news is that problem-solving skills can be woven into classroom content. Find ways to intentionally teach these skills to students—they *don't* acquire the skills on their own. The sooner we teach students how to resolve their own conflicts, the less we'll have to intervene in social battles. Here are programs and practical ideas:

> **Warning:** *Do NOT use conflict resolution with a bullying child and his or her target.* Bullying is not a disagreement but one-sided contempt, so there is no equality between a target and a bullying child, which is a crucial element of conflict resolution. Only if the targeted child requests the resolution process, then you might reconsider. (See chapters R5 and R6 for details on helping targeted children and children who bully.)

I Can Problem Solve (ICPS). One of the most widely respected children's problem-solving programs, I Can Problem Solve (ICPS) was developed by psychologists Dr. George Spivack and Dr. Myrna Shure. Over thirty-five years of research on the program's effectiveness found that students skilled in problem solving are less likely to be impulsive and aggressive, tend to be more caring and less insensitive, are better able to make friends, and tend to achieve more academically. ICPS can be incorporated into daily classroom activities or adapted by school mental health staff. Components are available for preschool, kindergarten, primary grades, and intermediate elementary grades, as well as for families. (See www.icanproblemsolve.info for more information.)

14. Cook et al., 2010.

Take a STAND to Solve Problems. Use the following as a guide to help students learn to solve social problems peacefully. Each letter in the acronym STAND represents one of five steps in conflict resolution.

- **<u>S</u>top, look, and listen to your feelings.** The first step to solving problems is to stay calm. Once in control, you can begin to figure out why you're upset and then find an answer to your dilemma. Teach students to take a slow deep breath to stay cool or walk away until calm. *Hint:* You might need to separate kids until their anger is under control.

- **<u>T</u>ake turns telling the problem.** Ask each child to say what happened, summarize each view, and then end with: "What can you do now to solve this problem?" Crucial communication rules are: No put-downs or name-calling. Listen to each other respectfully. No interrupting. Each person gets a chance to talk. You might even have each student repeat what the other child has said. If students are hesitant to talk to each other or trust is an issue, give them the option of writing or drawing their view of the problem instead (this is particularly helpful for younger or less verbal kids). The goal is to help students try to feel what it's like to be in the other person's shoes.

- **List <u>a</u>lternatives.** Now have children brainstorm options for finding a resolution. The basic rules work for any age: Say whatever comes into your mind, no put-downs, piggyback onto anyone's idea, try to come up with ideas that work for all those involved. *Hint:* Setting an oven timer for just three minutes can be invaluable for students with short attention spans. Stretch the time depending on the children's age and problem-solving skills.

- **<u>N</u>arrow choices.** Narrow options to a few choices using these guidelines: Eliminate solutions that are refused by either child, aren't safe or wise, or are in conflict with school rules or your values.

- **<u>D</u>ecide best choice and do it!** The final step teaches students to think about the consequences of the remaining choices. Two questions help their decision-making: "What might happen (both good and bad) if I tried that?" and "What is one last change to this solution that would make it work better for both of us?" Once students decide, the two shake on the agreement or take turns saying, "I agree."

Fight FAIR. While it's okay to disagree, the secret is to disagree *respectfully*, and it's a social-emotional learning skill you can teach. The acronym FAIR helps kids remember the four parts in getting your opinion across respectfully.

- **Focus on the behavior.** Teach kids to focus on the *behavior* of the person they're having trouble with and not on how they feel about the person. To help focus on the behavior, ask students to name what the person did that bothered them: "He cut ahead of me in line," "She grabbed my toy," "She made fun of me in front of the rest of the kids."

- **Assert yourself calmly.** Explain that messages are more respectful if delivered with a calm, firm voice and assertive posture: head held high, looking eye-to-eye, standing with feet slightly apart, and arms held loosely by your sides.

- **Use an "I-message."** An I-message helps kids stay focused on the person's behavior without putting down the recipient. See the SEL Skill: Use I-Messages below for details.

- **Remain respectful.** Though kids should not tolerate disrespect, they also should not act disrespectfully in response, so name-calling, insults, and sarcasm aren't allowed. Teach students to remain respectful when they assert a complaint about another's behavior, and then calmly walk away.

SEL SKILL: Use I-Messages

Tell students to describe their feelings by beginning sentences with "I" instead of "you." Next, students should describe the problem and how they want it resolved. Doing so helps the speaker focus on the conflict without putting the other person down. Example: "I'm upset because I didn't get a turn. I want to use the computer, too." Such I-messages help reduce normal peer conflict and are very effective in the class meeting format. *Note:* This strategy is *not* advisable for a target to use with a child who is bullying. Children who engage in bullying may have low empathy and a desire for control, and they may actually be glad that the target is upset. (See chapter R6: Replace for details on helping children who bully.)

Tip for ADMINISTRATORS

An effective way to train educators in a best practice such as class meetings or conflict resolution is to run a staff meeting using the method. Doing so builds competence so teachers are more likely to use the technique with students.

Ways to Involve PARENTS

You might arrange a workshop about problem solving, send home newsletters with tips on teaching kids to solve problems peacefully, or encourage parents to read a book such as *Thinking Parent, Thinking Child: How to Turn Your Most Challenging Everyday Problems into Solutions* by Myrna B. Shure, *Raising a Thinking Preteen* by Myrna B. Shure with Roberta Israeloff, or *Raising a Thinking Child Workbook: Teaching Young Children How to Resolve Everyday Conflicts and Get Along with Others* by Myrna B. Shure with Theresa Foy Digeronimo (for parents of children ages four to seven).

Classroom Practices That Encourage Student Cooperation

There are no silver bullets to the bullying problem. But research provides clear guidance about the most effective methods to reduce cruelty, and it turns out that the classroom climate and a teacher's behavior management style are crucial. What follows are evidence-based practices that can be used in the classroom and school-wide to reduce bullying and encourage cooperation.

> A systemic review of twenty-six years of intervention research found that three of the most important program factors associated with a decrease in bullying involved classroom practices—including disciplinary methods, classroom management, and classroom rules.[15]

RESPONSIVE CLASSROOM

Responsive Classroom is an evidence-based approach devised in the 1980s that includes four key domains: Engaging Academics, Positive Community, Effective Management, and Developmental Awareness. The approach uses rules and logical consequences to provide a consistent approach to discipline in order to foster responsibility and self-control. It also stresses: "Be firm, kind, and consistent"

---

15. Farrington and Ttofi, 2009.

and fits the Olweus premise that a "respectful, consistent, and firm" classroom management style is most effective in reducing bullying. Morning meetings build community and create a positive learning climate. It has been recognized by the Collaborative for Academic, Social, and Emotional Learning (CASEL) organization as one of the most well-designed, evidence-based social and emotional learning programs.

> A three-year, randomized controlled study that followed 350 teachers and over 2,900 students found Responsive Classroom to be associated with higher academic achievement, improved teacher-student interactions, improved school climate, and higher quality instruction in mathematics.*

THE JIGSAW CLASSROOM

Jigsaw is a cooperative learning technique developed in the 1970s by social psychologist Elliot Aronson and can be used across curriculum areas and grade levels. The class is divided into small learning teams of five or six students and assigned a task, such as learning about World War II. Just as in a jigsaw puzzle, each student's part in the assignment is essential for the completion and understanding of the total learning task. No student can succeed unless everyone works well together as a team.

The approach facilitates cooperation among all students and helps them value each other as contributors. Jigsaw is found to reduce racial conflict, promote better learning, improve student motivation and listening skills, and increase positive educational experiences. Because the approach encourages intergroup cooperation, it can be used to reduce victimization and encourage students to support one another in bullying incidents.[16]

KEY BULLYING PREVENTION POINTS IN PART I

- The most effective bullying prevention efforts address the whole school community, individual classrooms, and individual students.

- Research shows that bullying is far less likely to happen in classrooms and school cultures where caring and respect are the norms.

- Positive school climates are places that promote and teach prosocial behaviors.

---

* From responsiveclassroom.org/research.
16. Espelage and Swearer, 2003.

- All adults need to promote and model respectful attitudes and behaviors.

- Creating a caring school climate is *not* a quick fix, but a systemic, deliberate approach.

- Adults need to connect with students to create the trust that will help students come forward if they are bullied or witness bullying.

- Respectful relationships and caring people—staff, students, parents, and community members—are the ultimate antidote to bullying.

Part II

Getting Started to Make Real and Lasting Change

In Part II, you will learn:

- how to establish and organize a strong bullying prevention team
- four ways to build staff momentum and sustain team commitment
- why effective bullying prevention needs to be evidence-based
- eight components of an effective student bullying survey and steps to administer it to students
- tips for conducting a successful student focus group
- descriptions of the best proven school-wide programs for bullying prevention
- six steps to choose the programs and practices to fit your unique needs

The second part of effective bullying prevention involves creating a bullying prevention team, delegating roles and responsibilities to maximize your impact, and then selecting the best programs and practices to help reduce bullying in your unique school environment. You won't need to buy pricey materials, technology, or curriculum guides, or apply for grants so your staff or team can afford a costly outside trainer. Instead, I'll recommend cost-effective proven practices and programs you can implement—most of these ideas are a fraction of the cost of resources currently in the bullying prevention market. In fact, many of the surveys and reporting instruments are available free online. What your staff or team needs to do is examine what you already have in place at your school and then thoroughly analyze your data, current practices, values, and beliefs. This section shows you the steps to get started.

Note: Even if you are not building a bullying prevention team or you already have one in place, Part II offers a host of strategies to help concerned individuals cooperate and assist teams and school staffs to work more effectively to begin implementing the 6Rs described in Part III.

Create a School-Wide Team to Coordinate Bullying Prevention Efforts

"Creating a bullying prevention team is what jump-started our efforts. The members' commitment mobilized everyone to get on board."
—teacher, Edina, Minnesota

Developing a comprehensive, school-wide approach to bullying prevention is serious work and generally starts with the creation of a strong team. This small group will represent all stakeholders and coordinate the school's bullying prevention efforts. To succeed, members need to develop an understanding of bullying, assess their school's bullying problem, analyze best programs and practices, and then implement system-wide prevention plans. This section explains how to choose and organize the ideal school-wide bullying prevention team.

I've worked with dozens of schools and found that those with a strong team to coordinate their bullying prevention efforts are most effective. After all, a comprehensive, school-wide approach starts with a group of committed staff members and is chaired by a strong leader. The ideal team consists of energetic individuals who are passionate about creating a bully-free culture and represent a range of positions in the school and community. But desire alone won't cut it. Creating a safe and caring school culture takes a significant commitment. Here are six steps to creating a strong bullying prevention team.

Step 1: Determine if a new team is necessary. If your school lacks a bullying prevention team or task force, you will need to create one or designate another group to oversee, monitor, and plan efforts at your site. If you have a school safety committee or a professional learning community, they might assume those duties.

Step 2: Choose team members who are committed. Ideal members should be committed to creating a safe climate, be team players, and be willing to serve at least a year to maximize team effectiveness. Sensitive information may be discussed, so members should also be discrete. Simply wanting to serve does not guarantee membership.

Step 3: Create a team with a broad representation. Members should represent a wide range of stakeholders' positions and have staff credibility, since an important part of their role is to convince colleagues of the need to extend time and energy into bullying prevention efforts. Core members generally include:

- an administrator, a director, a principal, or an assistant principal to lead, distribute resources, and provide insight about school policy, budget, federal and state laws, and curriculum

- teachers to represent various grade levels, subjects, or departments

- psychologists, counselors, or social workers to share insights on assessment, mental health, and social and emotional learning

- special education teachers to offer insights on at-risk students or those with emotional and learning disabilities

- school resource officers to share facts about school safety and community trends

- members of the nonteaching staff, such as teacher's aides, bus drivers, librarians, secretaries, custodians, and cafeteria workers, to offer views on bullying outside the classroom

- parents or PTO officers to share the home perspectives and be liaisons to other parents

Step 4: Find members who offer different strengths and expertise.
Look for members who represent various grade levels, subjects, and staff positions, and offer a range of expertise on issues such as assessment, curriculum, leadership, psychology, social and emotional learning, school safety, presentation skills, technology, and people skills. Crest View School in Minneapolis chose members who shared a deep commitment to nurturing a safe, positive school climate but also offered diverse strengths, which proved enormously helpful in designing a comprehensive school-wide plan.

Step 5: Enlist part-time members. Based on the agenda for your team, some members can attend periodically and offer perspectives on certain topics as valuable part-time additions, such as:

- a student representative for upper grades or middle school to share prevention challenges

- a school nurse, who in most schools is on a rotating schedule with other schools

- other staff such as librarians, yard supervisors, secretaries, cafeteria workers, and bus drivers

"Including students on our team made a huge difference. Their ideas for reducing bullying were so on target and helped the team design a more realistic plan because they knew what kids needed to feel safe." —teacher, Corpus Christie, Texas

Step 6: Involve community liaisons. Consider including members of the wider community to help support and share your school's bullying prevention efforts. Ideas include:

- a representative from a youth group, Boys and Girls Club, YMCA/YWCA, or a scout leader
- after-school programs or organizations
- a coach in a community athletics organization
- a member of Kiwanis, Rotary, or another community-based organization that supports kids
- a member of the sheriff's department or law enforcement agency
- local media (newspaper, radio, television, bloggers)

Getting Started as a Team

"Taking time to figure out the roles and duties of our team was crucial to our success. Don't overlook getting organized!" —principal, Las Vegas, Nevada

This section provides the common questions, tasks, and duties that a strong team needs to address to get organized and begin the important work of reducing bullying.

QUESTIONS TO HELP YOUR TEAM GET ORGANIZED

Here are common questions team members often ask to help clarify expectations, their roles, and the team's purpose:

- What is our primary mission as a team?
- Who is our team coach, or how will we select that individual?
- When should we meet, how often, and where?
- What is our first, most pressing task?

- How will we communicate with each other between meetings?

- What are our individual roles? (recorder, chair, trainer, program reviewer, and so forth)

- Who will be our liaison to the district office, school board, or administrator?

- How will we create a timeline to succeed?

- What are our rules? (punctuality, confidentiality, regular attendance)

- What will be our decision-making process?

- How will we disseminate our decisions and progress to the staff?

- How will we prepare ourselves so we can train the staff?

> It is highly recommended that each bullying prevention team member receive a copy of this book so that readings and discussions can be done as a team. Download the PDF presentation provided in the book's digital content to facilitate team discussions. See page x for download instructions.

Tip for ADMINISTRATORS

Ongoing training is essential so that all stakeholders understand their role in bullying prevention. A national survey of 5,000 school staff found that fewer than 40 percent reported they were directly involved in their school's bullying prevention efforts.[1] Make sure your team plans include ongoing staff development and periodic assessment of that development.

THE TOP TWENTY ROLES AND RESPONSIBILITIES OF BULLYING PREVENTION TEAMS

Here is a list of typical responsibilities of bullying prevention team members. Determine the types of tasks, roles, and duties that will be needed for your team's success.

1. Review current bullying research and keep the staff updated on the latest findings.

2. Identify and preview evidence-based practices and programs that create safe and caring school environments.

---

1. Bradshaw et al., 2011.

3. Assess the staff's current understanding and views on the need for bullying prevention.

4. Review model anti-bullying policies in your region, state, or province.

5. Lead discussions or trainings about bullying and school climate at staff meetings.

6. Develop an anti-bullying policy based on survey findings and your school needs.

7. Investigate your state/province and district bullying regulations and utilize that language.

8. Connect with other schools in your district involved in bullying prevention.

9. Listen to parents, students, and community members to hear their perspectives about bullying.

10. Attend trainings in bullying prevention and share findings with your staff.

11. Offer bullying awareness training to staff and parents, if needed.

12. Conduct and review findings from school bullying surveys and assessments.

13. Roll out your bullying prevention policy to all your stakeholders.

14. Develop your discipline policy and sanctions for bullying behaviors.

15. Educate *all* stakeholders about bullying so everyone sees they play a role in stopping it.

16. Develop forms for students, parents, and staff to report bullying.

17. Ensure all stakeholders know where and how to use reporting materials.

18. Implement the school-wide bullying prevention plans or school climate initiative.

19. Evaluate bullying prevention efforts and refine them, if necessary.

20. Sustain your efforts so bullying is reduced and prosocial behaviors continue to increase.

Four Ways to Build Staff Momentum and Sustain Team Commitment

1. **Keep an open-door policy.** Continually invite interested stakeholders to join team discussions so they will be more likely to support your cause.

2. **Maintain communication with *all* your staff.** Use email blasts, brief staff meeting updates, notes in staff members' mailboxes, or in-person visits.

3. **Share progress.** Prepare brief updates that convey team efforts and progress so the staff recognizes bullying prevention is an ongoing commitment.

4. **Acknowledge success.** Developing a comprehensive, systemic plan takes time, so be sure to honor your gains and acknowledge staff contributions along the way.

Assessing Bullying Behaviors at Your School

"Many teachers felt bullying wasn't an issue until I showed our survey that reported two-thirds of our students witnessed bullying. Data convinced them!" —principal, Austin, Texas

Effective bullying prevention involves understanding the scope of the problem at your school. A useful way of gathering that information is to conduct periodic assessments with your stakeholders—particularly students—that can then be used to create evidence-based policies and procedures tailored to your school culture's needs. This section offers ways to gather crucial data about your school climate, inappropriate behavior, and bullying incidents so you can develop a "homegrown program" that reduces aggression and boosts prosocial behaviors based on your unique population and environment.

Your data will be instrumental in determining which types of programs to implement, behaviors to target, hot spots to monitor, and interventions to use with your students. Bullying assessments are critical and should include a range of formal and informal surveys and reports that identify bullying types, targets, children who bully, the prevalence and frequency of aggressive behaviors, as well as the spots and times bullying is most likely to occur. Measurements should assess bullying from multiple sources (students, parents, teachers, staff). Surveys might include confidential student surveys, staff and parent perceptions, self-reports, student identifications of hot spots on school maps or in photos, staff bullying reports, student focus groups, and behavioral referrals.

Those findings should then be shared with your staff to increase aware-ness of the problem and identify children who engage in bullying, targets, and students who might be switching roles. Data based on your school's culture is what you will use to help design your bullying prevention policies, procedures, and practices. Here are ways to get started collecting that data.

CONDUCT REGULAR STUDENT SURVEYS

While you can gather data in many ways, a formal survey to assess student perceptions and information about bullying is strongly recommended. Some instruments must be ordered through a publishing company and can be costly, while others are available at a minimal (or no) cost online. Select one instrument that can be given prior to implementing your prevention efforts and then again several months later to assess effectiveness. Ultimately the bullying prevention team or administrator should decide which information is most pertinent for your efforts. Don't overlook gathering informal data from your behavior referrals, tardies and absences, discipline records, detentions, suspensions, visits to the school nurse, and anecdotal observations from staff about student behavior incidents. This information can be valuable in helping you identify children who may be involved in bullying.

An effective student survey consists of (but is not limited to) the following components:*

- Prevalence or frequency of bullying behaviors
- Types of bullying (verbal, emotional, electronic, physical) that occur
- Locations (or hot spots) where bullying behaviors occur
- Attitudes about bullying
- Names of participants and their roles in bullying incidents
- Data collections prior to and following prevention efforts
- Age, grade level, and gender of student completing the survey
- An anonymous option for survey participants

See an example of a student bullying survey on pages 70–71.

---

* A compendium of bullying assessment tools is available free online: *Measuring Bullying, Victimization, Perpetration, and Bystander Experiences* by the Centers for Disease Control and Prevention's National Center for Injury Prevention and Control. See cdc.gov/violenceprevention/pdf/BullyCompendium-a.pdf. See also free assessment resources on StopBullying.gov.

"We didn't realize how much behavior data we already had. Once we compiled that information we didn't have to do as many surveys."
—counselor, Dublin, Ohio

TEN STEPS TO ADMINISTER BULLYING OR SCHOOL CLIMATE ASSESSMENTS TO STUDENTS

Collecting data about bullying or school climate involves several steps. Review these recommendations, choose those that apply to your site, and assign tasks to the most appropriate staff members.

"I wanted to tell the principal about bullying, but I couldn't read the questions on the bullying form and was too embarrassed to say anything."
—Derrick, age 7

1. **Choose staff members for the assessment committee.** Many schools use an existing school climate team, PBIS team, or bullying prevention team. Include the administrator and school psychologist because of their assessment and logistics training.

2. **Select assessments.** Select both formal and informal surveys (see the list of essential components on page 51). Ensure that your state/province and district regulations allow you to survey students about bullying and school safety without parent permission.

3. **Ensure age appropriateness.** Check that all questions are age appropriate for your students. Do any new students need clarification?

4. **Give all students a voice.** Identify ESL, nonreading, or learning-disabled students who may have difficulties completing the survey and find a solution so they can share their views. A staff member could read the questions, someone could translate questions into the child's native language or braille, or you might convert the questions to pictures for nonreading students.

5. **Data analysis.** Determine the most effective way to analyze your data (such as creating bar graphs or using a computer program) so reviewing results is manageable.

6. **Set timelines.** Decide the dates to administer the pre- and post-test to the same population using the identical instrument.

7. **Train staff.** The *same* directions should be given to all student participants or survey results will be invalid. Decide how to train staff so they use exactly the same procedure and read the identical bullying definition (altered to fit the students' ages and abilities). The school counselor, psychologist, or other bullying prevention team member can visit each classroom to administer the survey.

8. **Create safety.** Find ways students can divulge information so they do not fear retaliation. Allow confidential or anonymous reporting. See the "Tip for Teachers" box below.

9. **Sharing results.** Determine if/when/how results will be shared with staff, parents, students, the district office, or community members to enlist support for your bullying efforts.

10. **Act on the results.** Decide how to use the results to help you design bullying prevention policies, procedures, and practices, as well as school climate initiatives.

Tip for TEACHERS

Fear of retaliation is a top reason students don't tell adults about bullying. So give "safe" options for students to divulge information using three rules:

1. You do not have to sign your name on any bullying survey or report.

2. Print or type your responses so your remarks are indistinguishable from those of peers.

3. Cover your survey with a sheet of paper so no one but you can read your comments.

Using Student Focus Groups to Gather Bullying Data

One of the most effective ways to learn about school bullying is to hold student focus groups and ask kids themselves to tell you. I've used focus groups in dozens of U.S. schools as well as in Taiwan, Canada, Colombia, and in several of our department of defense schools on U.S. Army bases overseas. All in all, I've spoken with hundreds of students and each time I hear some of the best solutions for stopping peer cruelty I've heard anywhere. By asking students questions in a safe venue for thirty to forty minutes, a facilitator can learn how frequent bullying is, the most prevalent types, why it happens, where it occurs, students' concerns, and suggestions to improve school climate *and* reduce peer cruelty. The following guidelines and questions have been most effective for me in gathering focus group data, but adapt them to meet your objectives.

SEVEN GUIDELINES FOR CONDUCTING STUDENT FOCUS GROUPS

1. Explain the objectives of student bullying focus groups and the questions you will be asking to the school administrator. Ensure administrator permission is granted.

2. Choose an adult (no more than two) with facilitation experience, good listening skills, high student trust, and enough knowledge about bullying to pose questions that will generate answers for bullying prevention implementation. *Tip:* Students are often more open to sharing with an adult who is *not* on the staff. Consider using a staff member from a neighbor school as facilitator.

3. Ask counselors, teachers, or administrators to nominate students who are unafraid to voice opinions, have peer respect, and represent different peer groups (a cross-section of the school culture including race, cliques, activities, sports, and academic interests). Select eight to twelve students per focus group.

4. Pick a comfortable setting so students can sit at desks or long tables placed in "L" arrangements.

5. Set aside forty-five minutes to an hour or the length of one class period for the meeting.

6. Ask a staff member to take notes. I've found that students are more open if there is one adult leading the group and the adult notetaker is inconspicuous during the session.

7. Per student provide: 8½" x 11" school map (or photos of school locations for younger children); nametag; three 4" x 6" index cards; a pencil.

"No one ever asks us our ideas about bullying. Schools should have more of these focus groups. Kids have good suggestions, you know." —Kara, age 11

What Students Around the World Tell Me Will Help Stop Bullying

"Tell teachers to stand in the halls. That's where the bullying is." —*Jen, age 10, Queens, New York*

"Too many kids are in halls. They should switch the schedule." —*Kaila, age 11, Reno, Nevada*

"Mix up the cafeteria seating so there aren't cliques." —*Jeremy, age 9, Milwaukee, Wisconsin*

"Why don't adults just ask the kids how bad bullying is?" —*Krista, age 8, Taipei, Taiwan*

"Get a place where kids can go and feel safe!" —*Jeremiah, age 9, Colombia, South America*

"The school needs report boxes. You could save a kid's life, you know!" —*Jena, age 12, Iowa City, Iowa*

"Teachers should tune in to kids. Knowing someone cares makes a difference." —*Bill, age 8, San Diego, California*

"If teachers would just walk into the halls and look in the cafeteria they'd see a lot and maybe understand why many kids don't feel safe at this school." —*Alexis, age 11, Philadelphia, Pennsylvania*

"The principal should read what we write in the reports and take them seriously. Why fill them out if nobody reads them?" —*Mario, age 10, Corpus Christie, Texas*

"Students could stop the bullying if we knew what to do to help. We don't all like to be bystanders, you know." —*Sun, age 11, Taipei, Taiwan*

"There's so much bullying that we don't feel safe. No one believes us, so thanks for listening. We're hurting here." —*Mercedes, age 10, Cajon Valley, California*

STEPS TO CONDUCT A SUCCESSFUL STUDENT FOCUS GROUP

Greet students. Ask them to write their first name on a nametag to wear (wear one yourself) and sit where they feel comfortable. Give each student a school map (a simple facsimile depicting locations of classrooms, cafeteria, hallways, office, playground), three index cards, and a pencil. *Note:* Younger children may have difficulty marking a map, so you could provide them with photos of areas in the school they can easily identify.

Begin the session. Introduce yourself and your role. You might say why you are concerned about bullying or tell a story about bullying to break the ice. Ask students to make brief introductions with their name, grade, and anything else they'd like to add.

Briefly explain the meeting's purpose. Emphasize that you want to hear students' views and concerns about bullying and any solutions they may have and that those will be shared with the rest of the school staff. Explain to students that they were selected because their peers respect their opinions.

Define bullying terms. To ensure understanding, define bullying terms you will use based on the students' ages. You might write terms on chart paper. "Here is what I mean when we talk about *bullying* today . . ." (See chapter R2: Recognize for more information on how to recognize bullying and the different types of bullying.)

Emphasize: "There are no 'right' or 'wrong' ideas." Ask students questions about bullying. (See pages 72–74, "Twelve Key Questions About Bullying and School Safety," for a list of sample questions. Simplify them for younger students.) Students may verbalize their ideas or write them on the form or on a notecard. They may also share what they feel are their peers' points of view. Ask students to refer to the school maps or photos you provided them when answering the questions.

Emphasize confidentiality. Stress that the names of students will be kept confidential.

Close the session. Thank students for their time and suggestions and tell them how you will be using their data. Give kids the opportunity to talk to you alone following the session.

Tip for ADMINISTRATORS

Consider creating a list of "Top Ten Student Ideas to Stop Bullying" based on student suggestions and distribute to your staff and students so they know you listened. Then implement one simple idea so students know you take bullying prevention seriously.

How to Select Programs and Practices to Reduce Bullying

The bullying problem is nuanced and depends a great deal on individual as well as group factors, and generally requires more than one program or approach to reduce it. For instance, the best intervention for one child who bullies may be empathy building, but for another it may be anger management. One target may need social skill enhancement, while the next child needs cognitive reframing. The key to success is to determine what motivates the child's behavior and then to use the medical model: prescribe the antidote (or intervention strategy) that is designed and best proven to remediate the symptoms.

While this book does not endorse any one particular bullying prevention program, it does offer a host of researched practices and evidence-based programs that reduce aggression and increase prosocial behaviors. It also addresses common bullying problems such as mobilizing bystanders, supporting targets, improving school climate, and replacing bullying behaviors. The dozens of suggested practices and programs recommended in this book can be found in the index and in the section "Best School-Wide Evidence-Based Bullying Prevention Programs" on pages 59–65.

So how do you choose the most effective bully prevention approach? How do you know which programs and practices to select for your particular school, classroom, or student? Start with these six steps:

Step 1: Gather and review data. The first step is to use evidence to determine what issues need addressing. The section earlier in this chapter, "Assessing Bullying Behaviors at Your School" (page 50), offers ways to survey stakeholders about bullying perceptions, frequency, and locations. Then identify the specific issues that need addressing, for instance, how to mobilize bystanders, teach a specific SEL skill, replace aggression, or remedy a hot spot (see Part I for some suggestions).

> ## " Brave Staff Chat
>
> Crunch your data and analyze your school's behavioral trends and patterns. Then dig deeper: Can you use any individual behavior interventions (like anger management, aggression replacement training, or social skills) with the minority—generally 12 to 15 percent—of your students to drastically reduce bullying rates? How might you implement your findings? What would be your first step to getting started?

Step 2: Review the section of this book that addresses the problem. Each section in *The 6Rs of Bullying Prevention* describes a particular problem that is unique to bullying, offers up-to-date research, and provides recommended resources, programs, or practices to consider implementing. (Refer to the index and table of contents of this book.) Review the recommended approaches for each issue that matches your data and select the programs and practices (from this book or elsewhere) that are most appropriate for your culture and students' needs.

Step 3: Research the program or practice. Do an online check of the program or practice that you choose. Ensure that the approach is suitable to your students' ages, genders, grade levels, and abilities, and that it addresses your particular concerns.

Step 4: Verify that the approach is evidence-based. Choose *only* those methods that have been proven to work. You might search SAMHSA's (Substance Abuse and Mental Health Services Administration) National Registry of Evidence-Based Programs and Practices (NREPP), an online registry developed to help the public learn more about evidence-driven bullying and behavior interventions. See nrepp.samhsa.gov.

Step 5: Designate the facilitator. Who will implement the approach: a psychologist, counselor, or grade-level teacher? Ensure that the facilitator has the right training and knowledge and understands that the program or practice should be used *only* as directed by the source material (book, trainer manual, instructional video, website, and so forth).

Step 6: Determine how success will be measured. Student surveys? Focus groups? Bullying reports? Behavior assessments? Absenteeism? What will you use to discover if your efforts are making a difference or if another approach would be more appropriate?

Best School-Wide Evidence-Based Bullying Prevention Programs

This book is unique in that it offers the 6Rs (see Part III) as a blueprint of steps and strategies proven to reduce bullying, as well as recommending the best of the existing research-based programs that support bullying prevention. While numerous anti-bullying programs are on the market, few have been tested in rigorous scientific studies. What follows are programs that are evidence-based and proven to be the most effective as school-wide interventions. To achieve success, the program needs to be implemented as specified in the trainer manual; be used as a systemic, sustained endeavor; and fit the needs of your particular culture and students. Oftentimes, one program is not enough for a school; I've seen some schools use up to five different programs in tandem, while adhering to the 6Rs framework provided in Part III of this book.

POSITIVE BEHAVIORAL INTERVENTIONS AND SUPPORTS (PBIS)

Positive Behavioral Interventions and Supports (PBIS) was designed in 1996 by education professor George Sugai, who began his career teaching emotionally disturbed teens. The program targets all students in kindergarten through twelfth grade and aims to alter the school climate by correcting and improving four elements school-wide: 1) behavioral outcomes, 2) behavioral data, 3) behavioral practices, and 4) behavioral systems. Instead of using a piecemeal approach of individual behavioral management plans, a continuum of positive behavior support for all students within a school is implemented in all areas, including the classroom and nonclassroom settings (such as hallways, buses, and restrooms). It is a school-wide initiative, which means that every adult on staff who encounters students during the school day is trained in PBIS, so that all students hear the same message. Program initiation begins by a staff crunching their specific behavior data to analyze their student needs, deciding what needs to change, and then addressing those problem behaviors in a systemic fashion. A 2012 study found that children in schools that implemented PBIS display lower rates of teacher-reported bullying and peer rejection than those in schools without the program. The effects on peer rejection were strongest among children first exposed to PBIS at a younger age and suggest that this system-wide program may help address school bullying by improving school climate overall.[2]

---

2. Waasdorp et al., 2012.

For More Information

- *The PBIS Team Handbook* by Beth Baker and Char Ryan (Free Spirit Publishing, 2014)
- Positive Behavioral Interventions and Supports website: PBIS.org

OLWEUS BULLYING PREVENTION PROGRAM (OBPP)

The Olweus Bullying Prevention Program (OBPP) was developed by Dan Olweus in Bergen, Norway, and has been used in more than a dozen countries by millions of students worldwide. It is a school-wide program designed for students ages five to fifteen that uses a comprehensive, systems-change approach involving teachers, students, parents, and other school and community personnel in an effort to reduce existing bullying problems and prevent future problems from occurring. All students participate in most aspects of the program, while students identified as bullying others or as targets of bullying receive additional individualized interventions. OBPP is designed to improve peer relations and make schools safer, more positive places for students to learn and develop. Olweus attempts to restructure the existing school environment to reduce opportunities and rewards for bullying. Evidence-based outcomes have included a 50 percent or more reduction in student reports of being bullied and bullying others, with peer and teacher ratings of bullying problems yielding similar results. Also included were significant improvements in the classroom social climate as reflected in students' reports of improved order and discipline, more positive social relationships, and more positive attitudes toward schoolwork and school.

For More Information

- *Bullying at School* by Dan Olweus (Wiley-Blackwell, 1993)
- Violence Prevention Works! website: violencepreventionworks.org

KIVA INTERNATIONAL

KiVa is a research-based, comprehensive program developed at the University of Turku in Finland. The approach is holistic because it enlists support from the entire school community and aims to teach students the importance of their role in bullying. KiVa is used extensively in Finland as well as in Belgium,

Luxembourg, the Netherlands, New Zealand, the United Kingdom, Estonia, Greece, Italy, Sweden, and the United States. It addresses three age groups: six to nine years; ten to twelve years; and middle school transition. KiVa provides anti-bullying education via computer games and exercises to enhance empathy and empower students to help bullying targets by teaching safe strategies. The multilayered program has been evaluated in a large randomized controlled trial with 117 intervention schools and 117 control schools and has shown to significantly reduce both self- and peer-reported bullying as well as victimization.[3] An analysis in *Child Development* announced that KiVa instigated a 46 percent reduction in "victimization" and a 61 percent reduction in "bullying others" in only nine months. A positive impact on students' perception of their peer climate was also found. What's more, 98 percent of targets involved in discussions with the schools' KiVa teams felt that their situation improved.[4]

For More Information

- KiVa International website: kivaprogram.net
- "KiVa Anti-Bullying Program: Implications for School Adjustment," by C. Salmivalli et al., in *Peer Relationships and Adjustment at School* (Information Age Publishing, 2012)

SAFE SCHOOL AMBASSADORS (SSA)

Safe School Ambassadors (SSA) is considered one of the most effective bystander education programs. It focuses on the influence students have to stop bullying by changing the social norms of their school culture and has been implemented in more than 1,400 schools. The program equips and empowers socially influential and diverse student leaders with nonviolent communication and bystander intervention skills. Once trained, these student ambassadors help prevent, deescalate, and stop hurtful incidents within their peer group, school, and community. Over 70,000 fourth- through twelfth-grade students have been trained. A multiyear evaluation found statistically significant outcomes at schools that implemented the program as designed, including increased rates of intervention in bullying incidents by student ambassadors, improved school climate, and suspension rates that averaged 33 percent lower than pre-SSA rates (rates at demographically matched control schools rose 10 percent during the same years). The program is listed on the SAMHSA national registry of evidence-based programs and practices.

3. Ttofi and Farrington, 2011.
4. Kärnä et al., 2011.

For More Information

- *Safe School Ambassadors: Harnessing Student Power to Stop Bullying and Violence* by Rick Phillips, John Linney, and Chris Pack (Jossey-Bass, 2008)

- Community Matters website: community-matters.org/programs-and-services/safe-school-ambassadors

BULLY-PROOFING YOUR SCHOOL (BPYS)

Bully-Proofing Your School (BPYS) is a school-based intervention program for elementary and middle school designed to make the school environment safe for children both physically and psychologically while reducing bullying. The BPYS classroom curriculum features three major goals: 1) Heighten awareness of bullying by assessing the extent of the problem and creating classroom expectations and rules regarding bullying; 2) Teach protective skills for dealing with bullying and providing assistance to potential targets; and 3) Create a positive school climate through promotion of a "caring majority" in the school to alter the behavior of bystanders. All systems in the school are addressed and specific steps for implementing the school-wide program are included.

The BPYS curriculum consists of seven sessions (with two optional sessions on conflict resolution and diversity) taught once a week, from thirty to forty-five minutes per session with an abbreviated curriculum for first grade and kindergarten students. Complete implementation spans three years and appears effective as an intervention to reduce bullying and school violence, particularly at the elementary school level.

For More Information

- *Bully-Proofing Your School: A Comprehensive Approach for Elementary Schools* by Carla Garrity et al. (Sopris West, 2000)

- *Bully-Proofing Your School: A Comprehensive Approach for Middle Schools* by Maria Bonds (Sopris West, 2000)

- National Center for School Engagement website: schoolengagement.org/school-engagement-services/bully-proofing-your-school

BULLY BUSTERS

The Bully Busters program was developed in 2000 as a team effort committed to better understanding and addressing childhood bullying and victimization, childhood aggression, and the healthy development of children. The program is research-based and emphasizes both control and prevention and helps teachers increase their awareness, knowledge base, and intervention skills to attack the root causes of bullying behavior. The manual provides thirty-six activities designed to increase student participation in reducing and preventing bullying, as well as to strengthen the teacher-student relationship.

Several studies have evaluated Bully Busters on teacher knowledge and skills for responding to bullying and found that participants demonstrated significantly better results than the control group on several outcomes including their awareness of bullying, knowledge of prevention strategies that can be used in the classroom, identification of behavior characteristics of bullying children and targets, interventions for reducing bullying behavior, and ways to help targets of bullying.[5]

For More Information

- *Bully Busters: A Teacher's Manual for Helping Bullies, Victims, and Bystanders: Grades K–5* by Arthur M. Horne, Christi L. Bartolomucci, and Dawn Newman-Carlson (Research Press, 2003)

- *Bully Busters: A Teacher's Manual for Helping Bullies, Victims, and Bystanders: Grades 6–8* by Arthur M. Horne, Christi L. Bartolomucci, and Dawn Newman-Carlson (Research Press, 2000)

- *A Parent's Guide to Understanding and Responding to Bullying* by Arthur M. Horne, Jennifer L. Stoddard, and Christopher D. Bell (Research Press, 2008)

SECOND STEP

Second Step is a classroom-based, social skills program that teaches violence prevention curriculum that aims to reduce impulsive and aggressive behavior while increasing social competence and empathy. The program builds on cognitive behavioral intervention models integrated with social learning theory, empathy research, and social information-processing theories. Each curriculum contains five teaching kits that build sequentially and cover empathy, emotion management, impulse control, problem solving, and anger management in developmentally and age-appropriate ways. Lessons use interpersonal

---

5. Browning et al., 2005; Howard et al., 2001; Orpinas et al., 2003.

situations presented in photos or video format and are also available in Spanish. Training videos and teacher guides provide comprehensive and detailed instructions for use as well as ways to incorporate the program into the school community and integrate with the grade-level curriculum. Second Step is part of SAMHSA's national registry of evidence-based programs and practices.

Steps to Respect: A Bullying Prevention Program is another program, along with Second Step, designed by the Committee for Children. All of the components of the Steps to Respect program are included in the Second Step Bullying Prevention Unit. The program is designed to prevent bullying by changing multiple levels of the school ecology through intervention components that affect schools and classrooms, peer norms and behavior, and individual attitudes, norms, and skills. The program underwent the most rigorous evaluation of a school-based bullying prevention program done in the United States and was shown to be successful for reducing bullying while having a positive impact on the school environment at all levels.[6]

For More Information

Committee for Children website: cfchildren.org/second-step

SOCIAL-EMOTIONAL LEARNING (SEL)

More than a bullying prevention program, social-emotional learning (SEL) is an entire educational movement gaining steam around the world. SEL addresses the systematic development of a core set of social and emotional skills that are proven to help children handle life challenges and thrive in both their learning and their social environments. The Collaborative for Academic, Social, and Emotional Learning (CASEL) website has identified five categories of social and emotional skills: self-awareness, self-management, social awareness, relationship skills, and responsible decision-making. These core SEL skills are also the foundational competencies that students need in order to deal with bullying, reduce the likelihood of future incidents, and create healthier peer relationships that boost a respectful school climate. Many SEL skills (such as "I-Messages," "Brainstorming," "HELPS to Resolve Conflicts," "How to CARE About a Bullied Peer") are labeled as "SEL Skills" and set off in boxes throughout this book (see the index for a complete list). They can be taught by

6. Brown et al., 2011.

classroom teachers, counselors, or mental health professionals and reinforced by the rest of the staff. Many schools teach one SEL skill per month or integrate SEL with their character education program.

Three Ways to Implement SEL Skills School-Wide

1. **A school-wide theme.** Introduce a bullying prevention theme each month such as respect, peacefulness, empathy, and responsibility, and use it school-wide to match a SEL skill. For example, for courage, students could learn upstander skills. See pages 170–176.

2. **A monthly skill.** Teach one social-emotional learning skill from this book each month and review it with students a few minutes each day. Send an email blast to all staff or post a sign in the faculty room to read the specific pages that address the skill. A counselor or psychologist could reinforce the skill with students who need more intensive review.

3. **Student-led trainings.** Students could teach the skill in cross-age groupings. Older students read the book section (for example, how to calm down or disagree respectfully), and then teach the skill to younger students as part of a service-learning requirement.

For More Information

CASEL website: casel.org

Restorative Justice Approaches to Bullying Prevention

Interest in restorative justice is growing after repeated studies show zero-tolerance policies are ineffective in making schools safer and reducing bullying. The zero-tolerance approach actually appears to backfire: schools with *higher* rates of school suspensions or expulsions are found to have *lower* ratings on school climate surveys and *higher* rates of student misbehavior, alienation, anxiety, rejection, and distrust of adults. The American Psychological Association's Zero Tolerance Task Force endorsed restorative justice as a promising alternative to zero tolerance.[7]

7. American Psychological Association Zero Tolerance Task Force, 2008.

The following are three of the most popular restorative justice approaches being adopted by schools to reduce bullying and repair relationships.

RESTORATIVE JUSTICE CIRCLES

Restorative Justice Circles attempt to nip bullying in the bud with a more preventative approach. Students are asked to listen to and support each other, work out solutions, repair relationships, and restore the school community through "talking circles" that are generally led by a teacher. Asking wrongdoers to make amends before resorting to punishment is a complete paradigm shift from traditional discipline, which focuses on punishment. The core belief of the approach is that people will make positive change when those in position of authority do things *with* them rather than *to* them or *for* them. The idea is to hold students accountable for their behavior and bring them together in peer-mediated small groups to talk, ask questions, and air grievances. The model addresses misbehavior in a way that strengthens relationships, focuses on the harm done rather than only on the rule-breaking, gives voice to the person harmed, and engages in collaborative problem solving.

Research is promising: a UC Berkeley study of a restorative justice program in Oakland showed an 89 percent drop in suspensions from 2006–2007;[8] a high school in West Contra Costa Unified School District cut their nearly 500 annual suspensions in half;[9] and Denver Public Schools achieved a 68 percent reduction in police tickets in the schools and a 40 percent reduction in school suspensions.[10]

For More Information

- *Implementing Restorative Practices in Schools* by Margaret Thorsborne and Peta Blood (Jessica Kingsley, 2013)
- *Restorative Circles in Schools* by Bob Costello, Joshua Wachtel, and Ted Wachtel (International Institute for Restorative Practices, 2010)
- *The Restorative Practices Handbook for Teachers, Disciplinarians and Administrators* by Bob Costello, Joshua Wachtel, and Ted Wachtel (International Institute for Restorative Practices, 2009)
- *Circle in the Square: Building Community and Repairing Harm in School* by Nancy Riestenberg (Living Justice Press, 2012)

8. Henderson, 2010.
9. Lumpkins and Marshall, 2012.
10. Fix School Discipline, 2016.

THE "NO BLAME" APPROACH OR SUPPORT GROUP METHOD

Developed in England almost three decades ago by Barbara Maines and George Robinson, this nonpunitive approach is gaining popularity among users but deemed more appropriate for nonphysical forms of bullying. The method has four key elements: the absence of blame, the encouragement of empathy, shared responsibility, and problem solving. Students identified as bullying others are confronted at a group meeting with vivid evidence of the target's distress derived from a previous interview with the targeted child (who is not present). Those present include students who have been selected because they are supportive of the target. Seven steps are involved in the method, which is facilitated by a trained staff member.

1. A trained facilitator such as a counselor, psychologist, or other staff member privately interviews the target to discover what happened and how the child has been affected by the bullying. The target is invited to describe his or her distress from the incident and to identify the perpetrators.

2. A meeting is arranged for all students involved. The target does not come but is represented by student supporters. It is made clear that perpetrators will not be punished.

3. The facilitator tells the students how the targeted student feels. A drawing, poem, or other piece of writing by the target illustrating his or her feelings about the incident may be included. The actual details of the bullying incident or blame of any student involved is purposely withheld from the explanation.

4. Each participant is expected to assume responsibility to improve the situation and is asked how they can help improve the situation. The focus is on resolving the problem without blaming those involved.

5. Each child suggests a way she or he could help the targeted child feel happier. Solutions to improve the situation are generated.

6. The meeting ends with students expected to take action to solve the problem.

7. A follow-up meeting is scheduled, usually with individual students, to assess if the situation has improved, if the targeted child feels better, and if the bullying has stopped. The outcome is carefully monitored through interviews with the perpetrator and target.

For More Information

- *Bullying: A Complete Guide to the Support Group Method* by George Robinson and Barbara Maines (SAGE Publications, 2008)
- *The Support Group Method Training Pack* by Barbara Maines and George Robinson (DVD plus facilitator's manual) (SAGE Publications, 2010)

" Brave Staff Chat: Are We Teaching Our Students Social Problem Solving?

At a staff meeting address questions like: "What programs do we have in place that help students learn social problem-solving skills or restorative justice strategies? What percentage of our students is involved in these programs? Which classes, grade levels, or students are we overlooking who might benefit from this approach? How could we become better models of social problem-solving skills to help students become proficient in them?"

THE SHARED CONCERN METHOD

Another nonpunitive method is called the Shared Concern Method. Originally designed in the 1980s by Anatol Pikas, a Swedish psychologist, it has been employed in schools in Sweden, Finland, England, Scotland, Spain, Canada, and Australia. The method aims to resolve problems between the child who bullies and the target by empowering students who contributed to the bullying (or who become aware of the incident) to find an acceptable solution to prevent further bullying. The process involves a trained staff member holding a series of meetings and individual private interviews with students identified as likely to have taken part in the bullying or to have supported it in some way. No accusations, threats, or blame are made. As soon as the students acknowledge some awareness of what has been happening, they are asked directly what can be done to help improve matters, and then they are joined by the target to negotiate an agreed-upon solution. The goal is to produce a constructive response that will help change the situation.

Although this approach can be time-consuming and does not work as well for all forms of bullying, outcomes are reported by educators to be overwhelmingly positive. The intervention can cause a shift in the group dynamics and provide a climate in which the students may engage in a negotiation process to bring about a peaceful and sustainable outcome.

For More Information

- *The Method of Shared Concern: A Positive Approach to Bullying in Schools* by Ken Rigby (Australian Council for Educational Research, 2011)
- *The Kids' Guide to Working Out Conflicts: How to Keep Cool, Stay Safe, and Get Along* by Naomi Drew (Free Spirit Publishing, 2004)

KEY BULLYING PREVENTION POINTS IN PART II

- A comprehensive, school-wide approach to bullying prevention starts with a group of committed staff members chaired by a strong leader.

- Effective bullying prevention isn't a prepackaged program, rather it's driven by evidence.

- Bullying assessments are critical and should include a range of formal and informal assessments that identify bullying types, targets, children who bully, the prevalence and frequency of aggressive behaviors, as well as the hot spots and times.

- One of the most effective means of bullying assessment is to hold student focus groups.

- Student bullying surveys provide data about your efforts and whether they are preventing and reducing peer cruelty.

- For a program to be successful, it needs to be implemented as specified and then used as a systemic, sustained endeavor.

- Any bullying prevention practice or program should fit the needs of your particular culture and students' ages and abilities, and it should be based on your data.

STUDENT BULLYING SURVEY

Circle yes or no. *Note:* If your answer is "sometimes" or "maybe," circle "yes."

1. Have you ever been a target of bullying at this school? . . . . Yes   No

2. Is bullying a problem at this school? . . . . Yes   No

3. Do you feel safe going to school? . . . . Yes   No

4. Have you ever not wanted to go to school because of bullying? . . . . Yes   No

5. If bullying could be stopped, would school be better? . . . . Yes   No

6. Should a target walk away from a person bullying to keep the peace? . . . . Yes   No

7. If you have been a target of bullying, did you tell a school adult? . . . . Yes   No

8. If yes, did the adult help you? . . . . Yes   No

9. If you have been a target, did you tell your parents? . . . . Yes   No

10. Is bullying a problem on the playground? . . . . Yes   No

11. Is bullying a problem on the school bus? . . . . Yes   No

12. Is bullying a problem in the cafeteria? . . . . Yes   No

13. Is bullying a problem in the hallways? . . . . Yes   No

14. Is bullying a problem in the classrooms? . . . . Yes   No

15. Is bullying a problem in the bathrooms? . . . . Yes   No

16. Write the number of times you have been bullied this week at school:

_____

17. If bullying is a problem, where is it happening most of the time?

18. What could be done to make this school feel safer for you?

19. Is there anything else you would like to say about bullying at this school?

TWELVE KEY QUESTIONS ABOUT BULLYING AND SCHOOL SAFETY

1. On a scale of 1 to 10 (1 = hardly ever; 10 = daily), how often do you see or experience bullying at school?

2. If you have seen someone bullied at school, what type of bullying was it?

   What happened?

   Did another student or teacher try to stop it?

   Is what happened pretty common or rare?

3. Of the bullying types (verbal, physical, emotional, or electronic), what is the type you or your peers witness or experience most often? Why?

4. Is there one class or group of students that bullies more than others? Which one? Why do you think they do?

$\longrightarrow$

5. "Cool spots" are places in the school where students feel safest and bullying happens least. Look at a map of your school and circle each cool spot. Now, put triangles on the "hot spots"—places where bullying happens most.

6. What makes some spots safe or not safe?

   What would make hot spots become cooler, safer zones?

7. Imagine your friend is being bullied. Would he or she get help from someone, such as a classmate, teacher, or principal? Who would help or not help?

   Why are students more likely to go to some adults more than others?

   What do adults do or say that would make a student *not* go to them for help?

   Put an "H" on places on your school map where students can go for help.

8. Does your school have options for students to report bullying or safety threats? If so, do students use those reporting options? Why or why not?

What could your school do so that students are more likely to report bullying that they witness or experience?

9. If students at your school see bullying, do they try to help? Why or why not?

What could your school do so that students are more likely to help when they see bullying?

10. What skills do you think students need so they're less likely to bully or be bullied?

11. If you were the principal, what would be the one thing you would do to make students feel safer in your school?

What could teachers do to reduce bullying?

12. Is there anything else you would like to ask or do you have other suggestions about bullying prevention?

Thank you for your help!

Part III

The 6Rs of Bullying Prevention

Rules, Recognize, Report, Respond, Refuse, Replace

R1: Rules

Establish an Anti-Bullying Policy and Expectations for Respect

In this chapter, you will learn:

• how and why to write a strong anti-bullying policy (or improve the one you already have)

• six parts of an effective anti-bullying policy

• possible consequences and disciplinary actions to include for bullying behavior

• what an example of a strong policy looks like

• ideas for introducing your anti-bullying policy to all stakeholders

• how to use class rules and student pledges to mobilize support for your policy

The first "R," or R1, of bullying prevention is to create a school-wide set of rules involving bullying—an anti-bullying policy. An anti-bullying policy alone won't stop bullying, but it can be the first step toward mobilizing stakeholders to realize that together you can make a difference. An effective policy fits your school values and district and state statutes, focuses on prevention, features strong parental involvement, builds a respectful climate, and gets everyone onboard. Developing an anti-bullying policy or refining the one you have is a crucial part of bullying prevention, and it is often the most time-consuming task. But the benefits of developing a well-written and thought-out policy are critical for creating a safe and caring school.

The anti-bullying policy creates the basis for stakeholders' expectations for prosocial student behaviors (such as being caring, respectful, and responsible) and consequences for bullying or aggressive behaviors. The policy also communicates your school values and beliefs, and guides your decision-making process for your bullying prevention efforts and your approach for guiding students' behaviors and character. When all stakeholders—including parents, school personnel, students, and the community—agree on those expectations and can communicate the rationale that guides them, bullying prevention efforts are more likely to succeed. This chapter describes everything you need to write an effective anti-bullying policy and clearly communicate that policy to all your stakeholders.

> ## " Brave Staff Chat
>
> Ask your staff to pair up at a meeting. For five minutes, each member describes an experience of bullying, such as one that she or he may have personally endured, or one his or her child or student encountered. The sharing can set the stage for broader discussions—suggested throughout this book—about the need for bullying prevention.

Getting Ready to Write a Strong Anti-Bullying Policy or to Improve an Existing One

The process of writing an effective anti-bullying policy involves serious time and energy, but it is the document that will become the foundation for all of your bullying prevention efforts. If you already have a policy in place, this is the time to review it and ensure it includes the elements covered in this chapter and, most importantly, that all stakeholders are informed of it. Here are steps to get started as an administrator, a task force, a bullying prevention team, or a group of concerned stakeholders:

1. **Review your school, district, county, and state policy.** Begin by determining if your school or district (or county) already has a policy and investigate your district, state, or provincial bullying statutes and existing regulations so you can utilize that language if possible.

2. **Examine past history.** Next, review any past history or complaints from parents, staff, and students about bullying to ensure that your new policy will address them. The administrator should determine from the district or school legal counsel and district office if any pending legal issues, state laws, policy requirements, board requirements, or models under federal law should be addressed.

3. **Analyze your existing rules and touchstones.** Revisit your current handbook, rules, code of conduct, mission statement, disciplinary procedures, and any previous policy to see if existing information can be incorporated into the new policy.

4. **Gather resources.** Finally, gather resources that will help you write a strong anti-bullying policy. Ask to view neighboring school district's anti-bullying policies—especially those districts with demographics similar to yours (economic base, size, grade levels, culture, and so on). Discuss what strengths and weaknesses are in each policy to help you develop or improve your plan. An online search will reap a wide array of resources.

> ## " Brave Staff Chat
>
> Rent a documentary about bullying, such as *Bully, Bullied to Silence,* or *Rats to Bullies,* that you feel would appeal most to your staff. Watch it together and then have a serious conversation about the need for school-wide bullying prevention and how your own school's policy (or lack of policy) is working. All stakeholders need to understand the reasons and benefits of reducing bullying, and in doing so have much stronger buy-in and commitment to bullying policy. The form "Assessing Our School's Anti-Bullying Policy" on pages 103–104 is a list of questions to discuss among your staff or team to gauge their receptivity to bullying prevention.

The Six Parts of an Effective Anti-Bullying Policy

The process of writing your policy will give you the opportunity to reflect on current research, your own beliefs, and your staff and students' unique needs, which is why simply copying another school's anti-bullying policy is *not* recommended. However, it is helpful to peruse model policies. As of this writing, all fifty U.S. states and many Canadian provinces have passed anti-bullying statutes, and hundreds of school anti-bullying policies are available online. Begin your writing process by referring to these samples.*

Though each anti-bullying policy differs, the most effective statements are *always* tailored to the individual school or district, cite their state/provincial statute, and outline their own beliefs, procedures, and programs for reducing bullying. The six key elements of an effective anti-bullying policy are detailed

---

* For example, *New Jersey State Model Policy* from the New Jersey Department of Education is a free PDF available to provide guidance: www.state.nj.us/education/parents/bully.pdf.

on the following pages. You may want to include more elements, but include these core parts at a minimum.

1. Statement of purpose for your stance against bullying

2. Clear definition of bullying

3. Responsibilities of stakeholders and instructions for reporting incidents

4. Description of the support for targeted students of bullying

5. Discipline procedures for bullying and strategies for behavior reform

6. Prevention and training procedures to counter bullying

A suggested template for your policy, "Our School's Anti-Bullying Policy," is on pages 105–106, and a sample policy begins below. Following the sample is a description of each essential part of an effective anti-bullying policy.

Tip for ADMINISTRATORS

Brainstorm where you will post your final anti-bullying policy for easy reference so all stakeholders can access it. For instance, on your website, in your student handbook, or giving a copy to all parents at conferences.

Figure 1.1: Sample of an Effective Anti-Bullying Policy

Anti-Bullying Policy for U.S. Army Garrison and DoDDS-E Schools Europe*

The U.S. Army Garrison and DoDDS-E Schools are committed to making our community and school safe, caring, and welcoming places for all our children and teens. We will treat each other with respect, and we will refuse to tolerate bullying in any form in our community or at our school.

Our community and school define *respect* as follows: Treat others with the dignity and regard you would want to be treated with.

Our community and school define *bullying* as follows: Bullying is a mean and one-sided activity intended to harm where those doing the bullying get pleasure from a targeted child's pain and/or misery. Bullying can be verbal, physical, and/or relational; have as its overlay race, ethnicity, religion, gender (including sexual orientation), physical, or mental ability; includes all forms of hazing and cyberbullying. It can be and often is continuous and repeated over time, however, once is enough to constitute bullying.

---

* DoDDS stands for Department of Defense Dependents Schools. While this policy is for military base schools, I chose it because of its comprehensiveness, clarity, and specific language. The policy was developed in partnership with Barbara Coloroso, and the terminology was adapted from her book *The Bully, the Bullied, and the Bystander* (HarperCollins, 2008).

Bullying that happens off of school grounds, including all forms of cyber-bullying, can impact the feeling of safety the targeted child has upon returning to school with the perpetrator(s) and can create an intimidating, hostile, or offensive environment for all students. The school and the Civilian Misconduct Action Authority (CMAA) will address these actions when necessary for the well-being and safety of the community and all students involved. All suspension and expulsion documents, if forwarded to the CMAA, may be used as aggravating factors when considering administrative action in juvenile civilian misconduct under Army Europe Regulation 27-9.

Examples of bullying include but are not limited to:

- Taunting

- Using put-downs, such as insulting or making fun of someone's race, religion, physical ability or disability, mental ability or disability, gender— including perceived or actual sexual orientation

- Threatening or ganging up on someone

- Stealing or damaging another person's things (stealing or damaging can also be considered a criminal offense)

- Spreading rumors about someone

- Physically hurting a targeted child, including but not limited to hitting, kicking, tripping, pushing, shoving

- Unwanted touching, patting, grabbing, hugging, kissing, cornering, blocking passage, bumping (can be considered a form of assault which is a criminal offense)

- Shunning or purposefully excluding a targeted student or trying to get other students not to play with targeted child

- Using a cell phone, gaming device, the Internet, or other social media to threaten, stalk, ridicule, humiliate, taunt, spread rumors, lock out of a game, or hack into a targeted child's account

- Hazing, i.e., "any intentional, knowing, or reckless act by one person alone or acting with others, directed against a student, that endangers the mental or physical health or safety of a student for the purpose of pledging, being initiated into, affiliating with, or holding office in an organization"

Adults in our community and staff at our school will do the following to prevent bullying and help children feel safe:

- Closely supervise children and teens in all areas of the Child, Youth, and School (CYS) Services and the school (to include the school and playground)

- Watch for signs of bullying behavior and stop it when it happens

- Teach the Steps to Respect program and/or other supplemental social skills lessons to increase awareness and empowerment in all children and teens in our school and CYS Services (It is the school culture and social environment that these policies, procedures, and programs create as well as reflect)

- Provide training opportunities for students and families regarding awareness and prevention of bullying

- Take seriously families' concerns about bullying and create a procedure for reporting

- Look into all reported bullying incidents and respond quickly and appropriately

- Assign consequences for bullying based on the school discipline code

- Maintain open communication between CYS Services staff and school staff for optimal support of all children involved in a bullying incident

- Provide immediate consequences for retaliation against students who report bullying

Children and teens in our community will do the following to prevent bullying:

- Treat each other respectfully

- Refuse to bully others

- Refuse to let others be bullied

- Refuse to watch, laugh, or join in when someone is being bullied

- Report bullying to an adult

- Try to include everyone in play and social interaction, especially those who are often left out

Discipline Procedures for Bullying in School

Consequences for bullying will always include a procedure for holding accountable for their actions the perpetrator(s) and any bystanders who played an active supporting role in the bullying. Other procedures can range from positive behavioral interventions to expulsion from school. These consequences are dependent on the nature and severity of the behavior, the age of the student, and the student's past behavior. The purpose of these procedures is for holding student(s) accountable for the bullying, preventing another occurrence, and protecting the targeted child. Consequences for bullying may include, but are not limited to the following:

- Notify parents/guardian of the incident and consequences

- Assisting the perpetrator(s) to find more appropriate ways to relate to peers

- Conference with teacher, principal, and/or parent

- Referral to school counselor

- Corrective instruction

- Behavior management plan

- Temporary removal from the classroom

- Loss of school privileges

- Classroom or administration detention

- In-school suspension

- Out-of-school suspension

- Legal action

- Expulsion

Note: If the school can handle the behavior problem internally, it is within its right to do so. Should the behavior escalate or present a danger to the order, discipline, and safety of the Garrison, the individual should be referred to the Assistant Civilian Misconduct Action Authority (ACMAA). Any behavior that constitutes a criminal act or breaks the law *has to* be reported to the military police with a notification to the ACMAA.

Discipline Procedure for Bullying in CYS Services

Consequences for bullying will always include a procedure for holding accountable for their actions the perpetrator(s) and any bystanders who played an active supporting role in the bullying. Other procedures can range from positive behavioral interventions to removal from the program. These consequences are dependent on the nature and severity of the behavior, the age of the child, and the child's past behavior. The purpose of these procedures is for holding perpetrator(s) accountable for the bullying, preventing another occurrence, and protecting the targeted child.

Consequences for bullying may include, but are not limited to the following:

- Notify parents/guardian of the incident and consequences

- Assisting the perpetrator(s) to find more appropriate ways to relate to peers

- Conference with child and/or parent

- Referral to Social Work Services, such as Social Work Services, Garrison Chaplain, and Military Family Life Counselors

- Corrective instruction

- Behavior management plan

- Community Service—as determined by the CMAA

- Temporary loss of CYS Services program privileges as determined by program director and CYS Services coordinator

- Loss of logistical support as determined by the CMAA

- Legal action

- Removal from all CYS Services programs

Note: If CYS Services can handle the behavior problem internally, it is within their right to do so. Should the behavior escalate, or present a danger to the order, discipline, and safety of the Garrison, the individual should be referred to the ACMAA. Any behavior that constitutes a criminal act or breaks the law *has to* be reported to the Military Police with a notification to the ACMAA.

Support for a Target of Bullying

The effects of bullying on the targeted child cannot be overemphasized. Isolation, lack of friends and/or support, and a feeling of helplessness that targets of bullying experience can be devastating. The Garrison and School will ensure that targeted children receive all support necessary. Actions may include but are not limited to:

- Notify parents/guardians immediately of the incident. Give them the method to use to report any further targeting of their child.

- Take effective measures to keep the targeted child safe at school and at CYS Services; give him or her tools to stand up to the perpetrator(s), and support to keep the targeted child from succumbing to the bullying.

- Identify a person or persons to whom the targeted child can safely report any further bullying incidents.

- Should the targeted child appear to be in immediate danger of hurting himself or herself, parents will be notified without delay. If parents are not available, the Military Police will be contacted and asked for an immediate and emergency referral to Social Work Services.

- Should the behavior be a concern to the well-being and safety of the community, the ACMAA will be contacted.

- Provide referrals to counseling services, such as Social Work Services, Garrison Chaplain, and Military Family Life Counselors.

- Maintain open communication between CYSS staff and school staff for optimal support of the targeted child.

Important Note on Discipline vs. Punishment

Punishment is adult oriented, imposes power from without, arouses anger and resentment, invites more conflict, exacerbates wounds rather than heals them; is preoccupied with blame and pain; does not consider reasons or look for solutions; does something to a student; involves a strong element of judgment; and demonstrates a teacher's ability to control a student.

Discipline is not judgmental, arbitrary, confusing, or coercive. It is not something we do to students. It is working with them. It is a process that gives life to a student's learning. It is restorative, and invites reconciliation. Its goal is to instruct, guide, and help students develop self-discipline—an ordering of the self from the inside, not an imposition from the outside.

The process of discipline does four things the act of punishment cannot do:

1. Shows students what they have done.

2. Gives them as much ownership of the problem as they can handle.

3. Gives them options for solving the problem.

4. Leaves their dignity intact.

For mistakes, mischief, and mayhem that unintentionally or intentionally create serious problems of great consequence, the **Three Rs**—restitution, resolution, and reconciliation—are incorporated into the four steps of discipline: **R.S.V.P.** Consequences need to be **R**easonable, **S**imple, **V**aluable, and **P**ractical.

Signed on:

School Principal:

Adapted from "The Bullying Policy" created by the United States Government.

Part 1: Statement of Purpose for Your Stance Against Bullying

Begin with a strong statement that describes your school's position against bullying behavior because your purpose is to provide a safe and caring learning environment. Specify that bullying of any kind, form, type, or level is unacceptable since it counters that purpose, and clarify that all bullying incidents will be taken seriously by stakeholders. State the range of detrimental effects of bullying on students and staff such as safety, school climate, student mental health, character, learning, and academic engagement. Also consider including your mission statement if it stipulates your staff's beliefs about the rights of students to be treated with respect and learn in a safe, caring environment. Here are examples of model policy statements:

"The (district name) board of education recognizes that a school that is physically and emotionally safe and secure for all students promotes good citizenship, increases student attendance and engagement, and supports academic achievement. To protect the rights of all students and groups for a safe and secure learning environment, the board of education prohibits acts of bullying, harassment, and other forms of aggression and violence. Bullying or harassment, like other forms of aggressive and violent behaviors, interferes with both a school's ability to educate its students and a student's ability to learn. All administrators, faculty, staff, parents, volunteers, and students are expected to refuse to tolerate bullying and harassment and to demonstrate behavior that is respectful and civil."* —Michigan State Board of Education

"The district board of education prohibits acts of harassment, intimidation, or bullying of a student. The district board of education has determined that a safe and civil environment in school is necessary for students to learn and achieve high academic standards; harassment, intimidation, or bullying, like other disruptive or violent behaviors, is conduct that disrupts both a student's ability to learn and a school's ability to educate its students in a safe and disciplined environment."** —New Jersey Office of Education

"Bullying of a student creates a climate of fear and disrespect that can seriously impair the student's health and negatively affect learning. Bullying undermines the safe learning environment that students need to achieve their full potential."*** —Rhode Island Statewide Bullying Policy

Part 2: A Clear Definition of Bullying

A clear definition of bullying is a key part of an anti-bullying policy. The definition should be easily understood by school boards, policymakers, administrators, staff, students, families, and the community. Use the definition provided in your state statute so the policy is consistent with state law (state board of education anti-bullying policies are available online) as well as the most current definition used by researchers and leading experts. (See StopBullying.gov and apa.com). Here are examples:

"Bullying is unwanted, aggressive behavior among school aged children that involves a real or perceived power imbalance. The behavior is repeated, or has the potential to be repeated, over time." —StopBullying.gov

---

* From *Model Anti-Bullying Policy*, michigan.gov.
** From *Model Policy and Guidance for Prohibiting Harassment, Intimidation, and Bullying on School Property, at School-Sponsored Functions, and on School Buses*, www.state.nj.us/education/parents/bully.htm.
*** From *Statewide Bullying Policy*, sos.ri.gov.

"A person is bullied when he or she is exposed, repeatedly and over time, to negative actions on the part of one or more other persons, and he or she has difficulty defending himself or herself." —Dan Olweus, *Bullying at School* (Blackwell, 1993)

Most schools now also include a definition of electronic or cyberbullying in their policies:

"'Cyberbullying' includes the transmission of harassing communications, direct threats, or other harmful texts, sounds, or images on the Internet, social media, or other technologies using a telephone, computer, or any wireless communication device. Cyberbullying also includes breaking into another person's electronic account and assuming that person's identity in order to damage that person's reputation."* —Irvine Unified School District

In addition, include all the forms of bullying such as physical, verbal, and emotional bullying or relational aggression and provide clear examples of each such as the following:

- Physical violence such as hitting, pushing, or spitting at another student
- Interfering with another student's property by stealing, hiding, or damaging it
- Verbal bullying such as using offensive names when addressing another student
- Taunting or spreading rumors about another student or his or her family
- Ridiculing another student's appearance, way of speaking, or personal mannerisms
- Belittling another student's abilities and achievements
- Writing offensive notes or graffiti about another student
- Emotional bullying such as excluding another student from a group activity
- Cyberbullying such as misusing technology (Internet or mobile) to hurt or humiliate another person

---

* From the *Board Policy on Bullying/Cyberbullying*, iusd.org.

Part 3: Responsibilities of Stakeholders and Instructions for Reporting Incidents

This section of the policy clarifies what the staff, students, or parents should do if they witness bullying and the protocol used for reporting the incident in a timely and responsive manner. Specify that reporting may be done anonymously for protection against possible retaliation. Consider adding the clause: "Individuals who knowingly fabricate reports may be subject to disciplinary action." Include the procedure staff should take for promptly investigating and responding to any report of an incident. And stress that the goal is for all stakeholders to work together to combat and, hopefully, stop bullying. (See chapter R2: Recognize for more details on reporting.)

Some policies specify students' responsibilities in witnessing bullying incidents such as the Rhode Island Department of Education's *Statewide Bullying Policy*: "Students who observe an act of bullying or who have reasonable grounds to believe that bullying is taking place must report the bullying to school authorities. Failure to do so may result in disciplinary action. The victim of bullying, however, shall not be subject to discipline for failing to report the bullying."[*]

Include the stipulation that the policy applies to incidents that happen on the school site, in school-sponsored activities, on school-provided transportation, or on school-owned technology. The California Department of Education states in their *Sample Policy for Bullying Prevention*: "This policy applies to students on school grounds while traveling to and from school or a school-sponsored activity, during the lunch period, whether on or off campus, and during a school-sponsored activity."[**]

Part 4: Description of the Support for Targeted Students of Bullying

Specify the rights of children with respect to bullying at school and what stakeholders will do to keep targeted children safe. Stress that anyone who becomes the target of bullying should not suffer in silence and will be supported by the school. You might describe intervention and prevention strategies that will be provided to help students who are targets of bullying. Also include procedures for:

- Immediately intervening to protect a target from additional bullying or retaliation

- Notifying the parents of the targeted student

---

[*] From *Statewide Bullying Policy*, sos.ri.gov.
[**] From *Sample Policy for Bullying Prevention*, cde.ca.gov.

- Referring the target, perpetrator, and others to counseling or other appropriate mental health services, if needed

- Notifying law enforcement officials, if necessary

(See also chapter R5: Refuse for ways a school can support targets.)

Part 5: Discipline Procedures for Bullying and Strategies for Behavior Reform

The fifth section of your policy describes your investigative procedures and disciplinary action for bullying incidents. Clarify the action you will take to respond to the needs of both bullied and bullying students and how records will be kept. Include a plan for notifying students, students' families, and staff of policies related to bullying and contacting relevant professionals, such as a behavior management team, psychologist, social worker, nurse, or law enforcement official, if necessary. Include a detailed description of a graduated range of possible consequences for bullying. (Refer to chapter R6: Replace for specific ways to determine and implement consequences and interventions for the child who bullies.) Include disciplinary procedures and policies that are required by the state and district code of conduct. The *Model Anti-Bullying Policy* of the Michigan State Board of Education also describes factors for determining consequences for bullying (note their final clause regarding impartiality!):

> Specify that bullying of any kind, form, type, or level is unacceptable and all bullying incidents will be taken seriously by stakeholders.

"The following factors, at a minimum, shall be given full consideration by school administrators in the development of the procedures for determining appropriate consequences and remedial measures for each act of harassment or bullying: Age, development, and maturity levels of the parties involved; degree of harm (physical and/or emotional distress); surrounding circumstances; nature and severity of the behavior(s); incidences of past or continuing pattern(s) of behavior; relationship between the parties involved; context in which the alleged incident(s) occurred. *Note:* In order to ensure students' perception of fair and impartial treatment, a student's academic or athletic status is not a legitimate factor for determining consequences. Consequences must be perceived as fair and impartial."[*]

Stress in writing that the ultimate goal in bullying prevention is to take proactive steps to prevent bullying from occurring and help replace aggressive

[*]From *Model Anti-Bullying Policy*, michigan.gov.

behavior with prosocial behaviors. You might include strategies or programs you will use to promote healthy communication, conflict resolution skills, restorative justice, social and emotional learning, character education, respect for cultural and individual differences, assertiveness training, and appropriate online behavior.

Part 6: Prevention and Training Procedures to Counter Bullying

The final section of your policy describes what your staff will do to prevent bullying and help your students feel safe. Some policies describe the programs and procedures they will use to reinforce their anti-bullying policy and promote positive behavior and a safe learning environment. Stress you are using a comprehensive, research-based approach tailored to your population's unique needs.

You could state how you will offer *all* stakeholders training to prevent, identify, and respond to bullying and list the specific strategies that will be implemented to achieve those results. Include how you will monitor and review this policy and list specific ways your students, staff, and parents can prevent bullying and create safe and caring learning environments.

Possible Consequences and Disciplinary Actions for Bullying Behavior

The goal of imposing consequences is to stop bullying, send a message that aggression is unacceptable, repair relationships, and offer an intervention to prevent future bullying. All consequences need to be supported by the school board policies (as well as local, state/provincial, and federal laws) included in your anti-bullying policy and published in your handbook or posted on the school website so that stakeholders are aware of the consequences *prior* to the incident.

What follows are suggestions for types of consequences that can be imposed based on three levels of bullying: mild, moderate, and severe. Consequences may be combined in any order and should always be tailored to the child's age, ability, and intentions as well as the duration, severity, and frequency of the bullying incident.

At each level, the parent or legal guardian—of both the child *doing* the bullying and the child *being* bullied—need to be notified by the staff in the form of a written warning. In addition, children engaging in bullying can be required to notify (via note, phone call from school, or face-to-face conference) their parents to describe their bullying behavior. The form should be signed by the parent, returned, and then filed by school officials. Document and file all correspondence, consequences, and conferences, and thoroughly complete all bullying reports. *Note:* The actual consequence given to the child is to be kept confidential. Only the child who bullied, his or her parents or guardians, and appropriate staff should be aware of those specific disciplinary actions. (For more details, see "Five Steps to Setting the Right Consequences for Bullying" on page 223.)

LEVEL 1: CONSEQUENCES FOR FIRST OFFENSE, OR YOUNGER CHILDREN

Conference with the student about the incident: include behavior coaching by the counselor, teacher, or trained staff, and give a clear, strong message that bullying is unacceptable, that behavior will be closely monitored, and that if bullying continues, more severe consequences will be immediately assigned.

LEVEL 2: CONSEQUENCES FOR SECOND OR THIRD BULLYING OFFENSE

Issue a disciplinary referral to the child who engages in bullying as well as conferences with administrator involvement and appropriate staff members, which includes behavior coaching in addition to one or more staff-selected sanctions, such as:

Consequences That Require Reparation for Damages

- Make reparations for any items damaged or stolen: child required to pay for, replace, or repair the belongings if responsible for the damage.

- Deliver an apology to make amends to the targeted child (only *if* the targeted child agrees) and under the guidance of a staff member. (A written apology is recommended.) This should only be a consequence if the staff believes that the child engaging in bullying will deliver a sincere apology.

- Complete a "Think Sheet" describing what the child did wrong, how the action affected others, and what she or he will do to "right the wrong" and not repeat the scenario.

- Participate in (adult-monitored) restorative justice or no-blame approach. See page 65 for details.

Consequences to Educate Student About Negative Effects of Bullying

- Create a school PSA or poster about why bullying is wrong.

- Write a reflective essay describing the negative effects of bullying on the school and the targeted child.

- View a video of the school's anti-bullying assembly or training and write a report.

- Review the school's anti-bullying policy and write a paper describing specific values and rules that were broken in the incident and a plan for restitution.

- View age-appropriate bullying films such as *Bully*, *Mean Girls*, or *The Ant Bully*, and then answer teacher-designed questions about the harm of bullying.

- Read a children's literature selection about bullying and write a book report.

- Write a report describing how you will "retire" from bullying.

- Write a paper on the emotional and physical ramifications of bullying.

Consequences That Involve Social-Emotional Skill Remediation

- Conduct a lesson about empathy and present it to a staff member or class of younger students (it is not advised to have the student present a lesson to her or his own class).

- Participate in social-emotional skill training, such as impulse control, empathy building, or problem solving with the school counselor, social worker, nurse, or psychologist.

- Meet with a school counselor or psychologist for behavior coaching or intervention.
- Take a class on anger management from the school counselor or in an after-school program.
- Meet with a staff member to develop a behavior management plan and receive corrective instruction during recess and after school.

Consequences That Involve a Service Project

- Be a cross-age tutor (in an area of interest or ability) to a younger student.
- Read bullying prevention books to a younger student or group of younger students.
- Teach a younger student bullying prevention or anger management strategies.
- Do chores at the school or help the custodian, cafeteria worker, secretary, or librarian.
- Do monitored community service hours, such as helping at an animal shelter or food bank.

Consequences That Involve Deprivation of School Privileges

- Be removed from area where bullying took place and/or prevented from being near the target.
- Forfeit recess or school activities.
- Forfeit the privilege of eating in the cafeteria and eat lunch served in the office.
- Be temporarily removed from the classroom to spend time in the office or another classroom.

LEVEL 3: SEVERE BULLYING INCIDENT OR RECURRING BULLYING

- Undergo in-school suspension.
- Attend Saturday school or an after-school suspension (check district regulations).
- Undergo out-of-school suspension.
- Receive a police or community agency reference, if required.

- Face legal action, if warranted (via state/provincial code).

- Receive a recommendation for expulsion (maximum consequence).

See chapter R6: Replace for more information on selecting consequences for bullying behavior and determining interventions.

Ways to Roll Out Your Anti-Bullying Policy to All Stakeholders

In order to succeed in reducing bullying and creating a safe and caring environment for students, your staff and/or team need to clearly communicate the school's anti-bullying policy and procedures to *all* stakeholders: staff, students, parents, and community members. Remember, you need to reach out to embrace the entire school community: parents, students, administrators, teachers, counselors, psychologists, nurses, coaches, secretaries, bus drivers, custodians, paraprofessionals, after-school staff, yard duty, substitutes—everyone should be aware of your new policy and procedures and understand the seriousness of your stance against bullying behavior. Your first rollout is with your staff; your next step is to communicate the same message to parents, community, and students; your final step is to reinforce the rules to your students in classrooms or private conferences with individual students. Following are those key steps.

> 93 percent of school employees report their district has implemented a bullying prevention policy, but just over half (54 percent) said they have received training related to the policy.[1]

"Our staff always talked about bullying prevention, but it wasn't until our team handed out our anti-bullying policy that we worked as a united front and started to see real change in student behavior." —middle school teacher, Austin, Texas

INTRODUCE YOUR ANTI-BULLYING POLICY TO ALL STAFF MEMBERS

Once your policy is completed and approved by the higher levels (school board, district office, and perhaps county office of education), share it with your staff at a special meeting. Consider also inviting board members, district office administrators, and key community stakeholders. You may have to do several

---

1. Bradshaw et al., 2011.

sessions to accommodate many busy schedules. Some teams create a slide-show presentation depicting key points. Each participant then receives a copy of the policy and signs it to verify they have read and understand it. (I can't tell you how many times I've asked educators at my workshops whether they have read their school's anti-bullying policy. Though most raise their hands to say that their school has one, only a very small number admit that they have actually reviewed it.) Stakeholders need to recognize that once the policy is confirmed it may be legally binding. Buy-in to bullying prevention begins with the majority of your staff understanding each of the six elements in your anti-bullying policy and committing to honor those points.

> ## " Brave Staff Chat
>
> Some bullying prevention teams or faculties read and candidly discuss a short excerpt at a staff meeting from a stirring book that deals with memoirs of childhood bullying. A few that tend to resonate with adults include: *Bullying Under Attack: True Stories Written by Teen Victims, Bullies, and Bystanders; Please Stop Laughing at Me;* and *Vicious: True Stories by Teens About Bullying*.

ROLL OUT THE POLICY TO PARENTS, STUDENTS, AND COMMUNITY MEMBERS

Your next step is to announce the policy to parents, students, and the community at one big event. The whole school/community approach sends a clear "We're serious!" statement. Plaster your anti-bullying message on your marquee, fill balloons, and invite media, police department, youth coaches, school board, district office employees, scout leaders, and anyone else who touches your students' lives. Then hold a formal policy-signing assembly with *all* key stakeholders and community officials in attendance.

Ideas for Announcing Your Policy to Students

Over the years, I've witnessed dozens of anti-bullying policy rollouts, but the most effective always involve staff, students, *and* parents. You don't need to hire pricey, nationally known speakers; the best events are locally focused. This is your staff's opportunity to introduce their expectations for respectful behavior so that all stakeholders hear the same message. Here are a few suggestions:

Have students mobilize peer support. Enlist the help of concerned, willing students to mobilize the support of their peers for the school's anti-bullying policy. These students can design posters, quotes, buttons, T-shirts, and anti-bullying pledges. On the assembly day, they can enlist peers to sign the pledge with skits, songs, or speeches. (Parents are far more likely to attend an assembly if their kids are part of the agenda.)

Use a book. A former superintendent in Alberta introduced his district's bullying policy by reading the children's book *Hey, Little Ant* to students at an assembly. It's a wonderful parable about empathy that asks listeners to look at life from a small insect's point of view. He used the story to start a discussion about the district's policy on respect ("What would you do if the small ant you were about to step on looked up at you and started to talk?") It hooked students. Another principal scanned illustrations from *The Giving Tree* into a slide presentation (with necessary permissions) and read the book at an assembly as a catalyst for discussing the school's expectations for students to be "giving and caring."

Use a song. Many schools use the picture book *Don't Laugh at Me* (accompanied by a recording of the song) and play snippets of the melody over the loudspeaker to remind students of their policy. Other schools use the theme songs from TV shows like *Friends* or *Cheers* (a place "where everybody knows your name, and they're always glad you came"). Or have kids nominate their favorite songs.

Try a visual symbol. KLO Middle School in Kelowna, British Columbia, calls itself "The Blue Balloon School" after their principal shared the anti-bullying policy at an assembly. She held up a blue balloon and said: "We inflate people here, not deflate them," and then stated her expectations for respect on a large screen combined with images. Each student was given a blue balloon stapled to the policy to share at home. Staff members decorated the school with blue balloons and hung a huge blue parachute as visual reminders of the behavior expectations. Best yet, students learned them. "We're the 'Blue Balloon School' because we inflate, not deflate people," they told me. The mnemonic worked!

Tip for TEACHERS

Hold a contest for students to develop a motto for their classroom or school about what you stand for. A few student-created ideas I've seen: "We Care!" "The Builder-Upper School," and "The Place Where Kids Want to Be." Students then vote for their favorite motto and post signs on their classroom or school doors as a visual reminder.

Make a video. Students, the school principal, and the base commander at the school on the U.S. Army Base in Ramstein, Germany, made a video together that described their new anti-bullying policy. The video was then posted on their school website as well as shown at a school assembly and played over a PSA monitor in the school entrance. It sent a very strong message.

Develop a welcome packet. New students, parents, and staff are bound to move into your school throughout the year. Keep an extra copy of any video, pledge, rule book, or poster that your site introduces to your stakeholders and present it to any new community member. Doing so will help keep everyone abreast of your bullying prevention efforts.

Tip for ADMINISTRATORS

A powerful way to help students understand that acts of bullying will *not* be taken lightly is to use "the Airport Rule" developed by José Bolton and Stan Graeve in their book *No Room for Bullies*.[2] The rule is simple: "If you say hurtful words or make negative comments to others, you will be detained. If you engage in hurtful behaviors or make threatening gestures toward others, you will be detained." The metaphor conveys that the school's anti-bullying policy should be taken just as seriously as an airport's strict code of conduct, and violators will be held accountable for their actions.

Ideas for Announcing Your Anti-Bullying Policy to Parents

The best bullying prevention efforts always involve and educate parents on an ongoing basis. Let parents know that introducing your school's policy and helping them understand it is but the first of many events about bullying prevention that will involve them. Write a letter announcing the policy and mail it to each home inviting your students' families to the policy-signing assembly. Enclose a shortened version of the policy for each parent to review prior to the assembly and state that the longer version is at the school's website for their perusal. Here are more ideas:

- Have students write personal invitations to their parents to attend the assembly, which are far more likely to be read.

- Put a section in each school newsletter or correspondence piece about bullying.

2. Bolton and Graeve, 2005, p. 114.

- Ask PTO or parent groups to send email blasts or make phone calls to parents to enlist support for the policy.

- Post the date and time of the assembly on your outside school marque for the community to view.

- Involve students in the assembly in any way you can—this is always more likely to draw parents to the event.

- Make a video of the assembly and post it at your website for parents unable to attend.

- Give parents a list of questions about the policy to discuss with their kids.

- Assign the policy as homework: parents read it with their kids, sign a copy stating they've read it, and return it.

- Keep the signed copy in each child's file in case it needs to be reviewed with the parent.

Ideas for Sharing Bullying Prevention Efforts with Your Community

Reach out to introduce your policy to all community members, such as law enforcement, the city council, the mayor's office, pediatricians, local media, religious groups, Rotary members, scout leaders, Boys' and Girls' Clubs, YMCAs and YWCAs, youth coaches, and others. They can be instrumental in offering support for your efforts as well as spreading the message to your community. Invite these stakeholders to your assembly and then ask for their help. Here are a few unique ways I've seen schools involve communities in their anti-bullying policy rollout:

Create bullying prevention placemats. Middle school students in Cold Lake, Alberta, partnered with their local Denny's restaurant. The students made placemats by decorating construction paper sheets with anti-bullying logos that supported their school's new policy. Customers not only ate their meals on the placemats, but continued talking about the school's policy long afterward in the community.

Adopt a business. One principal divided students into groups and assigned each group to a local business (bank, store, real estate firm, etc.) with an adult mentor. Once a month the students designed posters describing the character trait the school was addressing that month (such as respect, kindness, and justice) to prevent bullying and create a caring learning environment. Businesses then hung the students' posters in their windows and the whole community came onboard to support the school's efforts.

Hold poster contests. Many schools give students a cooperative task of designing an anti-bullying poster that depicts why bullying should not be tolerated. Completed posters are hung in the school halls and a few prominent community members (such as the mayor or the sheriff) choose the winning entries, which are published in the local newspaper. Another city had a local print shop turn the posters into huge banners that were displayed around the city.

Tip for TEACHERS

Have your students make individual placemats to bring home that depict your class rules and the school norms for caring and respectful behaviors. Primary teachers have had students write simple manners and respectful comments ("Please," "Excuse me," "Would you like a seat?" "Please pass," "Thank you") on their placemats, laminated them, and used them at lunchtime in the cafeteria. Courtesy dramatically increased!

Help Students Develop Class Rules About Bullying

An important strategy in bullying prevention and reinforcing your school's anti-bullying policy is for teachers and students to agree on class rules about bullying. While each class may already have general rules that govern student conduct and work ethics (see Part I of this book for suggestions), these rules should focus *specifically* on bullying and treating each other with respect. And if students are involved in creating their own rules, they are more likely to follow them and take responsibility for creating a caring climate. Once created, teachers should continue discussing the rules with students throughout the year. In addition, any new student (as well as parent) should be introduced to the class rules as soon as possible. Here are some ideas to consider when creating class rules on bullying:

Discuss students' dreams for their classroom. Class meetings are a great venue for talking about bullying and creating a respectful classroom tone. First, review the "Class Rules That Create Respectful Classrooms and Reduce Bullying" on page 100 with students. Then discuss questions that elicit the hopes and dreams students have for the kind of class they want to be part of. See the form on page 107. Write the core traits on chart paper (such as safe, respectful, caring, nice, friendly); these can help generate your class rules on bullying. You might also give students pieces of paper cut into cloud shapes where they can each draw or write their dream for the classroom. Review the dreams to find similarities and then create a few rules for a caring classroom based on students' dreams. You might hang the "dream clouds" on your classroom wall. The children's books *I Have a Dream* and *My Dream of Martin Luther King* can help motivate the discussion.

Be a "Peaceable Classroom." Some teachers read *The Peaceable Kingdom* or display an image of Edward Hicks's famous 1832 painting *The Peaceable Kingdom* to initiate a class discussion about rules. Then ask: "What would a peaceable classroom where everyone gets along and helps each other look and sound like?" (Student answers might include: no bullying, smiling, feeling welcome, no put-downs, including everyone, no hurting others, feeling safe, no gossiping.)

Use the Golden Rule. Introduce the concept of the "Golden Rule" to students. (*The Golden Rule* by Ilene Cooper and *The Berenstain Bears and the Golden Rule* by Jan Berenstain and Stan Berenstain are helpful to introduce the concept to young students.) Then write the phrase, "In this room we treat others the way we'd like to be treated . . ." on the board or chart paper. On paper strips cut into 4" x 11" lengths, each student writes or draws the one character trait (older students can do up to four) that best describes how they hope to be treated (such as, respectfully, kindly, fairly, justly, compassionately). Students tape their virtues to the board at the end of the phrase. Review students' character traits and then create your class rules based on the "Golden Rule" and their wishes.

Students vote for their top three rules. Working in groups of four, each student draws or writes three rules they want for their class. In round-robin style, in each group students pass their papers to the person to their right, and students mark the rule on each paper they feel is most important to helping them get along and not bully. Students continue passing the papers until they have their own paper back, and then they tally which rule in their group received the most votes and report their findings to the class. Duplicate rules are eliminated and the top three rules gathered from the total group become the class rules.

Make a "Class Rule Pizza." Cut a large circle out of butcher paper then slice the circle into as many pie pieces as there are students in your class. Have each student write their number one rule to stop bullying on their pizza slice and then glue the whole pizza together with slices listing similar rules placed next to one another. Guide students to analyze results: "Did many students write the same rule? How are different rules related? Would these rules help us in our classroom?" The lesson usually reaps about five rules from a typical class and the group pizza can be referred to throughout the year.

Read books about rule-making. Here are a few favorite children's books that address rule-making and help generate a class discussion: *Know and Follow Rules* by Cheri J. Meiners, *Following Rules* by Cassie Mayer, *If Everybody Did* by Jo Ann Stover, *No Rules for Michael* by Sylvia A. Rouss, *Rules* by Cynthia Lord, *Rules for School* by Alec Greven, *The Golden Rule* by Ilene Cooper, *The Berenstain Bears and the Golden Rule* by Jan Berenstain and Stan Berenstain, and *What If Everybody Did That?* by Ellen Javernick.

Class Rules that Create Respectful Classrooms and Reduce Bullying

Effective class rules are clear, simple, age-appropriate and written in positive terms so they explain what to do instead of what not to do. The best rules help set a respectful tone and clearly state that bullying is not tolerated. They should address direct bullying (a face-to-face attack on the target) and indirect bullying (such as social isolation, gossip, or cyberbullying). And the optimum rules are ones that your students create themselves and are not copied from another class or published list. The more involved your students are in developing their own rules, the more likely they will own them. Here are some examples:

- We treat each other with respect and kindness.
- We listen to others' opinions and respect everyone's ideas.
- We think about the feelings of others.
- We try to help students who are bullied and speak out for those who need support.
- We include everyone so no one is left out.
- We say only nice things that build people up.
- We write only kind things off- and online about others.
- We look for the good in others and value their differences.
- We make everyone feel welcome.
- We are helpful, not hurtful.
- If someone is bullied, we report it to an adult at school or at home.

Use Student Anti-Bullying Pledges

Anti-bullying policies are written for adults and are often not very kid-friendly reading, so, in addition to writing class rules, many schools invite students to write their own school anti-bullying pledge. Pledges serve as a promise by students to their classmates not to bully others and to help support a caring, safe school environment. Numerous pledges are available online, but students can also develop their own. Some administrators roll out their school's bullying prevention efforts by having students sign the pledge and then start each school day by having students recite the pledge. The trick is to find a way to help students not only memorize the words but also take them to heart. Doing so requires repeated practice and repetition so students finally see the words as an integrated part of their classroom community.

One way to help is by commenting when students demonstrate the behavior: "Thank you, Kevin, for sticking up for your classmate and showing what our pledge looks like." "Jenna, I noticed how you made sure our new classmate had someone to sit with at recess. That's being a caring community member and demonstrating our pledge." Or, consider having your students acknowledge one another at your class meetings ("Did anyone see a member of our community who was demonstrating our school pledge today?") or in writing ("If you hear or see a classmate demonstrating our school pledge, please write his or her name on the board so we can discuss it later.").

Some examples of effective anti-bullying pledges:

"We will not bully other students. We will try to help students who are bullied. We will include students who might be left out. When we know somebody is being bullied, we will tell an adult at school and at home."

"I will not make anyone feel bad or afraid on purpose. I will not join others who are being mean, or hurting, or scaring another boy or girl and I will try to help anyone who is bullied to the best of my ability."

"I agree not to bully other students. I will try to help students who are bullied. I will include students who are left out."

KEY BULLYING PREVENTION POINTS IN R1: RULES

- Schools that are effective in reducing bullying involve all stakeholders (staff, students, parents, and community members), identify strong anti-bullying practices and procedures, and then develop a policy that fits their culture and students' needs.

- A clear definition of bullying is a key part of an anti-bullying policy. The definition should be easily understood and interpreted by school boards, policymakers, administrators, staff, students, students' families, and the community.

- The anti-bullying policy needs to specify tiered consequences for bullying, which consider ages, maturity, intent, and frequency.

- Introduce your policy to all community members who can be instrumental in offering support for your efforts as well as spreading the message to your community.

- Introduce parents to your policy and procedures and help them understand it is the first of many events about bullying that will involve them.

- An important strategy in bullying prevention and reinforcing the school's anti-bullying policy is for teachers and students to agree on class rules specifically about bullying.

ASSESSING OUR SCHOOL'S ANTI-BULLYING POLICY

1. Why do we need an anti-bullying policy?

2. What are the benefits for our students?

3. What is our timeline? How often can we meet and when should the policy be completed?

4. How will all stakeholders—staff, parents, students, and the community—be informed of the policy?

5. How will we generate buy-in and commitment from all of our stakeholders?

6. How will we train all our staff in the elements and to comply with the policy?

7. Which stakeholders need to approve our policy?

- ☐ State/provincial board of education
- ☐ County board of education
- ☐ District personnel
- ☐ School board
- ☐ School staff
- ☐ Students
- ☐ Parents
- ☐ Others? _____

8. Should our staff be involved in approving our final policy? If so, how?

9. If there is a disagreement in the language or elements, who will make the final decision regarding the content?

10. How will we verify that our staff has reviewed the policy?

OUR SCHOOL'S ANTI-BULLYING POLICY

The purpose of this Anti-Bullying Policy is:

Our school and staff are committed to:

Our school values and vision for our students are:

Our community and school define *respect* as follows:

Our community and school define *bullying* as follows:

Examples of bullying include but are not limited to:

Verbal bullying:

Physical bullying:

Emotional bullying:

Electronic bullying:

How All Stakeholders Will Prevent Bullying and Help Children Feel Safe

Adults in our community and staff at our school will do the following to prevent bullying and help children feel safe:

Children in our community will do the following to prevent bullying:

Discipline Procedures for Bullying in School

We believe:

Consequences for bullying may include, but are not limited to the following:

Support for a Target of Bullying

What our staff and community will do to support a child who is the target of bullying:

Important Notes on Bullying

This policy will be made public and may be read in the following places and sources:

Date: _____

Signature: _____

WHAT KIND OF CLASS DO YOU WANT TO BE PART OF?

1. What are your hopes for your class this year?

2. Describe the perfect classroom in which you can learn your best . . .

3. How would students treat each other in this classroom?

4. What kinds of things would kids say or do in this classroom?

5. What kinds of things would you *not* hear or see kids do?

6. What kinds of rules would help us have that kind of class?

7. Do you think there would be more or less bullying? Why?

8. How might class rules help us get along with each other?

9. If you could write *one* rule that would make your dreams come true for this class, what would it be?

R2: Recognize

Teach Stakeholders How to Recognize Bullying

In this chapter, you will learn:

• the most widely accepted definitions of bullying

• four elements of bullying behavior and five different types of bullying

• simple strategies to teach staff members how to recognize bullying behaviors

• ten ideas for helping parents understand and identify bullying

• five ways to help students review the types of bullying

• effective ways to teach students the difference between teasing and bullying

The second "R," or R2, of bullying prevention is ensuring that all stakeholders in the process—students, staff, parents, and community members—learn to recognize bullying behavior and use the same definition. Inconsistency in definitions is disastrous to prevention efforts since each adult and student may respond to and report bullying incidents differently. And if everyone interprets the situation differently, collecting evidence to help you develop prevention plans will be impossible. Effective bullying prevention teaches stakeholders how to identify bullying and provides ongoing training so that everyone can respond quickly, appropriately, and consistently.

But there's another reason why R2 is crucial: a staff's mixed and inconsistent response sends a troublesome message to students that the adults in charge aren't committed to bullying prevention. It may even convey to students who are bullying that they can get away with their behavior. It also breaks down parents' trust in the school's efforts to stop bullying and that means the staff—especially administrators—will have a backlog of complaints from parents concerned that the school isn't taking bullying seriously.

This chapter shows how to help all stakeholders get on the same bullying prevention page. When everyone uses the same bullying definition, responds to student aggression consistently, and demonstrates a serious tone, your school will be far more successful in stopping aggressive behaviors and replacing them with respect and caring.

"The teachers help kids sometimes if there's bullying but not always. I don't think they really care about stopping it." —Jenna, age 12

Helping Stakeholders Understand What Bullying Is

Bullying is one of the most widely used terms in the education world today, as well as in the general public: a Google search reaps over 94 million hits, and counting. A media story about the topic is a daily occurrence, and for good reason: bullying can be devastating to children's mental health and moral, emotional, and cognitive development. That's why educators, parents, experts, and citizens alike are concerned about bullying behaviors and searching for answers. But a big stumbling block to success is that people often use different definitions of the term *bullying*. Just recently, several parents contacted me about how to stop what they considered to be bullying behaviors:

"There's a girl at school who is always teasing my child. Why are so many kids bullying these days?"

"My son and his friends constantly fight over their toys. They have to stop bullying each other!"

"My daughter's best friend stopped talking to her and said she had a new pal. Bullying has got to end!"

"A kid smashed my son on the head with a bottle. Is that bullying? What do I do about it?"

While all of these incidents involve hurtful types of behaviors, none fit the recognized definition of bullying. Teasing, conflict, arguing, and even assault don't constitute bullying. This doesn't mean that the behaviors in each instance don't warrant concern or require any less attention, but responses to the issues are different from those that involve actual bullying behaviors. And therein lies the hurdle: if everyone uses a different definition, you'll always fall short in implementing effective bullying prevention.

"It wasn't until we had a staff training to understand bullying that we started to get onboard as a staff. What we needed was a common definition of bullying." —teacher, San Jacinto Unified School District

The first step of R2 is to help all stakeholders understand the definition of bullying used in your school's anti-bullying policy (see chapter R1: Rules) so they can respond to it as a unified team. A big mistake is assuming that everyone already knows the correct definition. This section describes ways to ensure that your stakeholders understand your definition of bullying, the four elements of bullying behaviors, and the five types of bullying.

"Our bullying prevention team spent weeks creating an anti-bullying policy. We posted it online, put it in the handbook, and hung it on our walls. And then I asked all the teachers how many of them could tell me the definition of bullying and only three hands went up." —middle school principal, San Jose, California

66 Brave Staff Chat

Stakeholders need to understand the following key points about bullying (the remainder of this chapter will explain all):

1. The widely recognized bullying definition and the specific definition adopted by your school in your bullying prevention policy

2. The four elements of bullying: aggression, repetition, power imbalance, and intentional cruelty

3. The five types of bullying: verbal, physical, relational, electronic, and sexual

4. The main players in most bullying incidents—bystanders, targets, and bullying students—and their roles.

If you were to give a quiz asking your team members or staff at your school about these four points, what grade would they receive? As you read through this chapter, discuss ways you might boost this grade.

"Everybody talks about bullying a different way. How can you stop it unless you know what it is?" —parent, Taipei American School

WHAT IS BULLYING?

Bullying is not always easy to detect. The behavior is often covert and perpetrated in situations where adults aren't present. Bullying behaviors can be subtle and difficult to recognize. It's also important to note that not every peer confrontation is bullying: social tiffs, arguments, teasing, and conflicts are inevitable among kids, and are normal.

"There are lots of times when classmates get into scuffles and somebody looks really hurt, but I don't want to step in because I don't know if it's bullying or just two kids arguing." —Jeremiah, age 8

"Kids need to know what bullying is before we're going to step in to help. We don't want to make things worse." —Karayna, age 10

As discussed in the previous chapter, a clear understanding of bullying is one of the first steps to turning around the behavior. Here are three of the most widely accepted definitions:

"Bullying is unwanted, aggressive behavior among school-age children that involves a real or perceived power imbalance. The behavior is repeated, or has the potential to be repeated, over time. Bullying includes actions such as making threats, spreading rumors, attacking someone physically or verbally, and excluding someone from a group on purpose." —StopBullying.gov, U.S. Office of Education[*]

"Bullying is a form of aggressive behavior in which someone intentionally and repeatedly causes another person injury or discomfort. Bullying can take the form of physical contact, words, or more subtle actions. The bullied individual typically has trouble defending him or herself and does nothing to 'cause' the bullying." —*American Psychological Association*[**]

"Bullying occurs when a victim is exposed to serious 'negative experiences' created by, or due to, another individual (or group), the bully or bullies. These negative experiences often involve physical discomfort or pain, but can also be social or emotional in nature and involve psychological pain. In bullying, these

---

[*] From stopbullying.gov/what-is-bullying
[**] From apa.org/topics/bullying

negative experiences occur repeatedly over a period of time. There is always an imbalance of power between the victim and the bully, and this power imbalance can also be physical, psychological, or social." —*Dan Olweus**

THE FOUR KEY ELEMENTS OF BULLYING

Bullying is a pattern of repeated, intentionally unjust, and cruel behavior that differs from normal peer discord. The most commonly used definition of bullying, stated in the previous paragraph, was developed by Norway's Dan Olweus, considered one of the world's foremost authorities on bullying, and stresses that it consists of four elements:

1. **Aggression.** Bullying is an act of aggression or cruelty, which can be delivered by the perpetrator directly or indirectly in a physical, verbal, relational, or electronic form. The bullying could also be homophobic, prejudicial, or sexual in nature.

2. **Repetition.** Bullying usually is repeated aggression, but it can also be a one-time occurrence.

3. **Power imbalance.** There is always an imbalance of power—physical, psychological, or social—which favors the perpetrator(s). The person bullying has more power due to strength, status, ability, age, or size than the target.

4. **Intentional cruelty.** The hurtful behavior is *not* an accident, but a purposeful act of cruelty.

THE FIVE TYPES OF BULLYING

All stakeholders at your school should understand the five different types of bullying because chances are they have seen or will see more than one of them, if not all. And some forms are more prevalent at certain ages or grade levels. Some types of bullying are also more subtle and harder to detect. A key to effective bullying prevention is to educate stakeholders in these five common forms of childhood bullying.

"A lot of grown-ups think that the only serious bullying is online. Things kids say to your face is the stuff you can't stop thinking about because it hurts so bad." —Carla, age 10

---

*DiPasquale, 2004, p. 6.

1. Verbal bullying. Perpetrators of this type of bullying use words or statements to intentionally cause a target pain or distress. Name-calling, making fun of the person, and delivering put-downs, racial slurs, hurtful comments, taunts, threatening statements, or insulting are all forms of verbal bullying. The intent is to use verbal means to belittle, demean, and hurt another person. Many adults say that verbal abuse has the least serious consequences on kids, but new research shows otherwise. Students with special needs are the most frequently targeted with verbal taunts for their differences in appearance or abilities. If taunts are discriminatory or aimed at insulting a child's race or culture, the bullying is sometimes called *prejudicial bullying.*

> In 2011, one national report found that 18 percent of students were verbally bullied; of all forms, verbal bullying is the most commonly used on school campuses.[1]

2. Physical bullying. This form is using physical power like pushing, socking, slamming, punching, hitting, slapping, shoving, grabbing, or spitting to gain control over targets and cause harm. Physical bullying is the easiest form of bullying to identify, yet it is actually the least common type on school campuses.

> Only 8 percent of students are said to experience physical bullying, and 5 percent are physically threatened by another student(s) during a typical school year.[1]

3. Relational aggression (sometimes called *emotional* or *social bullying*). This is an insidious form of bullying that often goes unnoticed because it is more covert, subtle, or manipulative in nature, and the methods are cold and calculated. The intent is to emotionally harm another child by attacking their relationships with other people. Shunning, excluding, or ostracizing a child from his or her friends; spreading rumors or mean gossip; threatening to stop talking to a friend (giving "the silent treatment"); creating situations to publicly humiliate a child; and trying to ruin someone's reputation are ways that young people engage in relational aggression to try to increase their own social standing. This form of bullying is generally most common among girls, especially between fifth and eighth grade. New research shows that boys also

---

1. Robers et al., 2013.

engage in relational aggression and that this form of bullying is now starting at earlier grades levels.[2]

> A large national survey found that 18 percent of students were the subject of rumors or excluded from activities on purpose during the school year.[2]

4. Electronic bullying (also called *cyberbullying*). Using any electronic device (such as a cell phone, camera, tablet, or computer) and/or the Internet to say or send mean or embarrassing statements about a person constitutes cyberbullying. While many people believe that electronic bullying is the most common type of bullying today, studies find the opposite: fewer students are bullied electronically than in person. Two large national surveys found that a higher percentage of students reporting in-person bullying than cyberbullying. Still, it is a very serious issue, and while most electronic bullying occurs off campus, schools are including sanctions against cyberbullying in anti-bullying policies.[3]

> A large national survey found that 28 percent of 12- to 18-year-olds reported being bullied at school compared to 9 percent who reported experiencing electronic bullying during the school year.[3]

5. Sexual bullying. Also called sexual harassment, this form of bullying consists of intentionally saying or doing repeated harmful, humiliating, lewd, or disrespectful statements or actions that are sexual in nature. It could include name-calling ("slut" "whore"), vulgar gestures, uninvited touches, bra-snapping, or crude comments about someone's appearance, sexual development, or sexual activity. Many states include statutes ruling that sexual harassment is against the law. *Note:* While sexual bullying is a grave and important issue, it is outside of this book's purview and is more prevalent in (although not exclusive to) the older teen population. This topic is so complex and nuanced that it warrants another book entirely. Many good ones are available.

2. Paul, 2010.
3. Paul, 2010; DeVoe and Bauer, 2011; Li, 2007; Williams and Guerra, 2007; Ybarra et al., 2012.

Cyberbullying Terminology

The following are some of the many cyberbullying terms that educators should know:

- **Sexting:** electronically sending or posting a naked, sexualized, or compromising photo of a person
- **Flaming:** posting angry, rude comments in an online forum
- **Harassment:** repeatedly sending offensive messages to someone
- **Denigration:** attacking someone online by spreading rumors or posting false information
- **Outing and trickery:** electronically disseminating intimate private information about someone or tricking someone into disclosing private information, which is then disseminated
- **Impersonation:** pretending to be someone else and posting material online to damage that person's reputation
- **Exclusion:** intentionally excluding someone from an online group
- **Cyberstalking:** creating fear by sending frequent threatening messages to someone

THREE PLAYERS: THE TARGET OF BULLYING, THE BULLYING CHILD, AND THE BYSTANDER

Every bullying episode has three victims: the target, the child (or children) doing the bullying, and the witnesses who watch the cruelty. All three children are at risk for mental health and moral development issues.

The target of bullying. Repeated bullying can cause severe emotional harm to a child and can be so serious that some school-age targets have committed suicide.

The bullying child. Aggression is a learned behavior that can become entrenched and increase in intensity. Each time a child uses bullying behavior it depletes his or her empathy reserve and teaches that cruelty is an acceptable way to manipulate relationships.

The bystander. Research suggests that students who witness their peers endure verbal or physical abuse could become as psychologically distressed, if not more so, by the events as the targets themselves.[4]

---

4. Rivers et al., 2009.

Nearly 60 percent of students who are identified as perpetrators of chronic bullying in middle school had at least one criminal conviction by the age of 24.[5]

Tip for ADMINISTRATORS

One of the most effective ideas I've seen for training a staff to recognize bullying was at a middle school on a U.S. military base in Vicenza, Italy. The moment I walked into the school, I knew their bullying definition. Students had created a fifteen-second PSA in their health class. The message clearly listed their definition of bullying, the types of bullying, and the school's anti-bullying policy in large text and played repeatedly on a large television screen attached to a wall. Simple, cost-effective, and consistent; every stakeholder saw it and learned it.

Strategies to Educate Staff About Bullying

Effective bullying prevention educates all school staff members about the definition and elements of bullying and how to recognize the different types. Much of this information is often new to staff, so take time to study it carefully. Next, discuss the best approaches to help everyone understand those key elements and types of bullying. Remember, your bullying definition should reflect the same terms that appear in your school's anti-bullying policy, so take time to review that section carefully. Only then will the staff be able to review the concept with students. *Note:* A one-time staff training is generally not sufficient for stakeholders to grasp the breadth of information on bullying. The most successful strategies are cost-effective, simple, and can be repeated so everyone hears and learns the same message as often as needed to stay united. Here are suggestions:

Create a brief presentation. Consider developing a short video or computer slide presentation that all staff members can review and share with students and their parents. The bullying prevention team at a school in Alberta, Canada, developed a short slide presentation on the computer that listed key points about bullying. The team then shared and discussed the contents at a meeting with all staff members. Each member was also given a flash drive of the presentation to review. Teachers used the presentation with parents at their

---

5. Smokowski and Kopasz, 2005.

back-to-school night and in their classrooms as a student lesson on bullying. New students and their parents viewed the session as part of the school orientation.

Start a book club. Your bullying prevention team, if you have one, may already have read books about bullying, but now the staff at your school needs to learn that information, too. A few favorite staff book club reads are: *Bully* edited by Lee Hirsch and Cynthia Lowen, *The Bully, the Bullied, and the Not-So-Innocent Bystander* by Barbara Coloroso, and *The Essential Guide to Bullying: Prevention and Intervention* by Cindy Miller and Cynthia Lowen.

Hold a movie night. Rent a movie (such as *Bully* directed by Lee Hirsch) to watch as a staff or find clips that depict types of bullying behaviors to show during a staff training.

Do a brief staff training. Several bullying prevention programs offer schoolwide training guides with an accompanying multimedia component that can be shown in shorter segments to staff and can be tremendous time-savers for a prevention team.*

Make a one-pager. Create one simple sheet printed on sturdy cardstock (consider laminating) that lists the most pertinent information a staff needs to know about bullying: school's definition, types, warning signs, and key elements, and hand it out to all staff members for easy reference.

Tip for TEACHERS

Send a flash drive of your anti-bullying computer presentation (if your team or staff creates one) home with students to share with parents as homework. The assignment is for the child to teach their parents "the definition and the different types of bullying." Parents sign a form stating they viewed the video with their child and then return the flash drives so another class can send them home until all parents have viewed the presentation. Posting the presentation on your teacher or school website is another option. New parents, staff, and students can also review the presentation.

---

* Examples: *Olweus Bullying Prevention Program: Schoolwide Guide with DVD/CD* (Hazelden, 2007) and *The ABCs of Bullying Prevention (DVD Bundle)* (National Professional Resources, 2011).

Ways to Teach Students How to Recognize Bullying

Adults aren't the only ones who need to learn to recognize bullying: if you want students to step in and speak out against peer cruelty they too need to learn the signs. The best student lessons are always done in a social context and woven into existing curriculum.

One of the most instructive student lessons I've seen was in Reno, Nevada. Teachers found the perfect scenes from three movies (*My Bodyguard, Bully Dance,* and *Monsters, Inc.*) and showed brief clips (no more than two minutes each) at a student assembly. Following each clip, teachers named the bullying type depicted in the scene (such as relational, verbal, or physical), and then asked students to describe what it looked or sounded like. Afterward, every kid in that audience understood not only the definition of bullying, but also could recognize it because they were shown it in context.

> Effective bullying prevention educates the whole school about the definition and elements of bullying and how to recognize the different types.

Here are five effective ways educators can help students recognize the types of bullying:

1. Watch film clips. As I just described in my example, film resonates with today's digital kids so using short clips of bullying scenes can be an effective way to help them recognize the types of bullying. Be sure to preview movies to gauge their appropriateness for your students. Common Sense Media (commonsensemedia.org) is a helpful source for ratings and movie suggestions. Here are some suggestions, along with the types of bullying depicted.

For lower elementary:

- *Chicken Little*: He's smart but afraid of everything and the target of bullying. (verbal bullying)
- *Dumbo*: Who can forget lovable Dumbo and not ache when everyone makes fun of his "big floppy ears"? (verbal bullying)

For upper elementary:

- *Monsters, Inc*: Lovable Sulley and his wisecracking sidekick Mike are at the top of the scare team. The scene with the birds on the clothesline is great for discussing bullying roles: bystanders, bullying figure, and target. (verbal bullying)

- *Billy Elliott*: Eleven-year-old Billy trades his boxing gloves for ballet lessons and endures the wrath of bullying. (verbal bullying)

For middle school:

- *Bully*: Lee Hirsch's eye-opening film about school bullying from an up-close and personal angle. (physical and verbal bullying)

- *Cyberbully*: A teen is subjected to a campaign of bullying through a social networking site. (electronic bullying)

- *Heathers*: Three "queen bees" bully another girl but don't get away with it. (verbal bullying, relational aggression)

- *Mean Girls*: The new girl is a hit with the A-list clique at her school until she makes the mistake of falling for one of their ex-boyfriends. (relational aggression)

- *The Karate Kid*: A New Jersey kid moves to California and finds himself bullied by a karate gang; an elderly gardener intervenes and teaches the boy karate so he can stand up for himself. (physical bullying)

- *The Fat Boy Chronicles*: An overweight teen transfers to a new school where he is mercilessly bullied by peers. (verbal bullying)

- *The War*: A Vietnam War vet father must deal with his PTSD and unemployment while helping his son stand up to a group of bullying kids. (verbal bullying)

2. Listen to song lyrics. Song lyrics are a powerful way to help students understand the harm of bullying, and they can also spur on a great class discussion about bullying types. Steve Seskin and Allen Shamblin's lyrics to "Don't Laugh at Me" are used in hundreds of schools around the world as an anti-bullying anthem and performed by celebrities including Mark Wills and Peter Yarrow. Countless educators use the song lines: "Don't laugh at me. Don't call me names. Don't get your pleasure from my pain" to help kids recognize that bullying is an intentional act of cruelty. The book version *Don't Laugh at Me* by Steve Seskin comes with a CD of the song. I know a Cincinnati principal who invited middle school students to work as a team to put together a presentation using photographs that depicted the song's lyrics and showed it at an assembly. The song became their school's anthem and was played over the loud speaker once a week to remind students of their anti-bullying pledge.

Other songs about bullying include: "You Had to Pick on Me" by Matt Kennon, "Hey Bully" by Morgan Frazier, "Mean" by Taylor Swift, "Who Says" by Selena Gomez, "Miss Invisible" by Marie Digby, and "Why's Everybody Always Pickin' on Me?" by Bloodhound Gang. Ask students for more song suggestions or, even better, encourage them to compose their own lyrics. Hundreds of YouTube videos are posted online of kids performing their own anti-bullying songs and many are superb! (Preview them for appropriateness.)

3. Read children's literature. Hundreds of children's and young adult books about bullying have been published in the past few years and many have become classroom staples. School librarians can stock the library with popular bullying titles, set up table displays in the library, and share new titles at staff meetings. Counselors and psychologists can use books about bullying for bibliotherapy (healing a child through a book). Teachers can use books as read-alouds to initiate class discussions about bullying or assign book reports requiring students to find key passages that describe different bullying types. Principals can require a child engaging in bullying behavior to report on how a book character reformed her or his ways. Here are a few selections that can be used specifically to help kids of all ages recognize bullying behaviors. (For many more ideas, see pages 249–257 in the Resources section.)

For younger students:

- *Spaghetti in a Hot Dog Bun: Having the Courage to Be Who You Are* by Maria Dismondy
- *The Juice Box Bully: Empowering Kids to Stand Up for Others* by Bob Sornson and Maria Dismondy

For upper elementary:

- *Taking the Bully by the Horns* by Kathy Noll with Dr. Jay Carter
- *Confessions of a Former Bully* by Trudy Ludwig

For middle school:

- *Stargirl* by Jerry Spinelli

- *Real Friends vs. the Other Kind* by Annie Fox

4. Make "Looks Like, Sounds Like, Feels Like" charts. These charts may be developed as a whole class during a class meeting or in cooperative learning groups. Adapt the chart for younger or nonreading children by using photographs or drawings that depict the words. An elementary school in Minneapolis created huge charts and hung them in the hallways, cafeteria, and school entrance—a powerful way to remind everyone about bullying.

Figure 2.1: Example of a "Looks Like, Sounds Like, Feels Like" Chart

Bullying is unwanted, aggressive behavior that is intentionally harmful, involves a power imbalance, and occurs repetitively. It is not tolerated at our school.

Bullying Looks Like	Bullying Sounds Like	Bullying Feels
Ignoring	Put-downs	Dangerous
Excluding	Taunting	Lonely
Shoving	Rumors	Destructive
Slapping	Threats	Hurtful
Bad finger gestures	Name-calling	Awful

"Everybody always tells us to help bullied kids, but we don't always know when it's bullying. Maybe they're just arguing. Teach us the difference."
—Kelly, age 10

---

5. Role-play the differences between bullying and normal conflict. Bullying behaviors and arguments are different and understanding the distinction is crucial. Child arguments are normal and expected while bullying should never be tolerated. Helping students understand the difference will help bystanders be more likely to step in to assist a targeted child who is being bullied. An effective teaching strategy is to role-play bullying and normal conflict scenarios or to have older students create scripts, videos, or screenplays depicting the two different dynamics. Role-play scenarios involve the following behaviors in Figure 2.2 on page 122.

Figure 2.2: Bullying Behaviors vs. Normal Conflict

Bullying	Normal Conflict
Cold, calculated, intentional cruelty	Disagreement or difference of opinion
Bullying person is fully responsible for the problem	Both people are responsible for the problem
One-sided issue (only the bullying person's viewpoint is represented)	Both people have the power to influence
Bullying person has intent to harm from the start	Neither person seeks to intentionally harm the other
Imbalance of power between people	Both people have equal power
Frequent, repeated negative actions	Occasional or ongoing conflict
Purposefully done, deliberate	May be accidental
Strong emotional reaction from target	Equal emotional response from both people
Bullying person seeks power or control over target	Neither person is seeking power or to gain anything
Bullying person makes no effort to resolve the problem	Both people make efforts to resolve the issue
Bullying person takes no responsibility for actions and often blames others	Each person takes responsibility and often feels remorse

HOLD CLASS MEETINGS TO DISCUSS BULLYING

The majority of students are clearly opposed to bullying and sympathetic to targets, but they don't get the opportunity to voice their opinions or express their disapproval of the behavior.[6] Class meetings are a perfect venue to help students hear the true views of their peers as well as learn how to recognize bullying behaviors. Students who bully often learn in meetings that peers don't support their behavior. And targeted students, who often believe that their peers support the kids who bully them, get a chance to hear that their classmates are in their corner. The right class discussions can even mobilize students to defend targeted classmates because they know other students will back them up.

6. Salmivalli and Voeten, 2004.

Your first learning objective is to clarify the school's definition of bullying. Post the definition on the board and review it with students. You can also refer back to the "looks like, sounds like, feels like" chart on page 121 and create a large poster chart for students to add descriptions. Then pose questions to students in your class meeting so they hear their peers' attitudes toward bullying. Use the form on pages 128–129 as a starting point and adapt questions as needed for your students. You can either have students fill out the form prior to the meeting or pass out the form during the meeting as a discussion guide. (See "Class Rules That Create Respectful Classrooms and Reduce Bullying" on page 100 for more information on holding class meetings.)

SEL SKILL: Friendly Teasing vs. Bullying—Know the Difference!

There are two very different types of teasing: friendly teasing and unfriendly teasing (bullying), and kids need to learn the difference. Doing so will help them recognize when a peer is bullying a child or teasing. Adapt the following script depending upon the children's age to help them grasp the difference:

"It's unfriendly teasing when a person makes fun of your accent, weight, or what you wear or look like. They're making fun *of you,* and they don't care if it causes you to feel sad. If you've told the person to stop and they continue being very hurtful, it *can* be bullying.

"It's friendly teasing when kids are just being playful *with* you and they don't mean to hurt your feelings. You can tell friendly teasers to cut it out or stop it, and they usually will."

Students may need lots of help as they learn to decipher friendly teasing versus bullying so discuss the difference frequently. You can also use books to help.

For younger students:

- *The Berenstain Bears and Too Much Teasing* by Stan and Jan Berenstain
- *Let's Talk About Teasing* by Joy Wilt Berry

For older students:

- *Simon's Hook: A Story About Teases and Put-Downs* by Karen Gedig Burnett
- *How to Handle Bullies, Teasers, and Other Meanies: A Book That Takes the Nuisance Out of Name Calling and Other Nonsense* by Kate Cohen-Posey

FIVE WAYS STUDENTS CAN TEACH PEERS TO RECOGNIZE BULLYING

We've long known that one of the best ways to learn something new is by teaching it to someone else. The same principle applies to helping students understand bullying. Over the years I've witnessed some great examples of kids teaching other kids about bullying. Here are a few:

1. **Homeroom sharing.** Student teams study the types of bullying, create a joint lesson, and then visit homerooms to teach a five-minute course on bullying to other students.

2. **Bullying bookmarks.** Encourage your students to find a simple way to educate their peers about bullying. Following a class discussion, students in Alberta, Canada, decided to make bookmarks to help the student body understand bullying. They researched the most common ways students bully, designed a 3" x 8½"–size template, printed over 600 bookmarks on cardstock paper, and distributed them to classmates. They also stacked copies in the school library for students to pick up as they checked out books. Their bookmark read:

   IF YOU INTENTIONALLY . . . Exclude kids, push kids, taunt kids, insult kids, kick kids, harass kids, hurt kids, put-down kids . . . YOU ARE BULLYING. Bullying is not tolerated at our school.

3. **Student-made charts.** Health and science teachers assigned upper-grade students to work in teams to research the definition of bullying and types of bullying, and the emotional impacts of each. Each team then created a large poster of their findings. Posters were displayed around the school. Lower-grade students created bullying "Looks Like, Sounds Like, Feels Like" charts and hung them in hallways for students to read during passing times.

4. **New-student education.** Middle school students in Boise, Idaho, decided to welcome incoming sixth graders by teaching them about bullying the first week of school. The older students worked in teams to create short presentations about bullying and then gave the presentations to groups of incoming students during lunch or homeroom period. Teachers claimed it helped older students understand bullying even more than younger students, and many bonds formed between the older and younger kids that lasted well into the school year.

5. **Cross-age tutors.** Assign upper-grade students to become "bullying prevention tutors" to younger students. The older student creates a five-minute lesson to help a younger child understand what bullying is and how to recognize it. Once the lesson is teacher-approved, the older student first practices teaching it to a peer (such as in cooperative learning groups), and then teaches it to a younger child.

" Brave Staff Chat: How Are You Reaching Parents?

Parents are a crucial part of bullying prevention, so take a moment to seriously ask yourselves what you've done to educate parents about bullying. Which parents are you reaching? Which ones are you missing? Have you surveyed parents to ask them when the most convenient time would be to come to a training session and what they need to understand bullying? What can we do as a staff to reach more parents?

A meta-analysis of over 600 studies found parent education was an essential piece for effective bullying prevention.[7] Involve parents!

Ways to Involve PARENTS

Bullying education needs to be extended to parents so they can be on the same page with the rest of the stakeholders. Look for simple ways to help parents learn your school's bullying definition, the key elements of bullying, and the five bullying types. Possibilities include:

1. Post bullying information on your school website or school marquee.

2. Write short educational blurbs and include them in parent email blasts and school newsletters.

3. Create a one-page sheet listing crucial information about bullying and give one to every parent at conference time or send as email blasts.

4. Involve your students. Have them write the newsletters, email blasts, or website posts about bullying. Parents are more likely to read information that their children write.

5. Set up a lending library of videos and books for parents, hold speaker events, or start parent book clubs on bullying led by parents or staff members.

---

7. Farrington and Ttofi, 2009.

6. Copy videos of your school assembly or pertinent classroom lessons about bullying onto flash drives so parents can share in their child's school experiences.

7. Enlist parents to be members of your bullying prevention team or staff group. They can reach out to other parents and mobilize their support via phone trees, email groups, or parent coffees held before, during, and after school.

8. Hold "make and take sessions" where students and parents work together at after-school events to create posters defining bullying to hang at home.

9. Print your bullying definition on bumper stickers, flyers, or refrigerator magnets for home reminders.

10. Create a page on your school website just for parents and continue to update pertinent information about bullying.

Strategies to Involve Your Whole Community in Bullying Prevention

Bullying happens inside *and outside* your school walls, so find ways to help everyone in your community recognize bullying behaviors. Here are some ideas:

Local businesses. Ask local businesses to display in their windows professionally printed or student-made posters that define bullying. Older students could be divided into teams to "adopt" a local business and keep them updated about the school's anti-bullying efforts.

School and community librarians. Coordinate with librarians to arrange book displays and encourage book clubs to read selections about bullying. An entire community outside Milwaukee read *Mindset* by Carol Dweck together. Let's get communities reading bullying prevention material!

Coaches. Bullying is also a problem in sports, so contact local coaches (AYSO, pee-wee football, hockey, and so forth) to support your anti-bullying policy on the fields and help parents, kids, and community members recognize bullying and stop it.

Youth organizations. Have students make flyers listing the signs of bullying and ways to report it. Distribute flyers to pediatrician offices, scout groups, Boys and Girls Clubs, YMCA/YWCA, youth groups, and places of worship.

Media. Your local newspaper can post ongoing news coverage about school and district bullying prevention events, including segments from principals' newsletters that list signs of bullying. Local TV and radio stations can coordinate with your school to publicize your bullying prevention events and review the signs of bullying. Assign upper-grade students to be your "local reporters" and provide ongoing news coverage of your bullying prevention efforts.

KEY BULLYING PREVENTION POINTS IN R2: RECOGNIZE

- Effective bullying prevention teaches *all* stakeholders to recognize bullying behaviors and be on the same page to respond quickly and appropriately to reduce it.

- Ongoing training is necessary to increase knowledge about bullying and ensure that your school's policy and processes are effective.

- Bullying happens inside and outside your school walls, so find ways to help everyone in your community recognize bullying behaviors.

- Only when staff, students, and parents are unified in their understanding of what bullying is can they respond as a unified team.

- Find ways to educate parents. Parent education is an essential piece of effective bullying prevention.

CLASS MEETING QUESTIONS ABOUT BULLYING

1. What does *bullying* mean?

2. On a scale of 1–10 (10 means it should be outlawed), how seriously do you rate bullying as a problem at our school? Is it right for someone to bully another person?

3. What are the four main types of bullying? Have you seen or experienced bullying at our school? What type(s)? Is there one type of bullying that happens more often at our school? Why?

4. *Social bullying or relational aggression* is when you deliberately leave someone out or spread mean or harmful stories about someone. Have you seen kids being excluded or left out on purpose at our school? Where were they and what were they doing? How does it feel to be excluded? What can you do if you see someone being excluded?

5. *Physical bullying* is kicking, shoving, hitting, or punching someone. Have you seen physical bullying at our school? How is physical bullying different from fighting? If you see physical bullying, how could you help without getting hurt?

6. *Verbal bullying* is putting down someone with mean words. How is verbal bullying different from friendly teasing? What kinds of things do kids say to one another when they bully? What could you do if you heard someone verbally bully another kid?

7. Tell me about a time you wanted to speak out and help someone who was being bullied but didn't. What stopped you? What could you do next time? How could you get other kids to join together to stop someone who's bullying? Would that make a difference? Why?

8. What can kids do to make this school a safer and more caring place? What can teachers do?

R3: Report

Create Procedures to Report Bullying

In this chapter, you will learn:

• the top reasons why students don't report bullying

• ways to help kids feel safe to make reports

• five steps to show students how to report bullying incidents

• how to teach students the difference between reporting verses tattling

• why you need to provide students with *multiple* reporting options

• how to create procedures for staff to report bullying incidents

• why frequently reviewing bullying reports builds students' trust

The third "R," or R3, of bullying prevention is to create solid, clear procedures for all stakeholders to report bullying. Anyone who is involved with your students needs to understand the importance of reporting bullying incidents—including your bus drivers, counselors, parents, custodians, teachers, school volunteers, and students. In some cases, law enforcement should be notified. As I stress in the introduction and throughout this book, there is no room in a caring school for an attitude of "Bullying is part of growing up," or "We can't do anything about it." Bullying has to be taken seriously and it *can* be reduced.

Reviewing bullying reports from students, staff members, and parents is an effective way to gain evidence of the frequency and duration of incidents and the names of the children involved. Studies show that if students know that they are being monitored and reported on, they are less likely to engage in aggressive behaviors.[1] Similarly, students feel safer when they know that school staff members and other students take bullying seriously. Bystanders

1. Unnever and Cornell, 2004.

are also more likely to report bullying incidents if reporting procedures are clear and students have positive relationships with adults in the school.[2]

Giving students a voice to share their concerns and acting on them is one of the best ways to reduce bullying. Your students need to know they *will* be heard and that you *will* back them up. I can't stress this point enough. One of the most common complaints I hear from students is that adults don't take student reports seriously. "I notice you have report boxes and online forms to report bullying incidents. Do you and your friends report bullying?" I ask students. The most common response is a loud, unified, "No!" "Why not?" I press. And the students bare all: "Why should we report bullying when the teachers don't take our reports seriously?" Or "We had a big assembly and the principal told us that we have to report bullying and our reports would be taken seriously, but that worked only for a few weeks."

> Giving students a voice to share their concerns and acting on them is one of the best ways to reduce bullying. Your students need to know they *will* be heard and that you *will* back them up. I can't stress this point enough.

One comment I received from a middle school student in Texas was especially poignant: "If I make a report because I'm concerned about my safety, it's not going to help if the principal waits until the end of the week to read it. The counselors and principal need to read our reports every day and then do something about them or what's the point of us writing them?"

The fact is that many children do not report bullying to adults due to embarrassment, fear of retaliation, or lack of faith in the adults. Sadly, that trend becomes more pronounced with age. Here are common reasons students give for not reporting:[3]

- feel ashamed and embarrassed about being bullied

- are afraid the person bullying will retaliate

- fear developing a reputation for being a "snitch" or a "rat" by peers

- are uncertain if what they experienced or witnessed is bullying

- don't want to get involved and make things worse for the targeted student

- feel pressure from peers to be quiet and not tell

2. Sojourner and Hyatt, 2013.
3. Stueve et al., 2006, p. 121.

- are concerned that "no one will believe me" so "what's the point?"

- believe they or the other child deserve to be bullied

- don't know where to go for assistance

- assume adults expect them to deal with bullying on their own

- are concerned for the well-being of the person bullying

- don't trust that adults will do anything about it or handle it correctly

- don't believe the perpetrator will continue bullying or act on his or her threats

> 18 percent of third graders don't report bullying to adults; by twelfth grade that number goes up to 47 percent.[4]
>   Only 4 to 13 percent of middle and high school students indicate that they would report an incident of bullying to a teacher, administrator, or another school staff member.[5]

Students need to understand the importance of telling an adult their legitimate concerns, and they need to be reassured that their reports will be taken seriously. This chapter discusses reporting and explains why students might not tell. The chapter also offers how to break the code of silence by building trust and using multiple reporting options and suggests ways educators can use those reporting strategies to reduce bullying and create safer learning environments.

" Brave Staff Chat: Why Don't Students Report Bullying?

Share with your staff the statistics in this chapter and the typical reasons why students don't report bullying to adults. Focus on why students say that face-to-face adult reporting is their least favorite preference. Ask staff members to recall times when they've received student reports of bullying, as well as times students should have reported bullying to them but did not. Then have a serious discussion about what you and your staff can do to build your students' trust so they feel comfortable sharing their concerns with you.

---

4. Olweus and Limber, 2010.
5. Hirsch and Lowen, 2012.

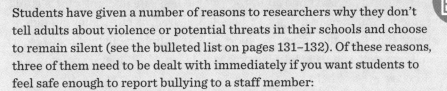

Tip for ADMINISTRATORS

Students have given a number of reasons to researchers why they don't tell adults about violence or potential threats in their schools and choose to remain silent (see the bulleted list on pages 131–132). Of these reasons, three of them need to be dealt with immediately if you want students to feel safe enough to report bullying to a staff member:

1. Students need to know where to go for assistance.

2. Students need to think they will be believed and taken seriously.

3. Students need to feel confident that adults can do something to help.

Consider holding several small focus groups with students in your school who represent different groups and ages. Ask them: "Step into the shoes of your classmates. Would they report bullying incidents to the staff? Why or why not? What can the staff do to help students be more likely to report bullying?"

How to Break the Student Code of Silence

"It's tough for kids to report. If we do, other kids call you a 'snitch.'"
—Ned, age 10

The "Silent Kid Code" is a big reason why schools need to provide multiple reporting options for students, including the option to remain anonymous. The idea that it's not cool to snitch is a large part of students' social scene. But you do not want students to remain silent about possible threats of abusive power. Over 75 percent of adolescents who commit harm to themselves or others *tell someone their plan before carrying it out,* and the most likely person they report their intentions to is a peer.[6] Most school shooters announce their plans to peers prior to carrying them out. Most children who commit suicide have been repeatedly bullied and at one point tried to share their trauma with someone.[7] But in too many cases no one believed the student or took action. The problem is that young people—especially those in middle school—often adhere to a strong, entrenched peer "code of silence."

If we want our children to report bullying and possible threats, we need to provide opportunities for them to do so. After all, students have the best pulse on their school's social climate and their reports can be instrumental not only

6. Zarzor, 2000.
7. Vossekuil et al., 2004.

in reducing peer cruelty, but also in saving lives. All students in a school should be able to identify at least one adult they would feel safe or comfortable going to if someone might be in danger, threatened, scared, or hurt. They should also know they have the option to report bullying anonymously, if they prefer. When it comes to school safety, kids may well be the best metal detector.

Here are ways to help kids feel safe to tell.

Nurture relationships with adults. Certainly one of the most successful tactics to reduce bullying is to increase communication and trust between staff and students. Doing so creates an environment where students feel empowered to come forward and discuss with those adults the bullying that they see or experience. We have our work cut out for us in achieving this goal. So take time to personally connect with students, ask how they're doing, and let them know you care—these small gestures can do wonders in creating a climate where students trust adults. Advisor-advisee programs can be especially helpful.

> ## "Brave Staff Chat: Which Students Feel Safe Coming to You? Which Don't?
>
> Meet with your staff and ask these questions: Which students are more likely to come to us, and which ones are we overlooking? What can we do to help special needs, ESL, and introverted kids feel they can report concerns to us? If we were in our students' places, what would we need to feel safe enough to report bullying?

Offer anonymity. Students need to be given the option to report anonymously. Assure them that their reports will be confidential and they may choose not to sign their names. This clause alone does a lot to boost reporting since it lets kids know they won't be considered "snitches" by peers.

Make your word good. The easiest way to let kids know you're taking their concerns seriously is to act on their reports. The word will spread among kids as to which staff members can and cannot be counted on to follow through. Emphasize that *threats need to be reported and will be taken seriously.* Repeat this announcement school-wide and/or in each classroom so that all students understand.

Convey your message as a unified team. Many schools hold an assembly (sometimes with police involvement) to convey the seriousness of reporting threats or bullying. Other schools have a building administrator meet individually with each homeroom class to explain reporting options. The key is to stress to students that all threats will be reviewed. An administrator of a private school in Taipei held a school-wide assembly and asked the student council to urge the student body to report bullying incidents and threats. The staff agreed that the students convinced far more peers to report than adults could have done.

Hold "Five-Minute Urgent Talks." One of the most powerful strategies I've seen was in a middle school where the student council asked the principal if they could go to each homeroom and give a "five-minute urgent talk" (the students' words) to encourage their peers to report bullying incidents. They were able to mobilize the majority of students to do so.

Make reporting a rule. Some schools institute a rule that it's against school policy (for all stakeholders except the targeted child) *not* to report bullying or threats. Check your anti-bullying policy to verify that the wording is there. After students understand that rule, they are more likely to report bullying incidents.

Initiate a student poster campaign. A team of middle school students in Arkansas asked their principal if they could start a poster campaign to encourage peers to report bullying. Dozens of colorful, student-made posters lined the hallways with captions such as "It's Okay to Tell," "Want to Stop Bullying? Report it!," and "Tuluka Kids Stop Bullying by Reporting."

STUDENTS TELLING STUDENTS

Research shows that students often are more comfortable telling peers about bullying than telling adults.[8] This reporting method is not utilized enough on school campuses. The majority of peers are also sympathetic toward kids who are frequently victimized by bullying, so mobilize them as "peer helpers." Here are suggestions for having students report to other students.

Report bullying as a duo. Many targeted kids who are uncomfortable reporting bullying incidents to an adult alone will do so with a peer. Another student can accompany the targeted child or bystander to report the bullying incident and serve as a supportive companion. Teach students to ask a child who has been targeted: "Would you like me to go with you to report this to a teacher?"

Use peer mentors. Train students to be peer mentors and give kids the option to report bullying to them instead of to an adult. Older students tell me

8. Smith and Shu, 2002; Menesini et al., 2002.

they are more likely to report bullying to a peer mentor than to a staff member. The peer mentors are instructed to then immediately report the bullying incident to a staff member and *not to deal with the incident or seek out those involved.* Some peer mentor programs to research online include: BullyBusters, National Peer Mentoring Anti-Bullying, and Beatbullying.

Role-play how to report. Many students may not know how to ask a peer for help reporting or feel insecure doing so. Role-play with students (especially younger kids or those with special needs) ways to ask a peer to assist them in seeking help. Students take turns playing the part of the child seeking help and the helper. For example, "Kevin, you be the helper. Jayla, pretend you want Kevin to help you tell the teacher that someone was mean to you and you don't feel safe. What would you ask Kevin?" Make sure you create a list of statements students can use to ask someone for help. (See "SEL Skill: Asking Someone for Help" below.)

Keep a class "helper's journal." Some teachers and counselors encourage students to track, either in a journal or on a large piece of chart paper, when they've helped classmates or observed peers helping each other. Periodically share the chart or journal entries with your students. Names of the students who were helped do not have to be included. This process inspires students to recognize that their class climate is about helping others. Acknowledging children's helping encourages their prosocial behaviors and conveys to kids who need assistance: "It's okay to ask. There are kids who will help me."

SEL SKILL: Asking Someone for Help

Asking for help is a critical skill for safety as well as problem solving. Some children don't ask for help because they feel threatened, are more passive, are too embarrassed, don't know how to ask, or don't know who to ask. Teach students how to seek assistance.

Tell students it's *okay* to ask for help. Help students know they shouldn't feel embarrassed to ask for help by using a few of these prompts: "Have you ever felt embarrassed because you couldn't do something? What did you do about it? Why is it hard to tell someone you need help? What can happen if you don't ask for help? Think about a time when you needed help. Who did you turn to? How did you feel asking for help?"

Tell students *when* to ask for help. Teach children (particularly young kids and those with special needs) when they should seek help, such as when they don't feel safe, they have a serious problem but don't know the solution, or they have trouble doing something important.

Teach how to ask for help using the steps: STOP, LOOK, ASK, and TELL. You might put the four steps from Figure 3.1 on a large chart to hang up or print on an index card for students to put in their backpacks. Then role-play the four steps until students can use them on their own.

Figure 3.1: Four Steps to Get Help: STOP, LOOK, ASK, and TELL

Step 1: STOP and identify your problem. What is the problem you can't solve? What do you need help with?

Step 2: LOOK for a person to help you. Who can you go to? (*Examples:* A teacher? A counselor? The secretary? A classmate? A parent?)

Step 3: ASK for help. Say to the person: "Can you help me? I have a problem."

Step 4: TELL your problem. State your problem simply and directly. (*Examples:* "I was bullied and I don't know what to do." "I'm scared to ride the bus because I'll get hurt.")

Remind students throughout the year: *If a classmate needs help, we give it, and if you need help, you ask for it.* Then keep repeating that mantra until students act on it.

Five Steps to Teach Students How to Report Bullying Incidents

Bullying reporting methods for students might be a paper form, a special hotline phone number, a Web page, or a downloadable PDF that can be printed off or emailed. Some schools are making apps available for students to fill out bullying reports via their smartphones. Regardless of the method, it is crucial that one is available to *all* your students, that it's convenient to find, that it provides an anonymous filing option, and that kids understand how to correctly complete it. It's also crucial that someone—an administrator, bullying prevention team, secretary, or other staff member—reviews the reports from staff, students, and parents *every* day; in higher-threat climates, review twice daily. The sooner you respond to a bullying incident, the greater the chance you can lessen the distress of the target and reduce the likelihood of a future incident. You also increase the chance that students will report future incidents and connect with staff to share their concerns. Here are the steps to meet those goals.

Tip for ADMINISTRATORS

Reporting forms can provide critical details about where and when bullying is happening as well as which staff members consistently report incidents. Periodically review your bullying reports to determine which members *never* report (as well as those who report too frequently or incidents that don't fit the bullying definition or your policy). Talk to those individuals privately to find out why they are not reporting bullying. One common reason is that people think the form takes too much time to fill out. If that's the case, then what can you do to create a simpler reporting option?

STEP 1: CREATE A *SIMPLE* STUDENT REPORTING FORM

The best forms are simple, age-appropriate, and ask questions that will provide the crucial information such as: who was involved, what happened, and where and when it happened. Modify the form for younger or nonreading children so they can draw their concerns and include picture cues. The form for ESL students should be in their native tongue. Visually impaired students will need one in braille. (See three sample student forms on pages 149–154.)

STEP 2: TEACH REPORTING VS. TATTLING

Many schools have broken through kids' "code of silence" by teaching students the difference between reporting and tattling: "Reporting is when a student tells to protect another student's safety or keep someone *out* of trouble. Tattling is trying to get a student *in* trouble." Some schools might use different terminology: *reporting* is sometimes called *informing* or *telling*, while *tattling* can also be called *snitching* or *ratting*.

Discuss tattling vs. reporting in age-appropriate terms. Here are three variations:

- For younger students: "*Tattling* is when you want to get someone *in* trouble. *Telling* is when you want to help a person stay *out* of trouble or help them so they don't get hurt. You should always tell an adult if someone is hurting you or if someone is hurting another person."

- For upper elementary students add: "*Reporting* is when you are trying to keep people safe; when you need help to solve an issue you can't resolve; or when the behavior is harmful, dangerous, or threatening, and done on purpose. *Tattling* is when you are trying to get someone in trouble; when the issue is unimportant, harmless, or accidental; or when you don't really need help to solve the issue."

- For older students add: "*Ratting* (or *snitching*) is *tattling* to get someone in trouble. The issue of safety is not considered when a person is ratting someone out. However, it is *not* ratting when your goal is to help someone who may be hurt—in fact it could be lifesaving."

Role-play "right and wrong" reporting scenarios. You might role-play with your students reporting and tattling scenarios. Here are a few examples to get you started: "My friend won't play with me." "Sara keeps telling all the girls not to sit by me at lunch." "Ralph accidentally tripped another student." "An older student punched me and says he'll do it again on the bus." "Sally cut in front of me." "Kelly and Juanita are arguing about who gets the first turn in dodge ball." "Tim won't share the ball." "A boy keeps threatening to hit me if I don't give him my money."

> Reporting is when a student tells to protect another student's safety or keep someone *out* of trouble. Tattling is trying to get a student *in* trouble.

Cornelia Elementary School in Edina, Minnesota, held a school-wide assembly and had students portray different "right" and "wrong" reporting scenes (such as the previous ones), vote on whether the scene was reporting or tattling, and then discuss why the scene should or shouldn't be reported. The students enjoyed watching peers act out the scenarios and it also helped them understand the type of incidents that *should* be reported.

Write class screenplays. Assign older students to write scripts or screenplays that depict peers involved in different social scenarios: bullying (verbal, physical, relational, electronic), teasing (friendly and unfriendly), and conflicts or arguments. Students then read their scripts out loud and classmates decide whether the scene warrants reporting (because it is bullying) or should be ignored (because it's friendly teasing or a conflict). Students can also work in teams to create school-wide PSAs or short videos depicting the student screenplays. The best videos can be shown in each classroom for everyone (staff and students) to learn when to report.

Hold class meetings. Consider holding class meetings to discuss the importance of reporting. When students hear peers open up and pledge to report bullying, other students are more likely to follow suit. Class meeting questions might include: "Have you ever watched someone be bullied? Did you try to help? Would it have helped if you knew how to report the incident to an adult? What stops kids from reporting incidents? What helps kids report bullying? If you were being bullied and saw people watching and not helping, how would you feel? Would it make you feel better to know that someone tried to get help for you?" (See page 33 for more information on holding class meetings.)

Use children's literature to guide class discussions. Here are a few books for younger students that teach the difference between telling and tattling: *Armadillo Tattletale* by Helen Ketteman; *A Bad Case of Tattle Tongue* by Julia Cook; *Telling Isn't Tattling* by Kathryn M. Hammerseng; *Don't Squeal Unless It's a Big Deal: A Tale of Tattletales* by Jeanie Franz Ransom; *Tattlin' Madeline* by Carol Cummings; and *The Tattle Tail Tale* by Tandy Braid.

Tip for TEACHERS

Once students understand the difference between tattling and reporting, establish a firm "No Tattling Rule." The best rules are simple, clear, and need to be used by all staff members. Consistently responding: "Is this helpful or unhelpful news?" often is enough to help kids realize you're only interested in hearing helpful information. The secret to eliminating snitching is to be consistent with your policy *every* time a student tattles.

STEP 3: PROVIDE *MULTIPLE* REPORTING OPTIONS

Educators need to provide students with multiple ways to report bullying incidents in order to meet all comfort levels. Keep in mind that the reporting method students prefer *least* is face-to-face reporting to an adult.

24-hour phone hot line. After school hours, a child's report can be recorded in a voicemail, directed to a security officer, or sent as a text.

Use peer mentors. Students often prefer seeking the counsel of peers versus adults to support them. However, peer mentors should never be used to remedy the bullying problem. Their role is to act as a liaison between the bullied child and bystanders and the adult staff member. (See page 135 for more on peer mentors.)

Email address or phone app. The police department in Lansing, Michigan, created a community website where anyone can send an email to report a concern or threat regarding students. The report is sent instantly to the school safety officer who acts on it. A mobile phone app could also be created for this use.

Designated staff. Designate particular teachers, counselors, or other staff members to receive student bullying reports. However, also remind students that they can always make reports to any adult on your campus—such as a cafeteria worker, coach, custodian, yard supervisor, or bus driver—because *all* staff are trained in reporting procedures and will help the student complete a form and then follow up with a written report filed in the office.

Online form posted on school website. Though online reporting forms can be purchased, you can develop your own and upload it to your school website for users to access. (See pages 149–154 for examples of reporting forms or see StopBullying.gov.)

Report box. Of all the strategies, the report box seems to be the most popular among students because of its convenience and the option of reporting bullying anonymously. The box should be about the size of a mailbox, be sturdy (made from wood or metal), have a slit large enough to insert paper (but not a child's hand), and have a clearly visible lock on the top. Blank forms and pencils can be hung on a nearby wall or in plastic sleeves on the side of the box. The boxes are locked at all times and placed in key locations such as in hallways, the principal's office, the nurse and counselor's offices, the library, the cafeteria, and the playground entrance. Many schools are adding reporting boxes on school buses, as well.

Rules for use are taped to the side of the box and encourage students to *"Fill out a form if you or another student is in need of help (being bullied, conflict with others, or safety concern, or you wish to inform the office of those who have done something good and deserve praise."* Note the last phrase: Students may refrain from reporting if they fear retaliation or think the bullying student(s) may be watching. Setting a practice for students to report good things about classmates as well as bullying incidents reduces the threat of retaliation. Many principals announce "good reports" to the whole school once a week and have discovered a pleasant surprise: prosocial behaviors rise as bullying decreases.

STEP 4: TEACH STUDENTS HOW TO FILL OUT A BULLYING REPORT

One common mistake in implementing bullying prevention is assuming students know how to fill out a bullying report form. The information will only be helpful if the form is filled out correctly—especially if the form is filled out anonymously and cannot be verified. For that reason, it's critical that all stakeholders are trained in the procedure so they can give students specific directions. Don't overlook staff members who do not have classrooms, such as school nurses, bus drivers, librarians, secretaries, counselors, and cafeteria workers—consider placing reporting boxes near them. One school discovered that students felt safest reporting to the custodian, so the staff placed a reporting box outside his door.

I've watched some principals explain how to fill out the reporting form using a slide presentation projected to hundreds of students during an assembly. An elementary school had a counselor visit each classroom so all students heard the same instructions. A middle school task force made a short video of the directions for each teacher to show in his or her classroom. The video was later shown at a parent night and was also part of the new students' orientation. Here are ways to help kids learn how to fill out an incident report:

Review the bullying definition. Remind students that bullying is a deliberate mean act and not an accident. (See page 111 for details on what bullying is and also review your school policy's definition.) Tell students they should only fill out a report if the incident is about bullying, a safety threat, or someone feels unsafe. It helps to provide each student with a copy of a blank report, and then project the report on a screen as students watch you fill it out.

Teach: "Use describing words." Explain to students that when someone reads the report they need to understand what happened or they won't be able to help. That's why *specific* details of the event are important. "She was bugging me" or "He bothered me" are too general and won't help the reader. And some classmates may choose to file the report anonymously so the person who reads it can't ask questions if they don't understand the content. Some teachers write a few "fake" vague reports, read them out loud, and then ask:

"If you were a teacher or principal reading this report, would you understand what happened? Would you be able to help the student? How can you make the report provide more information?" Some teachers create a list of sample phrases to help describe common incidents and keep them on a chart for students to refer to.

Consult children's literature. Several children's books do a great job explaining to young readers the importance of reporting bullying to trusted adults in their lives. *Tease Monster: A Book About Teasing vs. Bullying* by Julia Cook and *The Juice Box Bully* by Bob Sornson and Maria Dismondy are great for lower elementary students. *Just Kidding* or *Confessions of a Former Bully* by Trudy Ludwig are helpful for upper elementary students. *Words Wound: Delete Cyberbullying and Make Kindness Go Viral* by Justin Patchin and Sameer Hinduja is appropriate for teens.

Remind students again of the "confidential clause." Encourage students to sign their names and report the names of everyone involved. But also remind them that their reports can be completed anonymously.

STEP 5: REVIEW THE REPORTS FREQUENTLY TO BUILD STUDENT TRUST

The reality is that it's difficult for staff members to find time to review reports in addition to all their other duties, but timely review of bullying reports is crucial for students to believe that staff are taking their concerns seriously. The steps to review reports and thus build student trust do not have to take a lot of time, especially if the staff meets and plans simple ways to help students know that their reports *are* being reviewed.

Tip for ADMINISTRATORS

One way to send a clear message to students that the staff is taking their reports seriously is to assign one staff member to remove the reports from the locked report boxes during hall passing time. Students will see this simple act and know you are acknowledging their concerns.

What sabotages school bullying prevention efforts quickest is for students to report bullying incidents, but not see any changes being made around the school—or worse, for students to feel that their reports are being ignored by school officials. Students need to know they *will* be heard and the school *will* back them and recognize their concerns. Kids should be able to see changes happening at your school based on their reports. Those changes will happen if you train your staff in reporting procedures (see page 142).

Students often say that the moment they need help is the time that the staff member is too busy to help them (for example, he or she is about to start or dismiss a class or is conferencing with another student). Tell students that if they need support, to write a short note and put it on the adult's desk and the person will then follow up. Secretaries, librarians, nurses, counselors, teachers, and administrators can all provide a box near their desk or an envelope taped to their doors for students to place an urgent "I need to see you" note.

Tip for COUNSELORS

While students say that school counselors are at the top of their list of adults to seek help from, they refrain from doing so because their office is often busy. Kids also turn away because they are too embarrassed to knock on the counselor's door or too distressed to wait. One remedy is to put a special laminated index card on your outside door that reads "I need to talk to you NOW." Instruct kids to hold it up (if you have a window that views the outside waiting area) or slip it under your door. And then act immediately to help that child.

Create Procedures for Staff to Report Bullying Incidents

Since most bullying takes place when adults are not present, staff reports are crucial. Here are suggestions for developing procedures for staff to report and review incidents. The reporting can occur in two ways: by the staff member who actually witnessed a bullying incident and is reporting it OR by a staff member who received a report from another person about an incident.

Develop an effective adult reporting form. Save time by looking online to find hundreds of examples posted by schools as well as any existing forms used for student office referrals. Can any of those be used or updated? Essential information to include on any bullying report includes: name of the adult reporting the incident; date, time, and location of the incident; names and roles of students and adults involved in the incident; clear description of the incident; types of bullying used; physical injuries or property damage; adults notified about the incident; action taken (if any); other pertinent information. (A sample report form is on pages 155–156.)

Create staff reporting procedures. Next, instruct *all* staff members how to complete the form and where to submit it. Ideally, pair all staff members and have them complete a "fake" form together.

Designate staff to review reports. Establish which staff member(s), such as principal, counselor, dean, or social worker, will review bullying reports and how frequently. Handle all reports quickly, discreetly, and effectively. To save time, designate one staff member (such as the custodian, counselor, secretary, or assistant principal) to unlock the report boxes at least once a day, remove all reports, and bring them to the staff member designated to review those reports. In a high-risk area or in a middle or high school, it is strongly suggested that you do this twice a day.

Decide how to notify key players. Once a bullying report form is reviewed, student safety should be the top priority. For instance, if a bullying incident took place during first period, how will other staff members who need to know about the incident (perhaps the classroom teacher, bus driver, cafeteria worker, counselor, or nurse) be notified so they can monitor the target as well as the alleged child bullying? In middle school, it is essential that a system be established to report a bullying incident to each teacher. Some schools do email blasts to relevant members or a Web-based option for ease. Also, designate who will be responsible for contacting the parents of students involved since they should be informed of any bullying incident. Some principals also text, email, or call the parent after school to verify student safety.

Track evidence. Track all evidence and have policies in place guiding what investigative action will be taken for serious incidents. Reviewing and tracking all bullying reports will provide evidence for your bullying prevention plans. (For instance, if you note that more bullying is happening in the hallways, you could stagger the bell schedule; if buses are a new hot spot, bus drivers could meet to discuss new bullying prevention strategies.)

Follow up on all reports. Bullying is a repetitive behavior so follow-up meetings with the students involved are crucial. Check if the incident was verified by student witnesses, parents, or staff; if consequences or interventions were carried out; if the bullying stopped; and if the target feels safe. The frequency of follow-up meetings and the number of staff members involved will depend on the severity of the bullying. Here are a few items to consider as you create follow-up plans:

- *Identify key players.* Determine which staff members should be involved in the follow-up based on where the bullying took place, the type and severity of the bullying incident, and who is the responsible staff member for the child.

  - For instance, if the bullying took place on the playground, then playground supervisors should be contacted to keep a closer eye on the students during recess.

  - If the child's mental health or safety is in jeopardy, then often the school resource officer, nurse, counselor, or psychologist should be contacted immediately to keep an eye on emotional needs or conduct interventions.

  - If the child is engaged in bullying behaviors, then those staff members in direct contact with the student should be notified to monitor behavior. The teacher or administrator should notify parents of every bullying incident by written notice, phone, or personal conference (depending on the severity and frequency of the incident). Law enforcement or the school resource officer should be notified for any bullying action deemed to be an infraction of the law, an assault, or a threat.

- *Determine frequency of monitoring.* In some cases, a daily check-in with a bullied child is needed to assess mental well-being, as well as with a child who is engaging in bullying behavior to let him know that his behavior is being monitored.

- *Decide who should be the contact for the child.* For less serious offenses, a classroom teacher should be assigned to quietly pull the child aside and assess the situation and the child's well-being. Empathy is key. ("Are you okay?" "Do you need help?" "Is there a place you need to go?" "Are things better today?" "I'm here to help and will keep checking to make sure you're okay.")

- *Delegate follow-up personnel.* An administrator or counselor should also oversee the follow-up process, which could be just a one-time conference or a series of scheduled conferences between the child, parent, teacher, administrator, or other pertinent staff. Note that aggressive behaviors rarely change overnight and need to be continually monitored. The child who was targeted may have long-term effects that sometimes crop up a week or more after the incident.

- *Complete a follow-up report form.* A form is provided on pages 157–158 to help you manage the follow-up process. Adapt the form to meet your needs, and find ways to track the follow-up to ensure that all students' needs are met and that the bullying will be reduced.

Ways to Involve PARENTS

Clear procedures should be established so parents know how and where to report their concerns about bullying and to whom (the teacher, counselor, nurse, principal). Parents should also be instructed how to report possible school threats or safety issues. A key to success is using numerous ways to educate parents about reporting procedures. Here are some to consider:

Teach parents the difference between *bullying* and *teasing*. Doing so will drastically reduce irrelevant reporting, since parents frequently misconstrue teasing as bullying.

Create a one-pager. Many schools create a newsletter or a simple one-page description of how parents can report bullying. This is handed out at parent-teacher conferences and at the back-to-school open house.

Create a bulletin board. Designate a bulletin board outside the front office as well as above each student report box that describes how parents can report bullying.

Use the school website. Post a parent reporting form on your school website and tell exactly how parents should report a bullying incident and review the school's anti-bullying policy.

Hold an evening parent workshop. In an evening workshop, briefly describe for parents how to report bullying and strategies your school is using to combat the problem.

Reach out to new parents. Every parent new to your school should be advised about bullying prevention protocol and given a brief description of what bullying is and how to report it.

List reporting procedures in your school handbook. Reporting procedures should also be listed in your school handbook, student agendas, and parent bulletins, and verbal reminders should be given at parent-attended school events.

Provide parents a reporting form. Parents should be provided with the means to report bullying incidents. Ideally the form would be posted on your school's website as well as made available at the office and in the student handbook. A sample parent reporting form is provided on page 159.

Develop Ways for Parents to Report Bullying

Parents should be able to report bullying incidents to the school. Forms should be made readily available to parents in the office, on the school's website, in the school handbook, and in any other places you deem appropriate. Be sure to include the definition of bullying that your school or district has agreed upon, and then make sure that parents are contacted following a report by the administrator or teacher in a timely manner (ideally within two days), and a follow-up plan is developed.

When receiving a parent report of bullying, your first step is to determine if the incident is indeed bullying. A meeting with the adult and child witnesses may need to be scheduled. The administrator or teacher then decides whether to conference with the parent. Based on the information gathered at those meetings, the students involved in the incident may need to be interviewed and bullying intervention plans formed.

KEY BULLYING PREVENTION POINTS IN R3: REPORT

- Institute a policy requiring *all* stakeholders, including parents, to report bullying incidents or threats.

- Create multiple procedures (including anonymity) for reporting bullying incidents.

- Take measures, such as creating advisor-advisee programs, to nurture staff and student relationships so kids feel more comfortable making reports.

- Convince students that they *will* be heard and you *will* back them up if they report.

- Have student teams speak directly to peers about the importance of reporting bullying.

- Train peer mentors to receive reports of bullying from other students.

- Teach students the difference between *tattling* and *reporting* and mobilize them to help break the "do not snitch" code.

BULLYING REPORT FORM: PRIMARY STUDENTS

Note: An adult should fill this out with the student.

Today's date: _____

Your name: _____
(You do NOT have to give your name)

Name of person who was upset or hurt: _____

Name of person who was being mean: _____

Circle when this took place:

Before school   During school   After school

Circle where at the school this took place:

| Bathroom | Cafeteria | Playground | Bus | Classroom | Resource Room |
| Art Room | Gym | Library | Music Room | Hallway | Other |

Adapted from "Student First Grade Alleged Bullying Report Form," W. Reily Brown Elementary School, Dover, Delaware.
From *The 6Rs of Bullying Prevention* by Michele Borba, Ed.D., copyright © 2016. This page may be reproduced for use within an individual classroom or school only. For other uses, contact Free Spirit Publishing Inc. at www.freespirit.com/permissions.

Circle what happened:

Dictation to adult of what happened:

BULLYING REPORT FORM: ELEMENTARY STUDENTS

This form can be used to report a bullying incident. You may keep your comments anonymous. Please make sure what you are reporting fits the bullying definition: *The person was mean on purpose and there was a power imbalance.*

Name of student making report (optional): _____

Grade: _____   Date: _____

WHAT happened?

WHO were all the people involved?

WHEN did it happen? (time/date)

→

WHERE did it happen?

___ bus   ___ restroom

___ playground   ___ classroom

___ hallway   ___ gym

___ cafeteria   ___ other: _____

Did you tell an adult? ___ yes ___ no   If yes, WHO? _____

Do you need help? If so, what kind?

BULLYING REPORT FORM: MIDDLE SCHOOL STUDENTS

Please respond to only those questions you feel comfortable answering and can answer accurately. You may choose to include your name (which will be kept confidential) at the end of the form or submit this anonymously.

1. What happened? Describe the bullying.

2. Who was bullying? (Please give full names.)

3. Who was being bullied? (Please give full names.)

4. When did the bullying happen?
   Date: _____ Time: _____

5. Where did the bullying happen?

6. Who was the target of the bullying? (If you don't know the name, describe the person.)

7. Who else saw the bullying? (Please give full names.)

8. Have you told anyone about the bullying?

Yes ___ No ___

If yes, who? _____

9. Did anyone help you?

Yes ___ No ___

If yes, who? _____

Your name (*optional and confidential*): _____

Your grade: _____

Room number: _____

BULLYING REPORT FORM: SCHOOL STAFF

Adult making or receiving report:

Date and time:

If you did not witness the incident, who reported the bullying to you? (Check one):

☐ Bullied child _____

☐ Witness _____

☐ Staff _____

☐ Parent _____

☐ Other _____

Bullied student(s):

Student(s) who bullied:

Names of adult witnesses:

Names of student witnesses:

Where bullying occurred: _____ Date and time: _____

Description of bullying behavior:

Are there any immediate safety or mental health needs? Yes _____ No _____

Specify concerns:

☐ Physical injury _____

☐ Damaged clothing/property _____

☐ Transportation needs _____

☐ Retaliation fears _____

☐ Emotional needs _____

☐ Severity of bullying _____

☐ Cyberbullying _____

☐ Learning needs _____

☐ Other: _____

Action taken:

BULLYING FOLLOW-UP REPORT FORM

Student targeted in incident:

Student(s) reportedly engaged in bullying behavior:

Adult making or receiving report:

Brief description of the incident, date, and time:

Initial conference date: _____

Recommendations:

Follow-up conference date: _____ Time: _____

Conducted by: _____

Present:

☐ Administrator   ☐ Teacher

☐ Social Worker   ☐ Student

☐ Counselor   ☐ Parent

☐ Psychologist   ☐ Other

Current assessment of situation:

Recommendations:

Parents contacted: _____ Date: _____

Additional actions or notes:

Next steps:

Next follow-up conference date: _____ Time: _____

Person making contact:

PARENT BULLYING REPORT FORM

Note: A child is bullied when he or she is exposed to intentional negative actions on the part of one or more other people, and he or she has difficulty defending himself or herself.

Please print the following information:

Student's name: _____ Grade: _____ Teacher: _____

Parent's name: _____ Legal guardian: _____

Date of incident: _____ Time of incident: _____

Phone number for contact: _____

Exact location of incident: _____

Names (if any) of adults who were contacted or involved:

Names of any witnesses (child or adult):

Please describe what happened in your own words. Include as many details as possible to give a clear, accurate account of the events.

Parent signature: _____ Date: _____

School personnel receiving the report: _____

Procedures:

Date:_____

R4: Respond

Teach Student Witnesses How to Respond to Bullying

In this chapter, you will learn:

- the most common reasons kids don't help during bullying incidents

- four ways to combat the "bystander effect" and encourage witnesses to speak up

- six "Bully BUSTER" strategies witnesses can use to help during a bullying incident

- class meeting topics to mobilize students to help their peers

- ways students can reduce bullying if they become upstanders

- strategies schools are using to help kids adopt upstander skills so they *really* use them!

The fourth "R," R4, is devoted to the students who witness bullying. They are victims, too, and can be tremendous help in bullying prevention. The typical approach to prevention and intervention has been to deal individually with the child who engages in bullying and the target. But new insight into the roles student witnesses play in bullying incidents has generated a major shift in perspective. How spectators respond to the child who is bullying, the target, or other bystanders can dramatically *increase* or *decrease* the intensity and duration of the bullying. The right response can shrink the audience for the bullying, reduce the severity of a target's stress, mobilize kids to help the target, and even flip a school's norms so the majority of students support a bully-free culture. Activating the compassion and courage of student witnesses may be our best hope in reducing bullying and peer cruelty. But to succeed, students need the right guidance so they know *when* to step in, know *how* to help safely and effectively, and *believe* that adults will give them permission to do so.

Another reason we need to teach kids how to respond properly to bullying is *students are far more likely than staff members to witness bullying.* What's more, bullying almost always happens in front of other students and when adults aren't in the vicinity to help.[3] This chapter offers ways to arouse students' compassion and courage so they are more likely to help their peers, as well as a repertoire of upstander strategies and social-emotional skills to teach kids how to speak out against bullying and reduce peer cruelty.

A meta-analysis of twelve school-based bullying prevention programs that involved almost 13,000 students from kindergarten through high school found that bystanders taking action to stop bullying had a very positive effect in reducing the overall bullying incidences in schools.[1]

"I'd see a kid get slammed into the lockers by two boys and they'd say mean stuff to him every day. I couldn't think in class because I hurt so much for him." —Tim, age 11

"We'd step in to help, but adults don't teach us how." —Susan, age 11

"Just tell us what to say and we'll be more likely to help." —James, age 9

A 2013 study of more than 9,100 New Zealand students showed that schools with students who took action to stop bullying had significantly less victimization and fewer reports of bullying.[2]

"We want to help, but teachers need to tell us it's okay if we do." —Sara, age 8

"Kids don't want to make things worse." —Sosha, age 9

Nine Reasons Kids Say They Don't Intervene in Bullying

Here are the nine most common reasons kids tell me they don't help in bullying incidents:

1. *They feel powerless.* "I didn't know what to do." Intervening requires skills. If children are never taught upstander skills, they may hesitate to intervene because they feel incompetent.

---

1. Polanin et al., 2012.
2. Denny et al., 2014.
3. Padgett and Notar, 2013.

2. *They fear retaliation.* "The kid who is bullying will turn on *me* next." Kids worry they may become the next target or be singled out for revenge if they help.

3. *They distrust the system.* "The teachers won't help me." Kids say repeatedly that they worry adults will not support them if they intervene.

4. *They fear peer rejection.* "Kids won't think it's cool." Longing to fit in always factors into the student social scene. To some children, there's nothing worse than being called a snitch by peers.

5. *They assume someone else will help.* "Why do I have to help? Other kids saw it, too." Kids don't intervene because they figure someone else will help, hence the "bystander effect" discussed in the next section.

6. *They fear humiliation.* "I don't want to look stupid." Kids may refrain because they fear peer ridicule. Worse, what if they try to step in but the targeted child rejects their help?

7. *They fear losing social status.* "But he's my friend!" The child who is bullying may be the bystander's friend or a member of his or her clique or peer group. For some kids, keeping a pal can trump everything.

8. *They fear injury.* "I may get hurt." Kids who engage in bullying are often physically aggressive and bystanders worry they'll get hurt trying to help.

9. *They are scared of making things worse.* "I could get someone in trouble." Kids may worry that reporting the incident may result in disciplinary repercussions for pals or classmates or incite more bullying.

Fear or powerlessness is often what curtails kids' courage, but both can be overridden if kids learn *how* to respond properly and recognize that they *will* be supported by both peers and adults if they do.

Witnesses Can Suffer, Too

Children who watch repeated peer abuse often suffer from severe psychological and physiological stress, which over time can equal the level of distress felt by the target.[4] The effects of observing bullying on a child can include (but are not limited to):

Guilt: *"I should have helped."*

Fear: *"I could be the next target."*

---

4. Janson and Hazler, 2004; Rivers et al., 2009.

Powerlessness: *"I didn't know what to do."*

Desensitization: *"I guess bullying is just a part of life."*

It's another reason why reports need to list names of all students involved in any bullying incident, when possible, so educators can monitor the emotional needs of children who bully, targets, *and* witnesses.

What Is the Bystander Effect?

Bystanders: People who witness a bullying incident but remain uninvolved or inactive spectators.

Upstanders: People who witness a bullying incident and are willing to stand up and take action in defense of others.

The date: March 13, 1964

The place: A quiet, middle-class neighborhood in Queens, New York

The event: A young woman named Kitty Genovese was attacked, raped, and stabbed outside her apartment building while repeatedly screaming for help. Thirty-eight of Kitty's neighbors heard her scream or saw the beating but not one was reported to have intervened or called police,* and she died. The incident made world news and enraged citizens.

"How could witnesses be so complacent and not help?" everyone wondered. New York University professors John Darley and Bibb Latané were intrigued and conducted a series of experiments to uncover why some people don't help while others do. They discovered a phenomenon called the "diffusion of responsibility," also known as "the bystander effect." It seems the *more* witnesses present in an emergency, the *less* people feel responsible to help.[5]

The bystander effect also applies to children, and recent headlines of suicides due to bullying are sad reminders of what is at stake when student witnesses remain passive. One of the most shocking incidents involved a young girl named Phoebe Prince, who was a freshman at South Hadley High School in Massachusetts. The fifteen-year-old had recently moved from Ireland and became a target of "mean girls" at her school who viciously tormented, threatened, and humiliated her for nearly three months until she went home one day

---

* According to *The Witness*—a 2015 documentary film directed by James Solomon, featuring Bill Genovese, Kitty's brother—despite apparent indifference on the part of many witnesses, a few people *did* take action, such as screaming out the window, running after Kitty, and calling the police. However, for reasons unknown, these actions went unreported at the time. In light of these new facts, I chose to still use this story as an example of the bystander effect, due to the volume of witnesses who failed to act and also due to the important research the event inspired.

5. Darley and Latané, 1968.

and hanged herself from a stairwell. Particularly alarming was that students at her school were aware of the torment but did nothing to try to stop it. Why? How can educators help change this dynamic?

FOUR WAYS TO COMBAT THE BYSTANDER EFFECT

I've asked many kids over the years why they didn't help a bullied classmate, and their rationale often fits Darley and Latané's "diffusion of responsibility" principle to a tee: "I thought somebody else would help." "Someone else will tell the teacher." "I was late, but I figured another kid would get his back." So how do you overcome psychology to boost the odds that kids will be upstanders? Here are some ways:

Make helpfulness a requirement *not* an option. Be upfront and tell kids: "If you see bullying, you *are* responsible to help if you can do so safely. If you remain silent, you *are* supporting the person who is bullying."

Teach kids about the bystander effect. Studies find that people who attend lectures about passive bystander behaviors are less likely to demonstrate them.[6] So prepare kids for what to expect in bullying situations by teaching the diffusion of responsibility. Start by role-playing bullying situations involving large numbers of witnesses, and then reduce the numbers to just a few. Next ask students: "Why is it that the more witnesses, the less likely someone will step in to help if there's a problem?" Then role-play ways kids can leave a scene safely to get help.

Offer evidence that peers *want* to help. Combatting peer pressure is hard—especially for students in middle school. Along with the bystander effect, pressure from peers deters kids from stepping in to help a bullied child. ("I don't want to lose my friends." "The kids will turn on me.") The facts show that *most* kids are against bullying, but they don't realize that peers are as well. To demonstrate: give every student an index card and ask two simple questions: "Do you approve of bullying?" "If you were bullied, would you want your friends to help?" Instruct students to answer yes or no to each question and not sign their names. Tally the responses and you'll very likely find at least 90 percent of students disapprove of bullying and want their peers to help. Post those results on your school marquee, the school website, and huge banners across your school. For example: *At Markham Junior High: 99% of kids don't approve of bullying and 95% of kids* want *someone to help if they are bullied.*

6. Keltner and Marsh, 2010.

Step in and be an upstander! Such messages, along with the evidence, motivate students to help.

Set a consequence for aiding and abetting bullying. Many schools include a clause in their anti-bullying policy stating that there will be a consequence if students do not report bullying or remain passive during a bullying incident. If you choose to include this clause, announce it frequently so students clearly understand the rule and its consequences.

How to Build an Upstander Culture

A crucial part of motivating students to become upstanders is to help them realize that they *can* make a difference and that most peers *do* want their support. Here are six ways to encourage kids to step in and speak up when peers need their help.

1. Mobilize student support. Most students hate to see their peers treated cruelly and want to help ease their pain. Start mobilizing them by suggesting *easy* ways to make a difference in a bullying situation. Explain that one of the simplest ways is not to give the bullying person an audience. Use class meetings to encourage students to say to one another that bullying isn't cool and they want to help. Tell students: "If you want to be an upstander but you don't know what to do or you don't feel safe to help, you can always walk away, report the incident to an adult or peer mentor, or support the target *after* the incident."

2. Tell stories of "quiet" upstanders. Some students worry that they are too shy to speak up, so allay concerns by telling them about Rosa Parks and Pee Wee Reese. Parks's refusal to give up her seat to a white man—without saying a word—made a monumental difference in the civil rights movement of the 1960s. Jackie Robinson, the first black player on a major league baseball team, was booed mercilessly by fans because of his race. So Pee Wee Reese, his white teammate, walked over to Robinson, put a hand on his shoulder, and stared down the crowd until they stopped booing. Reese's silent gesture stunned the crowd into silence, and from that moment on, they never booed

Robinson again. (The book *Teammates* by Peter Golenbock, which describes this moment, is a must read-aloud.) Rosa Parks's and Pee Wee Reese's quiet gestures can show students that upstanders can make a difference without saying a word.

3. Expose kids to heroes. One way to encourage kids to be upstanders is to expose them to courageous people who help others. The website KidsAreHeroes.com honors real kids who are making a difference in the world. Students can also read stories of everyday kid heroes in books such as *Real Kids, Real Stories, Real Change* by Garth Sundem. Or, each day assign a different student to deliver a one-minute speech about an individual he or she knows or has read about who is a hero and why.

4. Try a pledge. Many schools incorporate pledges that encourage students to be upstanders. Younger students can pledge: "I will help my friends if they are in trouble." Older students might pledge: "Nobody is a victim. Everybody is valued." Upper-grade students at Northern Lights School Division in Alberta, Canada, say each morning to peers: "I pledge to act immediately to stop any type of bullying. You can count on me to help you if you are having any type of problem. I will take seriously your feelings and perceptions about being harassed or bullied." Better yet, have students write their own pledges!

5. Hold class meetings about upstanding. Class meetings can be a great way for students to hear peers voice their displeasure about bullying and their wish for students to help each other. Here are a few meeting topics to consider:

- "Have you ever seen someone bullied at our school? Without using names, can you describe what happened? How did you feel watching? Did anyone help? How?"

- "Have you ever been bullied? Did anybody step in to help you? If so, what did they do? Did it help?"

- "Is it right to stand by and do nothing if you see someone being bullied? Why? What would our school be like if no one ever stepped in to help?"

- "Do you think kids can make a difference in stopping bullying?"

- "Have you ever stopped someone from bullying? What did you do?"

- "Have you seen other kids try to step in and stop bullying? Did it work?"

- "What stops kids from stepping in? What would make kids help more?"

- "Is there something adults could do at school to make students more likely to help?"

- "What are things kids do to help someone who is bullied?"

6. Acknowledge upstandership! Don't forget to acknowledge kids who are upstanders. You and your team, colleagues, or students can seek out kids who "step in and speak out" to stop bullying and share their names publicly. Some schools announce students' names over the loudspeaker or at assemblies. A middle school in Cold Lake, Alberta, held a contest to design their "Be a Buddy" school logo. The winning design, chosen by kids, was printed on T-shirts, which are given to students who demonstrate upstandership . . . and coveted by all students!

Tip for TEACHERS

Important! Be sure to ask students for permission to have their names publicly announced, and then honor their decision. Some students do *not* want public recognition, in which case the principal could privately honor their upstanding efforts. If the school climate does not support upstanders or the student fears possible retaliation from the bullying child, public acknowledgment of a student's helping behavior could backfire.

Books That Show "Upstander Power"

The right books can be a wonderful tool to help mobilize students to stand up to injustice and bullying. Here are a few kid favorites:

For lower elementary:

- *Fat, Fat Rose Marie* by Lisa Passen
- *Hooway for Wodney Wat* by Helen Lester
- *The Bully Blockers Club* by Teresa Bateman
- *The Juice Box Bully* by Bob Sornson and Maria Dismondy

For upper elementary:

- *Nobody Knew What to Do* by Becky Ray McCain
- *Say Something* by Peggy Moss
- *Super Tool Lula* by Michele Yulo

- *The Bully Blockers: Standing Up for Classmates with Autism* by Celeste Shally

- *Teammates* by Peter Golenbock

- *Stand Up to Bullying!* by Phyllis Kaufman Goodstein and Elizabeth Verdick

For middle school:

- *Bystander* by James Preller

- *The Forgotten Hero of My Lai: The Hugh Thompson Story* by Trent Angers

BEWARE: UPSTANDING BEHAVIORS DECREASE BY GRADE

Ervin Staub, a psychology professor at the University of Massachusetts and renowned authority on bystanding behaviors, found that the practice of kids coming to the aid of their targeted peers actually *decreases* across grade levels. An especially large drop happens between third and fourth grades. What's more, older students receive *less* help if they are bullied from both teachers and from other students. And passive bystandership increases with grades. Staub theorized that the reason is that as children get older "they are expected by both their teachers and peers, and by themselves, to handle their own conflicts. The result of the decrease in active bystandership, however, may be that adolescents feel more endangered and abandoned, and their need for security and positive connection is less fulfilled." It's all the more reason that adults *and* children in all grade levels need to learn how to respond to bullying to reduce peer cruelty. Staub further states: "Training in constructive, positive bystandership and classroom and school climates that encourage students to be active bystanders will likely improve the list of all students."[7]

66 Brave Staff Chat: Take Your Students' Pulse

Students state that one of the largest factors that curtails them from being upstanders is that "adults don't listen or help." How do you think the majority of your students feel about the support they receive from the staff at your school? What can you do to convey to your students that you will support them in their upstanding efforts?

7. Staub et al., 2003.

SET THE RIGHT CLIMATE FOR UPSTANDERS TO THRIVE

While kids can learn ways to intervene, there is a caveat: the adults need to support the students' efforts. It's worth repeating again and again: Students need to know that the staff is serious about supporting them and will back them up. Here are strategies to help create a climate that empowers kids to step in, speak out, and stop bullying.

Review "tattling vs. reporting." Breaking the "code of silence" among students is a contingency to upstanding since there are times kids may need to seek help from an adult. Review the section on tattling versus reporting (pages 138–140) to help kids know there *is* a difference: Emphasize that "upstanders *report!*"

> It's worth repeating again and again: Students need to know that the staff is serious about supporting them and will back them up.

Stress safety. Kids need to realize that safety is *always* the primary goal, so stress to students: "If someone could get hurt, *report!* It's always better to be safe than sorry."

Identify specific trusted adults. "Distrust of the system" is one reason kids don't intervene, so convince them you *will* believe and support them. Principals (and select staff) can visit each homeroom to personally relate this message. Also, tell students that if an adult does *not* listen, they should keep reporting until they find one who will.

Teach "CAP" bullying. Frequently review how to recognize bullying with students so they are clear when they should and should not intervene. Teach the acronym "CAP" to help kids remember the three parts of bullying: **C**—Bullying is **C**ruel. **A**—It is *not* an **A**ccident. **P**—Bullies have **P**ower over targets who cannot make them stop on their own.

Encourage "Upstander Buddies" and "Talking It Out." Research has shown that kids in kindergarten and first grade are more likely to respond to distress sounds when in pairs.[8] Talking to one another about the situation and their concerns helps ease their worries and builds their confidence to help. "Talking it out" together can also build courage. Older kids tend to keep their fears to themselves and so are less likely to intervene since they lack peer support. So suggest that students pair up to support each other and share their

---

8. Ibid.

worries. Encouraging "upstander buddies" at young ages may help kids make a lifelong habit of talking through their fears and coming to the assistance of others in need.

SEL SKILL: The ABCs of Bullying Safety

While we hope students will intervene in bullying, we should always place their safety as the top priority. Teach the following ABCs of Bullying Safety so students learn protection strategies. Then, role-play age-appropriate scenes so they can use these strategies during an actual bullying incident.

Act safely. Look and listen. Use your instincts. Does it look like someone could be hurt? If so, act and get help! Don't wait.

Band together. There is safety in numbers, so stick together. If you're concerned that something is wrong, walk toward an adult or call/text for help.

Care for the person who needs help. Ask: "Are you okay?" Say: "I'm sorry that happened." "Can I walk you to the office?" "What can I do to help?"

Six "Bully BUSTER" Skills to Teach Students to Be Upstanders

"I always wanted to help but I never knew what to do when my friend was bullied. My teacher taught us Bully BUSTER skills and now I know what to do!" —Darlene, age 8

I've long been convinced that the most effective and under-used strategy in bullying prevention is mobilizing the compassion of the student majority and teaching them upstander skills. Doing so empowers children with tools to stop cruelty, help targets, create safer school environments, *and* reduce bullying. In fact, research finds that student witnesses are more likely to intervene if they know what to do and feel that they have the necessary skills and resources. Studies also show that when student witnesses do intervene correctly, bullying behavior stops more than half of the time.[9]

I developed the Bully BUSTER skills in this section after culling hundreds of articles on the bystander effect to determine the types of doable strategies that will disperse a crowd, stop a person from bullying, and help a target. I've since taught the skills to thousands of teachers and students around the world to

---

9. Stueve et al., 2006; Craig et al., 2000.

ensure success. The acronym BUSTER helps kids remember the six key strategies: each letter represents a way kids can be upstanders in a bullying incident.

The skills do work, but it's crucial to keep in mind that *not all strategies work for all kids or all situations.* The best teaching method is to introduce all six BUSTER skills, and then ask students to choose the ones that best fit their comfort level. The hardest skill is directly confronting the child who is engaging in bullying (that's difficult for adults as well). *Important:* Emphasize to students that "Safety is the first priority, so if there might be a problem, leave ASAP and get help."

Finally, be sure to teach these strategies to *all* stakeholders so adults can then suggest a Bully BUSTER strategy to a child to use as the need arises. You might invite all adult stakeholders (staff, parents, and community members) to view students demonstrating these lessons (such as at assemblies or in classrooms) or make extra copies of videos or handouts of the BUSTER skills they can review and learn themselves. A quick, simple outline of the skills is available on page 179. You could use this as a handout or post it in your school or classroom as a reminder to students. The section "How to Help Students Use Upstander Skills in the Real World" (page 176) offers ways counselors and teachers can help kids practice these strategies so they become lifelong habits.

"I am only one; but still I am one. I cannot do everything, but still I can do something. I will not refuse to do the something I can do." —Helen Keller

B—BEFRIEND THE TARGET

Students often don't intervene in bullying because they lack confidence or assume the target doesn't want help. But research shows that if witnesses see that a peer is upset and wants their help, kids are more likely to step in.[10] Kids tell me if just *one* bystander would help, the other spectators would be more likely to intervene. And they're right! Research finds that when bystanders have a positive attitude toward a targeted student, they are more likely to attempt to help the target, rather than to support the child who is bullying.[11] Here are strategies to help kids learn this skill:

10. Hawkins et al., 2001.
11. Snell et al., 2002.

Hold class meetings to generate ideas for how to befriend targets.
As discussed earlier in this chapter, class meetings are great venues in which
students can hear peers verbalize their wish to support targets. Ask students:
"What if you didn't do anything to help someone being bullied? Might you try
to help them after the incident?" "What can you say or do to help someone who
was bullied?" Then write the students' ideas on a poster to hang as a reminder.
Keep encouraging students to add more statements to the poster. Here are
ideas a fifth-grade class generated in a brainstorming session: *"That must have
felt so bad." "Are you okay?" "I'm sorry I didn't speak out." "That happened to me,
too." "Do you want me to help you find a teacher to talk to?" "You didn't deserve
that." "You didn't do anything to cause it." "It's not about you. That kid picks on
everyone."*

Start with *small* acts of befriending. Convince students that they don't
have to speak face to face with a person bullying in order to support a target:
their small, quiet acts can make a difference. An African proverb helps convey
the message: "If you think you are too small to make a difference, try sleeping
with a mosquito." Then role-play how small acts of befriending can help curb
bullying. For instance, have a witness move closer or stand next to the bullied
child. When kids see that one of their peers disapproves of the bullying, it gives
them permission to show support and do the same.

Role-play ways to support targets. Teach students ways to support targets
and then have them role-play the strategies. Ideas include:

- **Show comfort:** Put a hand on the target's arm or an arm around the
  target's shoulder.

- **Clarify feelings:** "She looks upset." "You don't want this, right?"

- **Ask if the target wants support:** "Do you need help?" "Are you okay?"

- **Wave peers over:** "Come help!" "We need you guys over here."

- **Empathize:** "I bet he feels sad." "I feel for her."

Encourage kids to befriend *after* the bullying. Be sure to encourage students to befriend a child who was bullied after the bullying episode.
Brainstorm specific things they could say or do to help. Although this strategy
won't reduce the bullying at the moment, it will help reduce the pain of both
the targeted child and the witness. Also, once witnesses recognize how appre-
ciative the targeted child is of their gestures, they may be more willing to help
the next time.

SEL SKILL: How to CARE About Bullied Peers

Having peer support reduces the likelihood of bullying.[12] So use this simple acronym to teach students ways to CARE about a peer who has been bullied or needs a pal.

Connect. Stand closer. Show concern. Invite and include. "Come be with us!"

Advise ways to help. "Don't go that way." "Sit in the front of the bus."

Report. Offer to tell an adult. "I'll go with you to the counselor." "I'll tell the teacher."

Empathize and **E**ncourage. "I'm sorry." "It must hurt." "You didn't deserve that." "That happened to me." "Stay with us—it'll get better."

U—USE A DISTRACTION

The right diversion can draw peers away from the scene, make them focus elsewhere, give the target a chance to get away, and induce the person bullying to move on. So tell kids: "Remember, a person bullying someone wants an audience, and witnesses can reduce it with a distraction." The best distraction I've heard about was a middle school boy who dropped his backpack on the ground in the middle of a group of bystanders and asked for their help to gather his belongings. Of course, the kids didn't know that it was a purposeful act, and many joined in to help him. Meanwhile, the person bullying lost an audience and the bullying stopped—exactly what the boy had hoped for. Here are more diversions to diminish an audience for bullying:

- **Make up an excuse.** "A teacher is coming!" "The bell is going to ring." "John, your mom is waiting at the office for you."

- **Ask a question.** "What are you all doing here?" "Don't you know you're breaking the rules and are going to get in trouble?"

- **Use a diversion.** "There's a great volleyball game going on! Come on!" "You should see what's going on in the cafeteria!"

- **Use an interruption.** "I can't find my bus." "Can you guys help me find the custodian?" "Hey, there's a cat stuck up on the roof. Let's get help!"

---

12. Salmivalli, 2010.

S—SPEAK OUT AND STAND UP!

Directly confronting a person bullying is intimidating, and it's a rare kid who can. This skill is the hardest of the six BUSTER strategies. But students can stand up to cruelty without speaking directly to a tormentor. Tell kids to instead turn and speak to one or more individuals in the crowd and encourage their support. Explain: "Speaking out can get others to lend a hand and join you, but you must stay cool, and *never* boo, clap, laugh, or insult, which could encourage the person bullying even more." Here are a few ways students can speak out to other bystanders.

- **Show disapproval.** Give a cold, silent stare. Signal a time-out. Put up your hand as if to say, "Stop."

- **Label the impact.** "That's mean!" "That's hurtful!"

- **Ask for others' support.** "Are you with me?" "Are you going to stand by and let this happen?"

- **Name it.** "That's bullying!" "That's against the rules."

- **Tell your disapproval.** "This isn't cool!" "Don't do that!" "Cut it out!" "This is wrong."

SEL SKILL: What to Say to Help Others

Students want to help friends who are marginalized or bullied but often don't know what to do. So help your students learn *specific* things they can say to help peers, such as the following statements. Students can print these on paper "dialogue bubbles," and then role-play different scenarios using them. You can also post these in classrooms or hallways as reminders. With practice, these will become default skills that they can use in a real bullying situation.

- Reduce the audience that kids who bully crave. "Let's move on."

- Encourage other students' support: "Come on, let's help!"

- Help the target: "Are you okay?"

- Seek adult help: "I'll get a teacher!"

- Affirm positive school norms: "That's not what we do here."

- Report incidents to adults to stop future bullying: "[Student's name] was bullied at recess again."

- Stand up to the person bullying: "Hey, that's mean. Cut it out!"

- Reduce a target's emotional distress: "You didn't deserve that!"

T—TELL OR TEXT FOR HELP

Bystanders sometimes don't report bullying for fear of retaliation, so make sure kids know that adults will support and protect them. Also reassure kids that their names will be kept confidential and that they have the option to report anonymously. (Review with students how to report bullying: See R3: Report.) Don't assume students know these "tell or text" options: teach them.

- **Find an adult to tell.** Walk to the nearest adult to report the incident. Tell the grown-up *where* the problem is and *what* needs fixing. "There's bullying going on in the hallway. Kids need help now!"

- **Keep telling.** If the first adult doesn't help, go to the second or third. Keep telling until you get help.

- **Call the office.** Call the school office from your cell phone and report the bullying to the secretary.

- **Send a text.** Send a text to a peer who is not at the scene asking him or her to get adult help. Text your teacher. Text the principal. Text your parents and tell them to call the school.

- **Use the school report line.** Text or call the report line if the school has one. Or find the school resource officer or security guard.

- **Call 911.** If someone could be seriously injured in the incident, call 911.

- **Set off the fire alarm.** Pull the fire alarm if there is a serious threat or injury and you can't get to or find an adult.

Tip for ADMINISTRATORS

Today's students would rather text than talk, and most students own cell phones. Texting also offers the confidentiality kids often prefer when offering a report. But most important, the text is sent in "real time"—at the moment the bullying occurs and when the child needs help most. So set up a system in your school for receiving and responding to texts from your students about bullying. Options include subscribing to a commercial service, using a tool such as the free Google Voice app, or setting up a system that connects to your local law enforcement agency. If you choose to set up a text system, advertise it on posters and on your school website so students are aware of it, and then assign a point person (or people) on staff to respond to each text. Remember that every complaint needs to be taken seriously and investigated.

E—EXIT ALONE OR WITH OTHERS

Tell students, "If safety is an issue or you can't persuade your peers to leave, exit the scene yourself. To stay and watch bullying means you are supporting it." Role-play ways kids can try to break up a crowd as they exit, while not drawing attention to themselves and inciting the person bullying. Ideas might be:

- **Direct.** "Come on, we're going to the gym to play basketball."
- **Ask.** "I'm leaving. Who's coming with me?"
- **Suggest.** "Let's get out of here."
- **Encourage.** "Come on, we shouldn't be here."

R—GIVE A REASON OR OFFER A REMEDY

Bystanders are more likely to intervene when they are told *why* the action is wrong or *what* they can do in a bullying situation to help. So offer ways kids can help peers "stop and think" about what they're doing.

- **Give reasons why the bullying is wrong.** "This is mean!" "You'll get suspended." "You'll hurt him." "Hey, that's exclusion. Let him play!"
- **Offer a remedy.** "Go get help!" "I'm going to ask the coach to work this out." "If we don't watch this, it'll stop."

How to Help Students Use Upstander Skills in the Real World

We can teach children upstander skills in a classroom, but they need to learn them so well that they can use them immediately, if needed, to help a bullied classmate in the hallway or on the playground. In that moment, they won't have time to look at a poster on the wall or have a teacher tell them what to do. Each of the BUSTER skills should be rehearsed, role-played, and practiced until it becomes second nature and kids can use it *without* adult reminders, coaxing, or reinforcement.

I've watched counselors role-play the skills with students and film each child reenacting the skill so they can watch themselves. I've watched teachers create charts of the strategies and post them around the classroom and school, while other teachers had students work in cooperative learning groups to create screenplays around each strategy. Counselors have saved lessons on flash drives for kids to bring home and practice with parents and siblings.

Here are four additional ways to teach upstander skills so students have the confidence and competence to use them in actual bullying incidents.

1. **Role-plays.** The staff at Cornelia Elementary in Edina, Minnesota, presented the BUSTER skills to students in a series of assemblies by a team of staff members and students who role-played them onstage for everyone to watch. Each assembly featured *one* Bully BUSTER skill. Teachers and counselors then had students practice skills repeatedly in class-rooms. Other staff members reinforced the skills on the school grounds.

2. **Cross-age buddies.** An upper-grade class at Katherine Finchy Elementary in Palm Springs, California, taught lower-grade kids each BUSTER skill, which helped both the younger *and* older students.

3. **Videos.** The staff on the U.S. Army base in Vicenza, Italy, had middle graders make brief videos depicting each BUSTER skill and then played them on a large television monitor outside the front office for all stake-holders to review repeatedly. The video can also be replayed for students who need more review time or missed the lessons due to absence.

4. **Homework.** Shipley School in Pennsylvania holds an open house during which students teach parents social-emotional learning skills and are given posters that depict the steps to practice at home. You could also invite parents to visit a classroom where students teach their moms and dads the BUSTER skills.

KEY BULLYING PREVENTION POINTS IN R4: RESPOND

- Bullying almost always occurs when adults aren't in the vicinity to help.

- Kids who watch repeated peer abuse often suffer from severe psychological and physiological stress, which over time can equal the level of distress felt by the target.

- The right response by a bystander can reduce the audience in a bullying incident, reduce the severity of a target's stress, mobilize other kids to help, and create an environment where the majority of students support bully-free norms.

- Students need to frequently practice Bully BUSTER skills so they can confidently use them during an actual bullying incident.

- To activate bystanders' courage, students need to know *when* to step in and *how* to help, and then *believe* that adults will give them the permission to do so.

- We need to place students' safety as the top priority and help them learn how to protect themselves during a bullying incident.

STOP BULLYING:

BE A BULLY B-U-S-T-E-R!

Befriend the target
Use distraction
Speak out & stand up
Tell or text someone
Exit the scene
Reason & remedy

R5: Refuse

Help Targets Refuse Provocation and Cope with Victimization

In this chapter, you will learn:

- warning signs a student may be experiencing bullying
- the "5A Staff Response" to assist targeted students
- seven interventions to reduce victimization
- three quick ways to identify marginalized kids
- what kids can say and do to support bullied peers
- how to create a safety PLAN for a targeted child
- ways parents can reinforce bullying prevention skills

The fifth "R," or R5, of effective bullying prevention helps educators identify students who are vulnerable to bullying and teach them skills to refuse provocation, increase their safety, and cope with the effects of bullying. Educators need to focus their efforts on not just intervention with targeted students, but also on helping them learn new habits of assertiveness and form healthy peer relationships to reduce the likelihood of continued bullying. Adults need to also recognize the importance of properly handling the targeted student's emotional distress to minimize long-term damage. Ongoing training is essential to help everyone identify and support present and potential targets.

How Bullying Affects Targeted Children

A child who is bullied hurts, and that hurt can last for years, even for a lifetime. What adds to the pain is that targeted children are often unsupported by witnesses, so they also feel isolated, humiliated, and exposed. The help these children should receive from adults is often never given—usually because the bullying they endure is never reported. Many bullied kids are too embarrassed, too full of shame, and too fearful of retaliation to seek help. They desperately need someone to believe them and tell them they did nothing to warrant the cruel acts they endured.

We can try to understand why children who bully target specific kids, but keep in mind there's no one profile of a target, just as there is no one cause of bullying. Many elements put kids at risk for being involved in bullying dynamics. We also might mistakenly assume that a target has somehow done something to trigger his or her tormentor: "She's too sensitive." "He's too impulsive." "She's a whiner—that always leaves kids open to bullying."

But the fact is that bullying has more to do with the social situation and less to do with a particular behavior or shortcoming of the targeted child. It's also a key reason why educators as well as parents need to tune in closer to social settings and learn possible signs of bullying so they can help prevent victimization. At the root of bullying are dysfunctional relationships and a lack of empathy.

Another bullying myth continues to endure that reduces a child's chance to receive needed support: "Bullying has always been a problem. It's no big deal. Kids get over it." The perpetuation of that belief is deadly to bullying prevention efforts. The reality is that bullied kids experience a wealth of negative effects that can be disastrous to their well-being in the short and long term, and scores of research from our most prestigious organizations prove it.

"It hurts so bad. I hate my life. I hate everything." —Dylan, age 12

"I'm so scared he's going to come after me again. I just can't think."
—Tyrell, age 8

"All the mean things the bully does keep flashing in my head."
—Kara, age 10

WHAT THE EXPERTS SAY ABOUT THE IMPACT OF BULLYING

StopBullying.gov. Kids who are bullied often suffer from depression, anxiety, increased sadness and loneliness, changes in sleep and eating patterns, and loss of interest in activities they used to enjoy. These issues may persist into adulthood. In addition, bullied kids can suffer from health complaints, decreased academic achievement—GPA and standardized test scores—and school participation. They are more likely to miss, skip, or drop out of school.[1]

American Academy of Pediatrics. A study of 4,297 children at three time points (fifth, seventh, and tenth grade) found that bullying at any age was associated with worse mental and physical health, increased depressive symptoms, and lower self-worth and those effects remain even after it stops.[2]

American Psychiatric Association. Children who are bullied can experience serious emotional difficulties. Bullying can interfere with social development, self-esteem, and school performance. Victims of bullying are also at increased risk for problems with anxiety and depression and suicidal thoughts. What's more, a five-decade-long nationwide study of more than 7,700 participants reveals that the impact of being bullied in childhood persists up to midlife.[3]

The damage of bullying to a child's mental, social, emotional, and physical well-being is undeniable. Though the target has done nothing to warrant such torment, the child begins to believe otherwise. "I guess I'm just a worthless person," one girl told me. "The bully must know something about me," another boy said. "I probably deserve to be treated like this."

The pain from being bullied can seem unbearable to a child: anxiety builds, fear mounts, confusion climbs, and self-esteem plummets. As the torment continues, anxiety and depression can set in, post-traumatic stress disorder symptoms can emerge, suicidal thoughts are possible, and bullying can become a life-and-death issue.

> Just 42 percent of students who had been bullied at moderate, severe, or very severe levels reported the bullying to a school official. Of those who told what was happening, only 34 percent admitted that things improved afterward.[4]

The good news is that concerned, committed adults can create a safe and caring school climate that greatly reduces bullying and helps children feel secure, connected, and respected. The task isn't easy, but it is a moral imperative. A key step is for all staff members to recognize the signs of bullying so they can identify bullied children and then work as a team to help them learn to refuse the provocation of the bullying child, recognize they deserve to be treated with respect, and acquire a cadre of skills so they have the confidence to circumvent victimization for the rest of their lives.

---

1. From stopbullying.gov/at-risk/effects.
2. Bogart et al., 2014.
3. Arseneault et al., 2011.
4. Davis and Nixon, 2010.

WARNING SIGNS A STUDENT MAY BE EXPERIENCING BULLYING

Most bullying signs go unreported or undetected. Many students are uncomfortable telling adults they were bullied for fear it will make matters worse, because the parent or educator will confront the bullying child. Fear of retaliation is a major concern of targets, and rightly so. Most bullying occurs in areas and times when adults are not present to protect targets. That's why it's crucial that educators learn specific warning signs of bullying so they can support potential targets. Every student can have an "off" day and display a sign or two, so look for a sudden unhealthy behavior that is not typical of the student and endures. Of course, the signs might also indicate other problems, but any signs warrant closer examination and discussing with other staff members and the child's parents. See the form on page 211.

Warning Signs of Possible Cyberbullying

Cyberbullying, as discussed in R2: Recognize, is a form of bullying by electronic means. A perpetrator uses digital media (such as texts, emails, IMs, website posts, tweets, videos) to hurt, threaten, embarrass, annoy, blackmail, or otherwise target another child. Though it is most common during the middle school years, the problem is making its way into the younger set. It is not surprising that cyberbullying has the potential to cause severe psychological damage in targeted children. Though most electronic bullying happens off school grounds, many students carry cell phones or tablets to school, so the staff should be aware of these signs. In addition to many of the signs just listed, a child who is being cyberbullied may:

- be hesitant to go online, or act nervous when an IM, a text message, or an email appears

- act visibly upset after using a computer or cell phone, or suddenly avoid electronic devices

- hide or clear the computer or cell phone screen when a peer or adult approaches

- spend longer hours online in a more tense, pensive posture

Tip for TEACHERS

It sometimes helps to keep a written record of your concerns about students. Mark the specific times the behavior occurs in your lesson plan or date book. Doing so may help you uncover a pattern that will be helpful in developing an intervention plan. For instance, you note that the child becomes more anxious in third period. When you dig deeper you discover that third period is the only time when two girls join your class roster. Could they be the perpetrators? Also be sure to share your concerns with other staff members.

Brave Staff Chat: Hold Five-Minute "Share Your Concerns" at Meetings

Consider instituting a brief weekly or monthly "Share Your Concerns" time at staff meetings for members to discuss students who are at risk for being bullied. Break up into grade-level teams or do a five-minute round robin style discussion in which each educator takes a turn to briefly describe a student who might be (or is) a target. Warning signs of bullying can be missed, but regular chats about vulnerable students can be a proactive way to generate staff support for them as well as identify those who may be overlooked. Bullying generally happens when adults are not there, so the more often educators can use their "collective eyes" to spot bullying and work together to create solutions, the more effective the bullying prevention efforts.

"Any kid can get bullied, but the ones who are 'different' get bullied more because they stand out. Too bad kids can't turn on an 'invisible switch.'"
—Jeremy, age 9

Factors That Increase a Student's Chances of Being Bullied

Any difference can set children apart from their peers and make them a potential target for bullying. I've held dozens of focus groups around the world and asked students: "Name why students are bullied," and their answers would fill an entire wall. The characteristics they named included: *short, fat, wears braces, wears glasses, has pimples, whines, stutters, geeky, gay, too tall, too skinny, colored skin, too white, has freckles, smart, new kid, cries easily, tattles, in special education class, in the gifted class, pouts, too popular, a different reli- gion or culture, shy, too loud, acts silly, annoying, too anxious, scared . . .* the list is endless.

The simple truth is that any child who is "different" from the norm can become the target of a child engaged in bullying. It's one reason why educators need to err on the side of caution and not use "profiles of kids most likely to be bullied" as guides, which can cause us to overlook other students. However, research does find that there are certain characteristics that make students especially susceptible to peer abuse. Staff members might tune in a bit closer to students with these characteristics in regards to bullying.

Autism spectrum disorder (ASD). Studies find that students with ASD are especially vulnerable to bullying and often intentionally led into meltdowns or aggressive outbursts by cruel peers. Children with ASD attending regular pub- lic schools are bullied at a rate of nearly 50 percent more than kids in private school or special education settings.[5]

Severe food allergies. In one survey, roughly a third of the children reported being bullied for their severe, sometimes life-threatening, food allergies— especially nuts, milk, and eggs.[6] Some schools suggest that cafeteria monitors be trained to intervene quickly to help prevent trading of food or bullying activ- ities regarding food.

Depression, anxiety, or aggression. Students entering first grade with signs of depression and anxiety or excessive aggression are at risk of being chronically victimized by classmates by third grade.[7] Also, children who have recently experienced trauma will appear more vulnerable and often become targeted. Alert staff members of those students who have experienced a recent trauma or a parent's deployment, illness, death, job loss, divorce, or family tragedy.

Lack of popularity or peer support. One student questionnaire found that kids who bully often choose unpopular kids to target who are less likely to be defended by their peers.[8] In bullying these kids, perpetrators can then keep their status and not lose the affection of popular peers.

LGBT. A Gay, Lesbian & Straight Education Network (GLSEN) national school climate survey of over 7,800 middle and high school students found that

5. Chen, 2012.
6. Saint Louis, 2013.
7. Leadbeater et al., 2009.
8. Veenstra et al., 2010.

nearly two thirds of LGBT (lesbian, gay, bisexual, or transgender) students heard homophobic remarks often or frequently at school. Almost one in five reported being physically assaulted at school, especially during middle school years. Over half of LGBT students reported feeling unsafe in school because of their sexual orientation.[9]

> ## " Brave Staff Chat: Who Are Your Vulnerable Kids?
>
> **Review the previous section, "Factors That Increase a Student's Chances of Being Bullied" and then hold a staff meeting to discuss what you're doing to identify your vulnerable kids. Divide staff into grade-level teams and make lists of kids you are concerned about. Then create a plan to help them be less likely to be victimized. How will you notify other staff members about those children?**

THREE SIMPLE WAYS TO IDENTIFY MARGINALIZED KIDS

Social exclusion or relational aggression (in which a child or group deliberately isolates a peer from the social scene) can be far more painful than many adults recognize. One team of researchers compared the effects of hitting, name-calling, and social exclusion and found that systematic isolation and exclusion had the most severe negative effects on kids and could even result in post-traumatic stress disorder.[10] Children who bully often target students who lack social networks since they are less likely to have peers come to their aid. So identifying your marginalized students and then building their social support is one element of effective bullying prevention.

Here are three easy activities to do with students to find out which ones may be prone to peer exclusion. *Important:* Only staff members who have developed trust with their students should gather this information. Students need to know that their responses will be kept confidential.

Circles of Support. Draw four concentric circles on a letter-sized paper (the center circle should be about an inch or so in width with the final circle outline almost touching the paper edges). Number each circle from one to four, beginning with the center circle. Ask students to answer the following questions either verbally or by writing down names: Circle 1: "People who you love most and can count on." Circle 2: "People you can count on, but not as much

---

9. Kosciw, 2014.
10. Mynard et al., 2000.

as Circle 1." Circle 3: "People you like to do things with." Circle 4: "People who you can count on but are required (or paid) to be in your life." Students with a strong support system generally have numerous names of people in each circle. Those who are marginalized often have limited names of peers and individuals who are not part of the school scene.

An Index Card Socio-Gram. Ask each student to write the names of two to four peers they hope to "play, work, or sit with in a cooperative learning group, club, recess, game, or lunchroom." Collect the cards and identify names frequently listed by peers as well as names of children left out. You will have a quick index of children with high and low peer support.

A Map of Social Networks. Provide a map of the school cafeteria or playground (or other locations where students congregate in large groups with few adults) and ask students to privately mark: "Where do you sit in the cafeteria (or play on the playground)?" "Who sits (or plays) around you?" Watch for those students who have limited or no other peers around them.

The "5A Staff Response" to Help Bullied Students

It's challenging for staff to know what to say to comfort a student who has been bullied. Train your staff in the "5A Staff Response," which includes five steps to comfort a traumatized child and gather information about the incident so you can report it and assure the student's safety and support. The severity of the incident, as well as the child's reaction to it, will determine the number of these five elements you need to address. You'll need to alter the scripts so they are appropriate to each incident. In some cases, the student may be so distraught that you will need to forgo any conversation, but instead accompany the child to a counselor, a nurse, or an administrator for immediate help, or notify the school security, police, and parents.

1. AFFIRM the student. Be empathetic and explore how the child feels about the incident, but also ensure the child that he or she was *not* responsible for the behavior of the child who bullied. A few script possibilities are:

- "You were right to report this and get help from an adult."

- "I'm glad you asked for help and came to me."

- "You did nothing to cause this. It's not your fault."

- "Nobody has the right to hurt other people. I'm so sorry, you don't deserve this."

- "I know it's hard to talk about it, but I'm so glad you did. I'm here for you."

Caution: Do *not* promise the student that you will keep the information confidential and not tell school authorities or parents. You will need to report the incident. You can promise that only trusted adult officials will be aware of the situation.

2. ASK the right questions. Posing the right questions will help gather critical information. A traumatized child usually is in a heightened state of anxiety and may have trouble remembering or focusing. Be alert to the child's distress level. You can always gather more data at a later time.

- "Tell me more about what happened."

- "Has this happened before?"

- "Who was there?" "What time did this happen?" "Where were you?" "Who did this?" "Did anyone else see what happened?" "Did anyone try to help you?"

- "Did the person do this on purpose?" "Did you tell them to stop?"

3. ASSESS the student's emotional and physical safety. Determine what the child needs to feel safe, while recognizing that the student may not have the answers.

- "What can I do to help?" "I'm going to make sure you're safe."

- "How are you?" "Do you need to go to the nurse?" "Can I call your parent?" "Do you want to go to a quiet place and sit for a while?" "Would you like me to stay with you?"

- "What do you need to feel safe?" "Let's think about what we can do about it."

- "Let's talk about what you can do the next time." "Is there anyone you'd like me to tell?"

- If the child is in emotional or physical distress, get immediate help from the nurse or counselor and report the incident to the administrator.

4. ASSIST the student on the road to recovery. Here are things to say that help the student recover and realize he or she is not to blame: (*Important:* While we certainly can help kids develop coping strategies or social skills, use caution in giving students the impression that their behavior *caused* the problem. Doing so can only make targeted kids blame themselves, and even believe they deserve to be treated in a demeaning way.)

- "Thanks for giving me that information. Let's use it to make a safety plan."

- "Let's think what would help you feel safer when you need to use the restroom." "Let's make a plan for how you can feel safer walking down that hallway." "I'm going to contact the bus driver so he knows what's going on. It's best for you to sit in the front of the bus on the right side so he can keep an eye on things."

- "Would you like to log these incidents so you can show us what's happening?"

- "I'm going to set up an appointment with the counselor who can help you learn ways to lower your stress so you can concentrate."

- "Let's think of some things you can say or do so you will be less likely to be bullied."

- "There are some things kids do that help them be bullied less. Would you like to learn them?"

5. <u>A</u>DVOCATE for the student to reduce future bullying. The goal is for the student to leave the meeting feeling more secure knowing that adults will ensure his or her safety. Tell the student what will happen to make him or her safer. Refer the child to an administrator, a nurse, a guidance counselor, a security officer, or a homeroom teacher as needed, and complete a detailed bullying report. (See R3: Report for details on reporting.)

- "No strategy works immediately, but I'm going to keep tracking what's going on."

- "You can find me in this room most of the day [name times] but if I'm not here, you can go to [list names and rooms of other staff members]."

- "Please come back [tomorrow or a certain time] and let's keep connecting until things get better."

- "Thank you again for coming to me. I know it took courage. Now I'm going to do all I can to help."

How to Encourage Students to Support Targets of Bullying

As I discussed in chapter R4: Respond, many bullied students have told me one of the best things that anyone did to help was when a peer supported them after the fact. "It made me feel I wasn't alone," one boy told me. "All I needed was to know that one of my friends cared," another child said. A big part of prevention is encouraging students to support a bullied peer even if it's later that night, the next day, or next week. Students should be encouraged to care.

"I saw my friend being bullied and didn't do anything to help. I felt so bad I couldn't sleep. Do you think it's too late to tell her I'm sorry?"
—Susan, age 12

Though we ideally want students to stick up for bullied students during an incident, doing so takes courage and is far less common than we hope. But encouraging students to support targets "whenever or wherever" has hidden benefits: It may help ease a bullied child's pain, as well as nurture peers' kindness, ease their shame and guilt of not aiding in the moment, and help them learn caring habits. Saying simple comments such as: "Do you need help?" or "I'm sorry that happened to you" are gateway behaviors that move kids from passive bystanders to active upstanders. Here are ways to encourage kids to support targeted students.

WAYS TO HELP STUDENTS BECOME SUPPORTIVE ALLIES

Write essays. Some teachers mobilize student support for bullied peers by having students respond to this essay prompt: "How do you feel when you see a student being bullied?" Then teachers select a few essays to read anonymously to the class. The activity almost always creates a passionate discussion in which students share how they want to support targeted kids but don't know how to help. Use it as a catalyst to brainstorm specific ways that kids can support bullied peers.

Hold a "We Support Each Other" assembly. Some schools hold a schoolwide assembly to confirm students' support for one another. Involve your students in the preparation, especially those with "peer clout" and representing each "clique," which can increase student support. The assembly is almost like a high school homecoming, with the band, cheerleaders, sports teams, and school colors all in high gear, except the theme is "We Support Each Other." I've heard student speakers mesmerize the crowd as they spoke on the topic. One group of Oregon students followed the presentation by distributing sticky notes to the crowd and asking every student to write one way to support a bullied peer. Within an hour the school walls were flooded with ideas and the students were mobilized to help.

Flood your walls (and screens) with ideas! Don't assume that students know ways they can offer support to a bullied peer. Brainstorm those possibilities and make a list of options visible. You might hold class contests in which each class suggests the best strategies, which are posted later on a bulletin board. The principal might read one of the "best caring strategies" each day over the loud speaker. Student ideas can be displayed on computer screensavers throughout the school, large video screens, or on posters hung in hallways and classrooms. Each staff member can also find a place to mount supportive ideas. For instance, secretaries might place them on their front ledger, cafeteria workers might prop them on a food line counter, and custodians and bus drivers can post on their doors. One of the best ideas I've seen came from a small school in Florida: yard supervisors wore colored vests that were printed with ways to support kids. Be creative!

SEL SKILL: What Kids Can Say and Do to Support Bullied Peers

Students can say or do dozens of things to support targets. Here are ideas that I gathered from my focus groups in Ohio, Texas, and California. If practiced often, they can become skills that kids can use to help and comfort others for the rest of their lives.

Things kids can **do** to help bullied kids:

- Call or text the person to say you're sorry.
- Send a note saying she or he shouldn't have been treated like that.
- Ask if the person wants to sit with you on the bus or have lunch together.
- Ask if he or she wants you to help report the bullying to a teacher or counselor.
- Let the person know she or he is not alone and that you've also been bullied.

> Things kids can **say** to help bullied kids:
> - "You don't deserve to be treated like that."
> - "I'm sorry that happened to you."
> - "Is there anything I can do?"
> - "That was really mean. He shouldn't do that to you."
> - "That happened to me, too. She does that to everybody."
> - "Are you okay?"

Ways to Provide Safety and Support to Targeted Students

"I'm just so scared. Every time I turn or go anywhere I think the bully is going to be there. Can't you tell the teachers I need a safe place to go?" —Kevin, age 8

If you suspect or know that a student is being bullied, safety and support for the child needs to be provided. Work as a team with staff members to develop a safety plan and ensure that all pertinent staff members are aware of which students are vulnerable, recognize the plan, and are onboard to help. A unified, consistent, systemic staff response to create safety and support for bullied students is essential for effective bullying prevention. Here are suggestions:

Develop a method to notify pertinent staff. Create a simple way to alert staff—coaches, nurses, school security officers, bus drivers, cafeteria workers, class teachers, counselors, or others—about the plight of a targeted student. It could be a confidential email blast, a text, a notification to the school counselor or security officer (who can then connect with involved staff members via text or in person), or a note delivered in a sealed envelope to pertinent staff. The key is to alert necessary staff *as soon as possible* to avoid further bullying incidents and undue trauma to the targeted child.

Identify adult allies for the bullied student. Brainstorm with your team or staff a list of adults a targeted student can feel safe to go to when bullied, such as the school nurse, second-period teacher, bus driver, librarian, or basketball coach. Kids who have even one person to confide in can deal with bullying better than those dealing on their own. Ask the student: "If you don't feel safe, who will you go to?" If the child doesn't know, identify allies for each time block. One boy told me his best friend at middle school was the librarian. "She knew I was bullied and made me feel safe. I don't know what I would have done without her."

Tip for ADMINISTRATORS

Bullying on the bus is a big problem. Here are a few ways to reduce it:

- Educate your bus drivers so they are aware of your anti-bullying policy and on the same page with your prevention efforts.
- Insert video cameras on the bus. Review footage periodically and following incidents.
- Ask an older kid to "watch out" for a more vulnerable student.
- Mandate assigned seating on the bus so that children who might be prone to bully other kids are separated from each other.
- Provide report forms and boxes on the bus so students can share concerns.
- Post "Bully-Free Area" signs on the bus.
- Have an extra adult ride the bus and monitor student behavior. Many schools require the parent of a student who is bullying to ride the bus until the child's behavior improves.

Create a safety plan for the bullied student. Sometimes the best way to spare a student distress is to avoid the bullying child all together—especially if the targeted child's emotional health is in jeopardy. Keep in mind that most bullying happens when adults are *not* present, so identify the place and time bullying usually happens and then brainstorm ways to reduce contact. Explain to the student that bullying often happens in unsupervised areas, so he or she should plan to be near others at lunch, recess, lockers, parks, in hallways, or other spots. Be sure to pass along your safety plan to other adults who will encounter the student and can stay vigilant about bullying activities. Here are common places bullying occurs and possible solutions for a targeted student:

- *On the bus:* "Sit across from the bus driver on the right side of the bus. Don't sit near the back where the driver can't see you."

- *At a locker:* "Carry your books in a backpack so you don't have to go to your locker between periods." "I'll leave an extra textbook here for you in class so you don't have to go to your locker."

- *In the restroom:* "Avoid using the bathroom during recess or before or after school. Instead, get a hall pass during class time or use the nurse's restroom."

- *On the playground:* "Play closer to the yard supervisors. Avoid the outside corners of the playground or right near the equipment. Teachers can't see you there. If you have a problem, walk toward an adult."

SEL SKILL: Have a Safety PLAN

While you can teach students how to reduce the chances of bullying, learning how to be safe is the top priority. Teach students the acronym PLAN and its four parts to keep students safe from bullying.

Pal up. Hang out with a large group, stay with one companion, or find someone older or bigger who can help look out for you. (Ensure that the child has a companion. If not, find one for her. For younger or special needs students, assign the bullied child a specific "buddy" to watch out for her in "hot zones," such as the playground, school bus, or cafeteria.)

Let an adult know. Talk to someone you trust and seek him or her out if you don't feel safe. (Discuss with the child his "go-to" people. Who will he seek out in case he feels unsafe?)

Avoid "hot spots." Stay away from areas where bullying is more likely to happen, such as bathrooms, the back of the bus, the far corners of a playground, or under stairwells. (Identify with the child the places where bullying has occurred, then encourage her to avoid those spots and remain in areas that are well-lit and adult-supervised.)

Notice your surroundings. If you think there could be trouble, leave that spot. Take a different route, but don't go off alone. (Advise the child to walk different routes with other children so he feels safe and knows what to do and where to go in case of a problem.)

Use "Safe Place" stickers. Some schools use stickers or posters to designate safety zones for students. Adults should monitor these zones and also invite allied students who are not bullied to enter the spot so it doesn't make bullied kids stand out. This strategy often works well with younger students or those with special needs. A high school in Bonnyville, Alberta, opened extra classrooms for targeted students to eat lunch with staff volunteers. An elementary school in Dublin, Ohio, made bright vests for playground supervisors to wear so students could easily seek them out. Identify your "hot spots" (see Part II, page 50 for details) and create safe zones with adults there to help.

Tip for ADMINISTRATORS

I've conducted focus groups with hundreds of children around the world and always ask: "Where at school do you feel safest?" Hands down, kids answer, "the school library," and their reasons are insightful. "Libraries are quiet." "The librarian is strict and watches kids." "You feel safe and can breathe." "Most kids who bully don't read so they don't go there." Kids need safe zones where they can breathe easy. Where might you create more library-like spots in your school?

Enlist peer helpers. Many schools are enlisting the support of peers to help targeted students. St. Dominic's School in Cold Lake, Alberta, calls these students "Guardian Angels"; other schools have named them "peer helpers." Regardless of the term, the strategy is the same: pair a supportive child to "watch out" for the target at set times during the day, such as at recess, in hallways, during assemblies, in the cafeteria, or on the bus. The strategy is particularly effective if you pair a younger or special needs child with an older student.

Have the student keep a log of bullying incidents. Most students are reluctant to discuss bullying experiences or seek support. One way to reduce anxiety is to ask the student if he would feel more comfortable logging each incident and submitting it to a staff member. If he or she is receptive, help the student create a simple tracking system that notes the location, time, and perpetrators of the bullying. The system often helps kids be more open about discussing incidents, provides important clues about bullying patterns, and may help the child discover that the bullying is slowly decreasing.

Create a private signal. In most cases, targeted students fear retaliation from a bullying child and do *not* tell adults that they were bullied. Developing a private signal between the staff and targeted student can be a safe, stealthy way for the student to convey a personal need (such as using the restroom or seeing the counselor about a bullying incident) without having to raise a hand and draw attention. Signals could include the student putting a certain textbook or colored index card on his or her desk or keeping a hand on his or her ear until the teacher recognizes the need.

Books for Kids to Help Ease the Pain of Bullying

For lower elementary:

- *Hooway for Wodney Wat* by Helen Lester

- *Fat, Fat Rose Marie* by Lisa Passen

- *Spaghetti in a Hot Dog Bun: Having the Courage to Be Who You Are* by Maria Dismondy

- *The Name Jar* by Yangsook Choi

- *Weird! A Story About Dealing with Bullying in Schools* and *Nobody! A Story About Overcoming Bullying in Schools* by Erin Frankel

For middle and upper elementary:

- *Blubber* by Judy Blume

- *Bullying Is a Pain in the Brain* by Trevor Romain

- *Super Tool Lula: The Kind Warrior* by Michele Yulo

- *Wonder* by R.J. Palacio

For upper elementary and middle school:

- *Fat Boy Swim* by Catherine Forde

- *Feather Boy* by Nicky Singer

- *Feathers* by Jacqueline Woodson

- *Inventing Elliot* by Graham Gardner

Provide a "help card." Middle school students in Elk Island School Division created a "help card" for students to use if they needed help from a staff member about bullying but were reluctant to ask. All students were given a 3" x 5" laminated card that read: "I need help, please," which they could turn in to any staff member and receive immediate help without saying anything.

Set up a text number. Most kids prefer texting as their form of communication and many students carry cell phones. If your school allows cell phones, set up a private number that a bullied child can text for help (it may reach the counselor, teacher, administrator, school resource officer, or other staff member) and that person will immediately respond.

Develop a "safe mailbox." Staff members can create simple mailboxes to attach to their doors or place on their desks, with a secure lock so that only the adult can access the contents. Then, encourage students to drop a note in the box if they need help or a time to meet with the staff person. You could do a text or email version of this as well. Just be sure to check the box frequently!

FORM A STUDENT STUDY TEAM

Many schools meet as a team (some call these groups "Student Study Teams") to discuss the best intervention strategies for a targeted child. If you do not have such a group, form a team which generally consists of: the child's teacher(s); a site administrator; resource or special education teacher (if applicable); a counselor, social worker, or psychologist (if available); as well as the parent and/or any other adult who can offer perspective about the child. In some cases the custodian, secretary, or cafeteria worker has been involved. The group size does not matter, what does matter is that participants can offer perspective about the child's situation. The team discusses the bullying situation and reviews any reports or pertinent evidence. Then the student is discussed: his strengths and weaknesses, his motivators and interests, and what might help this child. Would anger management, assertiveness training, social skills, stress management, or confidence building help reduce bullying? The team formulates a plan to help boost the student's safety needs and identifies the bullying prevention strategies deemed most appropriate for the child. (A list of bullying interventions is provided in the next section.) The team also discusses how to measure the plan's effectiveness, who will be responsible for implementing each part of the plan, and when to meet next to assure success. Some teams meet weekly, bi-monthly, monthly, or as often as needed to help the child.

Seven Interventions to Reduce Victimization

"The teachers and my mom tell me a lot of things to do but nothing works. I just want someone to tell me what to do to make them stop bullying me!" —Jessica, age 11

Some educators make the mistake of assuming that kids will "outgrow" their problem. However, research shows that bullying victimization is generally a pattern that continues as kids move to new social settings and often follows them through adulthood. So intervention is crucial. What is the best intervention to help a bullied child? It depends. Just as a child bullies for many reasons, a child is targeted for many reasons, which is why the same strategies won't work for all children who are bullied. The most effective interventions are not a one-size-fits-all approach; they meet the individual students' needs and always dignify the child. You cannot change a child's temperament, nor should you try. The purpose is to help the child find the strategy that works best for her or him.

> Keep in mind that some children will move in and out of their roles in the bullying dynamic, so the bullied kid in fourth period might start bullying others on the bus. Research that tracked students over three years in middle school found that less than 13 percent of students remained in their initial role of either a child who bullies or the target of bullying. That means that 87 percent of the sample changed their bullying/target roles during those three years.[11] Consider this possibility as you develop a plan for any bullied student.

What follows are seven intervention strategies that have proven helpful for targets, and you may discover some apply to children who bully as well. Choose those techniques that best help the student based on recommendations of your team or staff. In most cases, more than one approach will be required. Keep in mind that the ultimate goal is for the child to be able to use the new strategy *without* reminders, coaxing, or reinforcement from adults. Achieving that aim will require time, a lot of practice, and, ideally, sharing the strategies with other educators and school staff who can reinforce the child's efforts. The optimum approach is to have the parent also use and reinforce these same strategies at home. Of course, some parents, despite all your efforts, can't seem to be reached, and some parents are bullying their own child. This is all the more reason why you need to find ways to work together as a team at school.

I'll never forget Rene, a school custodian, waiting in the hallways each morning for the arrival of Billy, a student who had endured horrific bullying. Rene became Billy's safety net. Rene was aware of the bullying and watched out for the boy, but he also was pivotal in Billy's intervention plan—all because the counselor had wisely told Rene that Billy was working on assertiveness, and each week took one minute to share the lesson plan with Rene. As Billy walked by, I watched Rene give him a big high five and then heard him quietly say, "Strong body, Billy! I'll be watching for you. Use a strong body." Billy's smile

---

11. Swearer et al., 2009.

(as well as his discernible sigh of relief that somebody was looking out for him) was unforgettable. There's an important take-away here: work together with the *entire* school community to help your students.

Tip for COUNSELORS

While doing a parenting workshop on bullying in a Salt Lake City school, one parent came rushing up to describe how well the bullying prevention strategies were working for her child. The teacher, counselor, and mother had met to decide which strategies they would teach her son. They chose four, and took a photograph of the child practicing each strategy and glued the pictures to a poster as a visual reminder. They made copies of the poster to hang on the child's refrigerator at home and in the counselor's office, and made a mini version to keep inside his desk. The team approach worked, and his mom was ecstatic.

STRATEGY 1: STAY COOL

When targets look upset, cry, or flare up, bullying often escalates. Staying calm is tough—especially for sensitive or impulsive kids. Emphasize to targeted students that they have control over how they choose to react to bullying and they can't always rely on adults. You might say: "You can't control what another person says or does, but you *can* control how you respond." "You may not be able to stop that kid from being so mean, but if you practice, you can learn not to cry when he calls you names. I'll help you learn new responses." Here are some ideas for staying cool:

"Turn down" strong feelings. If students don't learn to "turn down" or "switch off" upset facial gestures, they'll never convince perpetrators they're not headed for a meltdown. And, unfortunately, kids who cry too frequently or become upset in public can become targets of bullying. So help students learn ways to postpone tears for a private moment or turn down a heated look and switch to a more neutral expression. You might take a photograph of a child using a facial expression that conveys little emotion (like when she's watching television or reading a book), and then another photo of the child showing heightened emotion. Help her study the two expressions and then ask: "Which face would make your classmates less likely to pick on you?" "Which one will make them more apt to pick on you?" Once the child identifies the expression that looks less vulnerable, help her practice achieving the more neutral look.

Emphasize to targeted students that they have control over how they choose to react to bullying and they can't always rely on adults.

(See the next point about distress replacers.) Clarify that emotions aren't "bad," but it's better not to display strong, upset feelings too publicly or too often. Kids with lower empathy levels might think strong emotions make someone vulnerable and an easier target.

Learn distress replacers. If a student tears up frequently in front of peers, he needs to learn how to hold back the tears until he's in private and learn other ways to release strong emotions in public. Being sad is normal, but a child needs to learn healthy, socially acceptable ways to handle distress in public. Ideas to help include:

- Think of a really fun place inside your head and make your mind go there.
- Clear your throat and hold your tongue.
- Count slowly to ten inside your head.
- Hum a song inside your head or very quietly under your breath.
- Take slow deep breaths.

In order for the distress replacer to become a habit, a child needs to practice it repeatedly. When teaching these skills, be sure to speak to the child privately to preserve his dignity. Frequent tears can also be a sign of depression (see depression signs on page 212) or other serious difficulties, so continue to monitor the child and seek the counsel of the school nurse, psychologist, or other resource.

Take a break. If the student has a tough time delivering verbal responses to the bullying child (see "Strategy 2"), sometimes a "walk off" is the best approach to regain self-control. Tell the targeted child to walk away without even a glance at her tormenter, pretend the tormentor is invisible, glance at something else, look completely uninterested, or pretend not to hear the abuse. "Take a break" works best in places where the child *can* escape her tormentor such as at a park or playground. This strategy doesn't work in close quarters such as on a school bus or at a cafeteria table.

STRATEGY 2: APPEAR ASSERTIVE

A student with timid body language and a soft voice can be seen as an easier target for bullying because he or she appears vulnerable. In fact, some studies, which reviewed hundreds of hours of video of kids on playgrounds, found kids who demonstrate less confidence are often more likely to be targeted. So it's important to help kids look assertive and confident and not passive. Of course, some kids may be in heightened distress while they're being bullied, but using the right comment or expression can reduce targeting and even stop bullying. Also, how the child responds the *first* time to a verbal barb can make a big difference to whether the bullying continues and is a reason why early intervention is so crucial. Students will need lots of practice to appear confident in their own skin so when they do need to stand up to bullying, they can succeed. Here are a few tips to choose from, based on the child:

Use strong body posture. Help the child use a posture that appears strong and confident: shoulders down, back straight, and head up. Eye contact helps kids hold their heads higher, which makes their overall body language appear more assertive, even if they're trembling inside. Of course, looking assertive isn't easy for kids who have been targeted or whose self-esteem is plummeting. It may be helpful to tell kids: "Always look at the color of the talker's eyes." Or, a bit less-threatening variation: "Always look at the bridge of the talker's nose." I've also taught kids to look at a point *behind* the head of the talker since eye contact can be so scary.

Tip for COUNSELORS

Take a photo of the student using "strong body" posture and then tell her to keep it in her backpack or inside a notebook (where only she can see it). Remind her to look at the photo to help her recall what confident body language looks like so she can use it when needed.

Use a strong, steady voice. Children who engage in bullying often do so to seek power or control. Targets who use soft, whimpering, whining, or quivering voice tones make these children feel like they've won. Convey to kids that, "It's not what you say that matters as much as how you look and sound." Demonstrate this by saying, "Cut it out" first in a strong, firm voice and then in a soft, quiet voice. Ask: "Which voice do you think another kid would listen to more? Yes, a strong voice is more effective. So let's practice using that stronger tone." You might role-play vocal variations, and have students practice until they can speak with stronger, more confident tones. For some kids, this technique may not work, so find a different strategy that is more effective and honors the child's temperament. Don't criticize a child's natural voice.

Say a firm "No." If a student needs to respond to a child who is bullying him, short, direct commands work best: "No," "Cut it out," "Stop," or "Back off." The response should be delivered with the strong, determined voice encouraged in the previous intervention.

Walk away confidently. Once the response is delivered, tell the student to walk off with shoulders back and head high so as not to look like a victim. Even though the child may be shaking inside, a strong appearance helps sell the response.

STRATEGY 3: USE PASS COMEBACK LINES

Most bullying begins with verbal harassment, so if a child can defuse a verbal grenade the first time, the bullying is less likely to advance to the next level. The right comeback line—a one-line assertive response—delivered using a firm voice and strong body language has that potential. A rehearsed response to an anticipated barb can also boost confidence and reduce stress because the target knows what to do. Usually the best comeback is a simple, "Cut it out." And the delivery is crucial: the line needs to be said with the least emotion possible. Annoying, agitating, insulting, threatening, or making fun of the bullying child can make things worse. It's better for the target to deliver the comeback and exit the situation with dignity still intact. (Refer to Strategy 2 for tips to help students stay calm and be assertive in delivering the comeback lines.)

These comeback lines are best for defusing name-calling or other nonviolent bullying. The optimum delivery is to sound sincere—never sarcastic—accompanied by an unfazed expression. Kids say that using humor, not sarcasm, is one of the best comebacks to defuse teasing or taunting. If students can try these lines when exposed to friendly teasing (not bullying) they will be more confident to try them in bullying incidents. Teach students the acronym PASS (as in "Let the taunt PASS by and not faze you"), and then have them practice delivering lines assertively to maximize effectiveness. Delivery is everything! The following suggestions were culled from my focus groups. I asked students, "What are the best ways to stop a kid from *teasing* or *taunting* you?" Here's what dozens of fourth through seventh graders told me:

- Be **p**olite and use manners. "Hey, thanks. I appreciate that!" "That was really nice of you to notice." "Thanks." "Thank you for that comment." As odd as it may feel, be sure to say the comeback in a normal voice *without* sarcasm.

- **A**cknowledge and move on. "I hear you and I'm ignoring it." "I heard you and I'm moving on."

- Say "**S**o?" "Whatever." "Okay." Say it matter-of-factly.

- Say "**S**top." "Cut it out." "No." Firmly let the person know that you won't take it.

> **Important:** Comebacks are not effective in every situation and in some cases may even increase the taunting. They should be taught with great care and used with discretion. Also, comebacks do not work for every child and can be especially difficult for kids with shy temperaments or speech and language difficulties. Offer a repertoire of options that fit the children's needs, abilities, and temperaments; help them identify the strategy *they* are most comfortable using; then help them practice it until they can use it confidently in the real world.

STRATEGY 4: USE AFFIRMING SELF-TALK OR COGNITIVE REFRAMING

Bullying can damage a child's view of self, so I teach targets to say a line inside their head (never out loud) to combat the pain of victimization. Internalizing a comforting self-statement is one coping strategy a child can use to prevent feeling helpless. These strategies are especially helpful for anxious children. Possible statements could be:

- "I'll be okay."

- "I don't deserve this treatment."

- "The person doesn't know another way to get her needs met, so she's picking on me."

- "This is not my fault."

- "This person needs to change, not me."

- "I can get through this."

- "I'll be home soon and can tell Mom or Dad about this."

Tip for COUNSELORS

Once you help the child choose his or her comforting statement, print it on a few index cards and encourage the child to put the cards in accessible places that only he or she can see such as in a backpack, locker, notebook, and bathroom mirror at home. Or suggest that older children can put the statement on their cell phone, tablet, or computer screensaver. Remind the child, "The more you read it, the more you'll remember to use it when you need to."

STRATEGY 5: USE COPING SKILLS

All kids benefit from learning ways to handle the inevitable bumps in life, but bullied kids also need to learn ways to cope with the injustice of peer abuse. Also, children who bully can pick up on cues when a targeted child is distressed and it can fuel their desire for power and to continue bullying. If a targeted child is quick to anger or stress, then intervention techniques might include anger management or stress or fear reduction. Options include:

Journal it. Have the child write in a journal about his or her worries or the pain of bullying.

Stop and breathe. Show the student how to inhale slowly to a count of five, pause for two counts, and then slowly breathe out while counting to five. Repeating the sequence creates maximum relaxation and reduces stress that can turn into anger. Yoga or meditation can also be effective in curbing stress.

1 + 3 + 10. Explain the formula: As soon as you feel your body sending you a warning sign that you're losing control, do three things. First, stop and say: "Be calm." (That's "1.") Next, take three deep, slow breaths from your tummy. (That's "3.") Finally, count slowly to ten inside your head. (That's "10.") Put them all together and you have 1 + 3 + 10, and doing this helps you calm down and get back in control.

Imagine a calm place. Again, as soon as the child feels the body warning signs of distress kicking in, tell her to close her eyes and imagine a calm spot while breathing slowly. For instance: the beach, her bed, her grandpa's backyard, a tree house.

Self-talk. Teach a simple, positive message the child can say to himself in stressful situations. For example: "Stop and calm down," "Stay in control," "I can handle this."

Seek the support of a school mental health provider for additional options.

STRATEGY 6: DEVELOP SOCIAL SKILLS

Children who bully tend to target kids who are isolated from their peers. Kids don't need a lot of friends to be socially healthy; one loyal buddy can help buffer the pain of peer rejection and abuse. Also, studies show that kids who know how to join a peer group; have a sense of humor; are friendly, cooperative, agreeable, and willing to share; and can control their anger are less likely to be targeted in school.[12] Social skills do matter when it comes to buffering bullying and they are teachable.

Child development experts Sherri Oden and Steven Asher worked for years with children who had problems fitting in. They discovered that social successes dramatically improved when kids were taught specific friendship-making skills.[13] You can use these steps, based on their research, to help students learn *any* social skill:

1. **Focus on one skill.** Watch the child in a social context to determine which skills would improve her social competence and choose one skill to teach, such as listening, taking turns, asking a question, or joining a game. For a list of key social skills, refer to *Skillstreaming in Early Childhood, Skillstreaming the Elementary School Child,* and *Skillstreaming the Adolescent* by Ellen McGinnis and Arnold Goldstein.

2. **Coach the skill.** Find a private moment to model the new skill with the child. Discuss why it is important, and confirm that the child can show you how to do the skill correctly. It's helpful to go with the child to a schoolyard, so she can observe other kids using the skill to get a visual reference to copy.

3. **Provide practice opportunities.** Telling a child about the skill is not enough, she needs to try out the skill with other children. It's best to practice with kids she doesn't already know and who are younger or less skilled. Keep practice sessions short. Offer suggestions privately—*never* in front of other students.

4. **Review and offer feedback.** A critical part of teaching social skills is evaluating the performance with the child. Discuss: "How did the practice go? What did you say? How do you think you did? What would you

12. Coloroso, 2015; Barker et al., 2008.
13. Oden and Asher, 1977.

do differently next time?" Don't criticize what the child didn't do; instead praise what she did right. If she was not successful, talk through what didn't go well, so she can try it differently the next time. As soon as she feels comfortable with the skill, you're ready to teach another one.

Tip for COUNSELORS

One of the best ways to teach social skills is in a small group setting. Consider setting up a social skills group of similar-age students to meet once a week where you can teach them a new skill, using Oden and Asher's four steps (see page 205). Then have students practice skills together. For the group, choose kids who have been bullied, have poor social skills, and/ or have difficulties making and keeping friends.

STRATEGY 7: BUILD PROBLEM-SOLVING SKILLS

Research published by the American Psychological Association found that teaching kids how to solve problems can help prevent bullying and even reduce children's chances of being victimized. Their analysis of 153 bullying studies over the past thirty years found that children—especially boys—who demonstrate difficulties solving problems are more at risk of bullying, becoming targets, or both.[14]

Take a few minutes to privately help a bullied child learn to solve his problem: "You seem upset, tell me what's bothering you." (You might need to help him find the words: "I can't get Kevin to share the ball.") Express confidence that he can work things out: "I know you'll come up with a solution." Then encourage him to brainstorm ideas. "Don't worry about how silly an idea sounds, it may help you think of other ideas." And finally, help the child eliminate any ideas he doesn't feel comfortable doing or that wouldn't be safe. Remind the child that he can use this same strategy whenever he encounters a problem.

Note: Do not use conflict resolution with a bullying child and his or her target. Problem-solving skills are intended to build the personal efficacy of a child and thus help the child avoid victimization.

---

14. Cook et al., 2010.

SEL SKILL: Brainstorming

Here are four simple rules to brainstorming. You might post them in your classroom to remind kids to "storm their brain" to find options. One counselor told a student: "Brainstorming helps you think of all the different choices you can use to solve your problem. Start by naming your problem and then asking, 'What are my choices?' The rules help your brain think of lots of alternatives, so you can choose the one you like best."

1. **Don't put down or judge any idea.** No criticism is allowed!

2. **Piggybacking onto other ideas is fine.** You may change or add onto anyone's idea at any time. It's now a new idea.

3. **The more ideas the better!** Say the first thing that comes into your mind. Don't worry if it doesn't seem practical or realistic.

4. **Never limit your thinking.** Turn your brainpower on, and let your mind go.

Ways to Involve PARENTS

Parents play a pivotal role in reinforcing the school's efforts to help their children learn bullying prevention skills. A few ideas for involving parents, especially the parents of targeted children:

- **Demonstrate skills at a student-parent conference.** Have children *show* their parents exactly how to do a new bullying prevention skill while the counselor or teacher explains the steps.

- **Create a skill poster.** Each time a new skill is taught to the child, make a mini-poster showing the steps to send home. Some educators take photographs of the child doing each step and then paste them on a poster for kids to bring home as a visual reminder.

- **Encourage "skill-building homework."** Each time the child is taught a new skill, require homework in which the child needs to teach a family member the skill and then practice it daily. The parent can sign a sheet that states the child practiced at home.

- **Make a video of the child.** As the child practices the skill correctly, make a video of it and save the video to a flash drive to send home. The parent and child can view the skill together, and the parent can help reinforce the child's skill-building efforts as well as correct any mistakes.

Seek Immediate Help for a Depressed Student

"I go to sleep and pray I won't wake up." —Sue, age 11

"The bullying hurts so bad that I want to die." —Joaquin, age 12

If a student has been bullied repeatedly, chances are he will need professional help, and you may need to be his advocate to ensure that he receives the unconditional support he deserves. Suicide and depression are possible tragic outcomes for children who are repeatedly traumatized by bullying. Here are possible steps to take:

Find support services, ASAP. Report your concerns about the student to an administrator and *document them in writing*. Seek the perspective of the school counselor, psychologist, and teacher. Contact the parent. Share your specific concerns.

Get staff perspective. Staff members may have varied concerns (or none at all) about a student's mental health based on their relationship and contact with the student.

Watch for depression. Bullying can cause feelings of immense sadness, loneliness, and rage, and even lead to depression. Some students hold their pain deep inside while others may release it in bouts of anger or rage. If you notice that a student is suddenly a "different kid," no physical problems can explain the symptoms, and those symptoms continue for several weeks with no improvement, seek the guidance of a school mental health professional. Report your concerns!

Learn the signs of depression. The rates of childhood depression are not only increasing but are also impacting younger kids. Understand that some of these signs could also be due to issues other than bullying, but they are concerning and should be monitored. See the form on page 212.

> **Brave Staff Chat: Does Your Staff Know Depression Signs?**
>
> Have the staff members at your school been trained in recognizing the signs of depression? Don't assume they know the signs: discuss them. Post the warning signs in your faculty room and provide a list to every staff member to keep in their desks.

Know when to intervene. If the child makes alarming statements (such as "What's the use?" "I'd like to shoot everybody," or "Nobody will miss me."); if the child is preoccupied with death or feelings of hopelessness; if the child tells others about or posts a death or threat "plan" electronically (via Facebook, Twitter, Instagram); if the child draws, writes, or asks about death; if the child makes or posts threats about peers, teachers, or the school; or if your instinct tells you something isn't right, report your concerns immediately to the administrator, school psychologist, counselor, or social worker. This person will be responsible for contacting the parents. You may need to submit a report to the district office and give a copy to your administrator. If at any point you believe that the child is endangered (abuse at home or elsewhere), call your local Child Protective Services and report your concerns. You are liable and the child's safety may be at stake.

> **Important!** If you have *any* reason to suspect that a student is suicidal, homicidal, or a possible threat to himself or others, DO NOT WAIT. Seek *immediate* help from your school mental health professionals and administrator. Post a suicide hotline number in the school office. Visit the Suicide Prevention Resource Center's website at sprc.org.

KEY BULLYING PREVENTION POINTS IN R5: REFUSE

- Review reports to gather names of targeted students. Notify appropriate staff, psychological services, and parents. Develop a safety plan together so you can provide support.

- Build adult relationships with targets so they are more likely to seek help.

- Provide "I Need Help" cards for nonverbal or shy students to present to an adult for help without saying anything.

- Create "peer buddies": older students who can watch, protect, or help targets on the playground, on the bus, or in the cafeteria.

- Teach targets strategies to reduce victimization, such as assertiveness training and ways to cognitively reframe events. Other staff members and parents need to reinforce those efforts.

- Recognize the hidden signs of bullying and identify targets or potential targets.

- Make certain your school colleagues know the warning signs of depression and how to intervene if necessary.

WARNING SIGNS OF BULLYING

Sudden disinterest in school. Child refuses to attend a certain class or activity

Sudden change in behavior or personality. Child is more sullen, evasive, moody, angry, anxious, or sad with no known cause; starts new behaviors such as bed-wetting, tics, nail-biting, stammering, stuttering

More anxious or fearful. Child may fear riding the school bus, suddenly takes a new and unusual route to school or to a class; tries to avoid the playground, cafeteria, or other location; may seek refuge in the library, school office, or stay next to a certain staff member

Unexplained damaged or missing school supplies. Child is missing electronic items, clothes, lunches, or money, and may report mysteriously "losing" possessions

Afraid to be left alone. Child seeks out a staff member at class dismissal, recess, in the lunchroom, or other times

Suddenly clingier. Child acts more insecure and noticeably less confident at certain times; wants an adult or peer present constantly

Starts to bully others. Child begins bullying younger or more vulnerable students or siblings, suddenly acts more aggressive or rebellious

Withdrawal from the social scene. Child stops talking to peers, withdraws from the social scene; uses derogatory or demeaning language when describing peers; remarks about being lonely or sad; complains that "nobody likes me"

Frequently ill or absent. Child is suddenly absent frequently from school or makes frequent visits to the school nurse's office

Physical injuries. Child has bruises, scrapes, or other marks not consistent with explanation

Appears exhausted. Child is tired, falls asleep in class, yawns, or complains of an inability to sleep

Sudden drop in grades. Child has trouble focusing and completing schoolwork

Carries protection. Child starts to carry "protection," such as a heavier backpack, a large flashlight, box cutters, forks, knives, or weapons

Talks about running away or committing suicide. Child may try to run away, describes life as "worthless," writes or talks about giving up, or has a plan for death or destruction

WARNING SIGNS OF DEPRESSION

- The child has an increase in physical ailments such as headaches, stomachaches, nausea, sweaty palms, change in weight, fatigue, or sleepiness.

- There is a marked, sudden, or intense change in the child's personality, temperament, or behavior.

- The child is unable to focus, demonstrates marked nervousness, and her grades and schoolwork are affected.

- Signs last longer than two weeks, become more intense, or come and go, and nothing eases the child's pain.

- The child is preoccupied with death or feelings of hopelessness, as is evident in his drawing, writing, or asking about death; giving away personal belongings; or saying things like, "What's the use?"

- Sadness or apathy interferes with the child's daily life; her social, academic, or family life is also affected.

- The child tells you something is wrong and he needs help. Or, your instinct tells you something isn't right. Trust your instinct. Chances are you're right.

R6: Replace

Help Students Replace Aggression with Acceptable Skills

In this chapter, you will learn:

- what bullying looks like age-by-age
- nine signs a student may be prone to bullying
- six ways educators can monitor students who bully
- the most effective adult responses to bullying
- five steps in setting the right consequences for bullying
- evidence-based interventions to reduce and replace bullying

The sixth "R," or R6, of effective bullying prevention focuses on replacing cruelty with kindness. It is perhaps the most important R to get right, since it addresses the root of the problem: bullying behaviors. Though a default profile doesn't exist, all kids who bully use repeated patterns of aggression steeped in contempt and intentionally dealt out in cold, deliberate ways. Whether the method is direct or indirect, or delivered physically, verbally, electronically, or emotionally, bullying is *always* laced with behaviors that are the antithesis of compassion, empathy, and respect for others. Because aggressive, cruel behaviors are learned and can become entrenched at an early age, we need to uncover as early as possible what is motivating a child to bully so we can address those specific issues and teach her or him healthier ways of relating.

While no single intervention or program will stop cruelty, a combination of proven interventions along with a no-nonsense approach to bullying delivered by a caring, committed staff can have a sizable impact. Educators may well be the last hope to help students unlearn harmful habits.

This final chapter offers the latest information about children who bully, what may be driving their behavior, and how adults can respond and replace aggression with prosocial behaviors. While chapter R4: Respond addressed how student witnesses should respond to bullying, this chapter describes the adults' response. The best chance at curtailing childhood aggression and breaking a potential cycle of violence is when *all* adult stakeholders respond in the same proactive way.

The New School Bullying

Even though bullying has always existed, today it is now arguably more intense, starts younger, and pervades both the offline and online worlds. The child who bullies today is far from yesteryear's image of "the big, unpopular thug on the block." The child who engages in bullying may be male or female; a preschooler or teen; rich or poor; a lone actor or part of a group. Kids who bully—even in the elementary school years—are often intelligent, self-assured, sociable, and sometimes among the most popular kids in school.[1] Of course, they are just as to likely to be disruptive, impulsive, rejected, and marginalized.

One thing is certain: kids who engage in bullying don't lend themselves to a one-size-fits-all description, and—contrary to what many adults believe—they are *not* necessarily easy to spot. A child who bullies may be a quiet second grader, an ostracized fourth grader, a middle school teen with a disability, the senior class president, or that adorable kindergartner. His or her calculated methods may be delivered directly with slams, threats, and verbal taunts, or with more covert, indirect approaches like exclusion, spreading rumors, rejection, or delivering disapproving looks.

And children today don't always play the same fixed roles at the bullying scene. The child who bullies at lunchtime may be the target on the bus. The target in fourth grade may be bullying others by sixth grade. The third grader who taunts kids face to face may be throwing verbal grenades online by middle school. Bullying is situational, roles can switch, and labels can become problematic.

"I was always in trouble for bullying last year, but this year things are different. My teacher told me that she knew that wasn't who I really am. I stopped because I didn't want to let her down." —Dahali, age 9

"Kids called me 'Bully Boy' at my other school, but it stopped when I got here. Teachers showed me how to make better choices and watched to make sure I did." —Josh, age 10

---

1. Rodkin et al., 2008; Orecklin, 2000.

NINE SIGNS A STUDENT MAY BE PRONE TO BULLYING

Here are nine signs to watch for, but keep in mind that no child will demonstrate *all* of them. A single profile of a child who bullies doesn't exist, so look for repeated and intentional patterns of aggression.

1. **Lacks empathy, sensitivity, or compassion.** The child shows little regard for others' feelings, takes pleasure in seeing another in distress, or acts unconcerned if someone is upset.

2. **Likes to dominate and craves power.** The child enjoys controlling others through power or manipulation, or uses people to get his way or gain attention.

3. **Feels entitled or has a positive view of self.** The child wants or expects the focus to be on her needs, rights, and feelings, and not on others. New research shows that contrary to previous thinking, most children who bully do *not* have low self-esteem. That said, some children who bully appear to have a positive view of self but actually are insecure and masking insecurity with false confidence.

4. **Obsessed with status.** The child is consumed with social status, power, fitting in, and staying popular.

5. **Intolerant of differences; excludes or shuns others.** The child shows contempt for those who are somehow different (whether in sexual orientation, culture, belief, gender, religion, race, status, appearance, age, or ability). He refuses to include certain kids in activities.

6. **Doesn't accept responsibility.** The child denies wrongdoing despite clear evidence to the contrary; may belittle, denounce, or blame the target, or say the child "deserved it"; or is used to being let off the hook.

7. **Impulsive or quick-tempered.** The child is hotheaded or easily frustrated if she doesn't get her way.

8. **Taunts, intimidates, or harasses those more vulnerable.** The child preys on those weaker or younger than him.

9. **Aggressive toward others physically, electronically, verbally, or emotionally.** The child has a positive attitude toward violence, believes it to be acceptable, or uses aggression to get her way.

"Bullying stops if teachers respond every time." —Susan, age 12

WHAT BULLYING LOOKS LIKE AGE BY AGE

Children's behaviors will vary based on their developmental levels and will not always match up neatly to expectations for particular ages or grade levels. Still, some bullying scenarios are more likely to occur at certain grade levels than others.

Early grades. Egocentric by nature, young kids often have difficulty considering the feelings and needs of others. However, new research carried out with preschool children shows bullying is a serious problem, even at very young ages. Bullying in early childhood is likely to be physical such as hitting, biting, pinching, poking, or tripping. Also watch for children who consistently exclude others from play; studies suggest that this can actually be a precursor to and represent the earliest forms of bullying. Though bullying at this age is usually not malicious, if it is allowed to continue, it can become a habit of cruelty.[2]

Elementary school. Don't assume that because students are still in elementary school that they are immune to bullying; in today's culture, even sexual harassment and cyberbullying can be issues at elementary ages. Bullying increases as children move through the school-age years, and verbal insults and put-downs become prevalent. Intentional social exclusion becomes a marked issue around fourth grade, and active bystanding takes a nosedive around the same age.

> The child who bullies today is far from yesteryear's image of "the big, unpopular thug on the block."

Middle school. Bullying peaks during the middle school years and becomes more covert and difficult to spot. Kids are transitioning into a new setting and trying to establish power within their peer groups. This is also the age when kids tend to blame the target. Three-quarters of the preteens who were interviewed said bullying is a regular occurrence; and girls are more prone to use "relational cruelty" by deliberately shunning another girl or spreading vicious rumors.[3] Boys—and increasingly girls—again resort to more physical means (hitting, shoving, intimidating body postures, threats of violence) to bully others.

2. Vlachou et al., 2013; Fanger et al., 2012.
3. Coloroso, 2015.

Why Adults Need to Consistently Respond to *Each* Bullying Incident

"Bullies change if teachers aren't wishy-washy and step in." —Josh, age 11

You see one child push another. You watch kids taunt a peer. You overhear students use foul insults with one another. You notice one child being excluded. I call those "code yellow" behaviors: they are clearly inappropriate but aren't necessarily clear-cut bullying incidents or serious safety issues. Do you intervene?

Many adults won't stop these types of milder behavior issues or lower-level bullying because: "I didn't see it." "It takes too much time." "I'll have to fill out another report." "I wasn't sure if it really was bullying." But *not* to respond to what may be construed as milder bullying, aggression, or disrespect is a mistake. Studies show that students view no response or a neutral response by adults as explicit permission for—and even approval of—the behavior.[4] Kids (and especially those who engage in bullying) begin to realize they can get away with inappropriate behavior, and so they try again and again, and they succeed again and again. Behavior incidents can become more frequent and more severe, and kids learn that aggression helps them get their way.

> Though almost 90 percent of teachers believe they should be trained in how to respond to bullying, most admit they lack confidence in their ability to do so.[5]

The simple fact is that bullying thrives in inconsistent environments, which is why a consistent, direct adult response to inappropriate behavior is essential for curbing bullying. This response does not have to be time consuming or difficult. But all staff members should be trained to recognize bullying behaviors and how to respond. Adults need to be committed to using this response *each and every time* to address any and all inappropriate student behaviors.

FOUR STEPS TO STOP MILD BULLYING

You see a child deliberately exclude a peer from the lunch table. You hear a student say mean, taunting comments to another child who cannot hold his own. These examples of relatively mild or lower-level bullying still require adult intervention as soon as possible to let kids know the behavior will not

4. Englander, 2013.
5. Harris and Willoughby, 2003.

be tolerated. The four-step response described here takes less than fifteen seconds and is enough to halt bullying. See page 239 for a quick-reference form listing these steps you can distribute to your team or staff, post on your school's intranet, place in staff lounges, or otherwise share with the adults in your school. (*Important:* This model is designed for mild bullying only or behavior issues that do not pose a safety threat. If serious bullying, aggressive behaviors, or safety issues are involved, refer to "How to Respond to More Serious Bullying Incidents" on page 219.)

Since bullying can happen anywhere on a school campus, all staff members should know and practice these four steps so they are prepared to intervene. The main message to convey to staff is: "Don't be wishy-washy! Step in and speak out *every* time to stop milder inappropriate, aggressive, or rude behaviors from becoming the gateway to serious bullying." Inconsistent staff responses are roadblocks to prevention and increase the chances of more frequent bullying and aggression.

Step 1: Stop it. Interrupt kids on the spot with a calm, firm statement such as: "Excuse me, *stop!*" "Let's put an end to this right now." "We don't do that here." "Please stop that immediately." "What's going on here?" or "I don't like what I'm seeing/hearing." Be loud enough so that other students hear you. They'll spread the word that the staff is serious about stopping bullying.

Step 2: Name it. Call out what you saw or heard like a sportscaster. Keep the focus on the inappropriate behavior, *not* on the child. For young kids, say: "I heard name-calling." "That's leaving someone out!" "I was hearing not-nice words." For older kids say: "I see you shoving to get your way." "It's not cool to whisper about someone, especially when they're standing right there." "I just heard some things that are inappropriate." Use the term *bullying* very cautiously, especially if you didn't witness the scene or you're with younger students. The word *bullying* can set off an emotional reaction or vehement denial. If you do use the term, provide the context based on your school's anti-bullying policy: "I'm concerned that what I heard was bullying, because your words were mean. Joshua is younger than you, and I don't think this was an accident." Direct your words quietly to the offender in a calm and dignified manner.

Step 3: Describe it. Give a clear reason why the behavior is inappropriate, against the rules, and harmful. For young kids: "Leaving people out is *not* what we do in this school." "That was unkind and it really bothers me." "That was hurting another person's feelings." For older kids: "Our motto here is 'Treat everyone with respect.' I didn't hear respect." "At this school we do *not* put down others." "Our rules are clear: we include everyone." Feel free to add: "I am offended by that language and I'm sure other people at this school are, too." Elizabeth Kandel Englander, founder and director of the Massachusetts Aggression Reduction Center, suggests you ask: "How do you think your behavior affects our school?" so the child considers that his behavior also has implications beyond the interaction with the target.[6]

Tip for COUNSELORS

Many kids who engage in bullying have diminished empathy, and a small percentage lack empathy. The response most likely to stretch empathy is called *induction*, in which the child is asked to reflect on how her behavior affects others and impacts the targeted person. It may take several "How would you feel" queries to activate empathy in some children, but keep asking. At the very least, the child will know that she is being held accountable.

Step 4: Alter it. Deliver a short, firm reminder that explains the behavior you expect. For young kids: "I expect you to be kind at all times." "Please pause and think before you speak." For older kids: "I'll be watching to make sure this doesn't happen again." "You have a choice with your words. I'll be listening for respect." "Let's try that again the right way."

Use your judgment about whether a formal bullying report is warranted based on your policy. (Refer to chapter R3: Report for more information on reporting.) But don't let inappropriate behaviors slide. Even if you don't file a report, seek out the kids over the next few days and let them know you are watching their behavior and listening to their words. Remain vigilant!

HOW TO RESPOND TO MORE SERIOUS BULLYING INCIDENTS

When serious bullying occurs and emotional or physical safety is at stake, a different staff response is required. Examples of serious bullying include a child hitting, kicking, scratching, shoving, or using (or threatening to use) a

6. Englander, 2013.

weapon on another child; vicious, alarming verbal attacks and humiliation; and systematic peer exclusion or blacklisting. Here is how to respond during and after a serious bullying incident. Again, I've included a quick-reference form listing these steps for distribution to your team or staff (see page 240).

During the Incident

Intervene immediately. Use the motto: "When in doubt, act." Never assume the incident is an isolated event.

Stay calm. Kids take clues from adults. If you're calm, kids are more likely to be calm.

Use a de-escalating statement. In a firm voice, say a comment to curb tenseness and break friction: "Everybody okay?" "Let's take a deep breath." "Do you need some help?"

Separate those involved. If it's safe to do so, stand between the target and the child bullying to block eye contact. If you cannot do this, separate them by saying something like: "Come here please. I need to talk to you." Request another adult to join you by alerting pertinent staff (administrator, security guard, counselor, secretary) via text, page, or student courier. Send students to separate predetermined locations.

Ensure safety. Call immediately for the school security guard, police, or medical attention if a weapon, sexual abuse, serious physical injury, illegal activity, or a threat of violence or extortion is involved. Direct children to safety or take whatever action is necessary to reduce the threat. In an imminent threat, pull the fire alarm or take whatever steps are necessary for safety.

Describe what you see. If safety is not an immediate issue, state what you see and why it is unacceptable. This also helps you gain clarity about what is happening. "I see behavior here that is against school rules." Then describe the bullying in age-appropriate terms using the school's definition. For younger students: "I heard you say mean words about Robby and then tell the others not to let him play. Our rules are to be kind to everyone at this school." For older students: "You shoved Jamie into the locker. I heard her tell you, 'Stop,' and you continued to hurt her. That's against what we stand for at this school."

Use the four A's: <u>a</u>ssess, <u>a</u>cknowledge, <u>a</u>ssure, <u>a</u>ssist. Assess the target's well-being and acknowledge her or his discomfort. Assure all students involved that adults will help them be safe. Assist any student who needs help.

Don't label. Specific roles each student played in the incident can be determined later, so don't label students at the scene as a "bully," "victim" or "bystander," or accuse students of bullying. Keep tension at bay and the scene as calm as possible.

Don't make students apologize or require conflict resolution. The students involved should *not* be told to make amends or attend a conflict resolution session. Bullying is *not* a conflict; it's about contempt and intentional cruelty. Requiring an apology is almost always an ineffective consequence.

After the Incident

Encourage active bystanders. If student witnesses spoke up or tried to help, reinforce their efforts. Let them know you admire their courage and appreciate their support.

Continue gathering pertinent information. Do *not* interview students in front of one another; separate them. Try to gather essential information from those at the scene. Listen to all sides without blaming or being judgmental. Collect the names of everyone involved—adults and students—as well as witnesses to use in your report.

Notify pertinent stakeholders. Alert necessary staff members with a brief review of the incident to ensure that they are aware and can monitor students. Parents of both the target and of the bullying child should always be alerted about a bullying incident.

Complete and file a bullying report. Supply as much pertinent information as possible in the report. See the staff bullying report form on pages 155–156.

Be vigilant. Seek out students involved—especially the target and the bullying child—so they know you care and are monitoring their behavior.

BEWARE OF ZERO TOLERANCE

A zero tolerance policy toward bullying is one in which harsh punishments are immediately enacted, such as school suspension or even expulsion, in hopes of setting an example for students. However, *no* credible evidence shows that a zero tolerance policy reduces violence. In fact, not only is zero tolerance ineffective in reducing bullying, it could cause negative outcomes for both schools and students.[7]

---

7. American Psychological Association Zero Tolerance Task Force, 2008; Casella, 2003.

Here is why zero tolerance isn't effective:

- It does not mend torn social relationships, so the culture of disrespect continues.

- Peers may fear retaliation for "causing" the bullying child's suspension or severe punishment.

- Peers may underreport incidents, believing the potential punishment is too harsh.

- The approach fails to teach *how to* replace aggression, so bullying often continues and even increases in severity.

- A child who is suspended or expelled may be at risk at home due to lack of adult monitoring.

- The child feels even more disenfranchised and isolated when he returns to school.

No credible evidence shows that a zero tolerance policy reduces violence. In fact, not only is zero tolerance ineffective in reducing bullying, it could cause negative outcomes for both schools and students.

Bullying should *never* be dismissed or taken lightly, and kids who bully need to be held accountable. But a more effective discipline approach than zero tolerance is the medical model: prescribe consequences to remediate the specific behavior and work toward curing the ailment permanently. Instead of imposing harsh, ineffective punishments, require kids to do intervention strategies that encourage healthy relationships. Instead of chastising kids for their lack of skills, show them how to change inappropriate behavior. The next section offers ways to select the best sanctions to achieve those results and reduce bullying.

66 Brave Staff Chat: Why Not Zero Tolerance?

Have a discussion with your staff about whether zero tolerance is effective as a deterrent to bullying. Analyze how often your school suspends or expels students. Assess which students are disciplined more frequently than others. What can you do to be more proactive in preventing bullying and teaching "repeat offenders" how to replace aggression?

Five Steps to Setting the Right Consequences for Bullying

The purpose of imposing a consequence is to help the child recognize that bullying is *not* acceptable. But imposing consequences for bullying should be carefully considered: consequences should be restorative and respectful for both the targeted student and the child who bullies, fall within the guidelines of the school's code of conduct determined by the school and/or district, and ultimately help the disciplined child learn more acceptable ways to behave. Only the student involved, his or her parents, and appropriate staff members should be made aware of imposed consequences. Here are five steps for choosing the right consequences (see chapter R1: Rules for a complete list of possible consequences).

Step 1: Carefully review all reports. Check that all witnesses—students and adults—were interviewed and that evidence shows a consequence is warranted. Review the child's behavioral history for any previous interventions. For more serious or repeated bullying offenses, call for a Student Study Team meeting to address your next steps. (Refer to chapter R5: Refuse for how to set up a Student Study Team.)

Step 2: Select the consequence that fits. Review "Possible Consequences and Disciplinary Actions for Bullying Behavior" in R1: Rules, or approved school or district disciplinary guidelines. Keep in mind that the discipline ideally should help teach the student a more appropriate way to behave. Then choose the most appropriate consequences based on these seven factors *and* on your common sense.

Factors to Consider When Choosing Consequences

- Age, ability, and maturity of the student(s) involved
- Bullying type: verbal, physical, electronic, or emotional
- Frequency, severity, intensity, and duration of the bullying
- Student's disciplinary history and bullying pattern
- Context in which the bullying occurred
- Clarity of the evidence in all reports
- Extent to which the student demonstrates remorse in interviews

CONSIDER CONSEQUENCES THAT REMEDIATE BULLYING

The primary goal is for the child to learn from the sanction so she does not repeat the same behavior. Educators once set consequences that were primarily punitive ("You lose the privilege of the cafeteria"), but many schools now set consequences that are instructive and help the child learn a healthier new behavior to replace the bullying. For instance, instead of sitting on the bench for verbally abusing a peer, the student is required to attend a class on anger management. Or instead of missing a school activity, the child must do a service project in an after-school club.

Here are ideas from schools of remedial consequences:

- Hilltop Academy in Washington has a classroom (called their "window room") for students to go to during class, before school, at lunchtime, or at recess to work with a trained aide on behavior management strategies.

- Epiphany School in San Diego designates a counselor to help children with lessons on empathy, impulse control, or aggression.

- Murray Elementary in Utah has an aide help students brainstorm alternate behaviors during their recess and then create a "What I Will Do Next Time" sheet of five better choices to replace their offensive actions.

If needed, you might combine two remedial consequences or pair a more severe disciplinary action with a lower-level remedial one. For instance, the consequence could be viewing the film *Bully* and writing a report about the impact of bullying, *and* notifying his or her parents about the behavior. Or, researching the emotional effects of online bullying and creating a poster that describes the findings, *and* losing a school privilege for a prescribed amount of time. See R1: Rules for more ideas of specific consequences.

Step 3: Notify the students' parents and pertinent staff members. The parents of students doing the bullying as well as receiving the bullying should be notified of *each* bullying incident by phone or written form. The student could also be required to notify (via phone call, email or written note) his parents about inappropriate behavior. A conference with the parent, teacher, principal, and necessary staff should be required for every serious bullying incident. Keep written notes of all meetings: at a minimum list the date, time, attendees, and the key points that were discussed.

Three Ways for Students to Notify Parents About Bullying

Consider having the student notify his parents about mild bullying offenses as part of the consequence. Doing so keeps the parents abreast of their child's behavior, and the child recognizes that the school and home are working together to monitor his behavior, which is a critical part of reducing aggression. The student could write a script, email, or essay in picture form, dictated, or handwritten (depending upon the child's age and ability). The child describes his offense, why it was wrong, and the steps he will take so it is not repeated. It's important these strategies are done under supervision of a staff member, who proofs the student's note, script, or email and listens to the phone call. A system should also be in place to ensure that the parent receives the school message. Possibilities include:

1. The student uses a school computer to email parents about the incident.

2. The student writes or dictates a "Dear Parent" letter as a short paragraph or full essay.

3. The student phones home in the presence of a staff member, reading from a script he or she completes (and staff reviews) prior to the call.

Warning: This strategy can be effective in helping a student learn accountability but should *only* be used with supportive parents who want to work with the school to help reduce the behavior. It will not work with noncompliant parents or those who you suspect may be using unduly harsh punishment with their child.

Step 4: Determine if additional intervention is necessary. For repeated offenses or more severe bullying, the child may need more intensive, individual interventions. Discuss mental health assistance and other counseling or psychology services that the school district can provide, as well as possible referrals for family or individual counseling if needed.

Step 5: Follow up with the student. The final step to effective discipline is following up with the student. Was the consequence successful in halting the negative behavior? Is staff monitoring or further intervention required? A brief meeting sends a message to the student that you care enough to check how things are going. If there is improvement, praise the student's efforts. Encouragement can do wonders! *Note:* Keep in mind that bullying behaviors can become entrenched if the child has used them for a while. Change will be gradual. Follow-ups with the child may need to be weekly, daily, or even hourly depending on the situation, but brief "check-ins" are essential.

Six Ways Educators Can Monitor Students Who Bully

Assuring student safety is paramount, which is why monitoring kids who bully is essential. Adult monitoring is also a proven way to reduce aggressive or at-risk behaviors. The reason is simple: when students know they are being watched, they are less likely to bully. Here are six effective, no-cost ways to let kids know adults are watching to ensure everyone's safety.

1. **Develop a notification system.** Create an efficient, prompt method to alert staff members as soon as possible about bullying incidents. Methods include a confidential email blast, text, or note to the counselor or security officer (who can connect with all teachers), or a memo in a sealed envelope delivered to pertinent staff members who oversee the students involved. Also, make sure to notify substitute teachers who may have contact with the bullying child or target. (See R3: Report for more on creating a staff notification system and united response.)

2. **Designate adult monitors.** Monitoring is more difficult when students have multiple teachers and/or class changes and attend larger schools. Some schools designate a different staff member per period to monitor the bullying student. Notify and utilize bus drivers, cafeteria workers, yard supervisors, librarians, custodians, secretaries, nurses, and counselors to help. *Note:* Using students to monitor a child who is bullying is generally *not* advised.

3. **Require parental monitoring.** In more severe cases, some schools require the parents to monitor their child in the location of the bullying incident (in the cafeteria, on the playground, or on the school bus) for a specified number of days, including escorting the child to and from classes.

4. **Send an "All Points Bulletin."** When safety is a concern, immediately send an email blast to alert pertinent staff members. Include names of all

students involved, a description of the issue, and what to do if a problem ensues. Some schools send an intercom message ("All staff please check your email") or sound an alarm bell.

5. **Designate "inbound" and "out-of-bounds" areas.** Identify secluded areas that are more difficult to view (like bathrooms, stairwells, and lockers) and make those spots out-of-bounds for kids who bully and need closer monitoring.

6. **Establish a "No Contact Contract."** Allan Beane, in his book *Bullying Prevention for Schools*, suggests having the child who bullies sign a "No Contact Contract," which requires her to avoid all contact (visual, physical, and auditory) with her target until the behavior improves. The contract could also specify how far away she must stay from the targeted student and, if broken, require that more significant consequences be applied.[8] *Important:* Please use dignity and privacy when applying this or any consequence for bullying behavior.

How to Choose the Right Interventions to Replace Aggression

"My brother always picked me on, and I just thought picking on kids was the way to get friends. My counselor showed me a better way."
—Stacey, age 9

We can design elaborate anti-bullying policies and create long lists of sanctions and consequences—both of which are important—but the pivotal piece in reducing bullying is often missed: *replacing* the aggression of the child who bullies with prosocial behavior. Without that piece, the bullying often continues and may become more frequent and intense. To succeed, the bullying intervention needs to match the child's needs, be evidence-based, and be implemented by a trained professional. Do *not* make the mistake of thinking that bullying is just a phase that will eventually go away. Without intervention, bullying students are often marked by more school failure, depression, anxiety disorders, substance abuse, premature sexual activity, violence, and crime than their non-bullying peers. What's more, these students often adopt aggression as a way to deal with life. The risks of unaddressed bullying are too serious to ignore.

8. Beane, 2009.

As discussed in R5: Refuse on page 197, the first step toward replacing bullying behaviors is to create a Student Study Team made up of the staff members who have a "pulse" on the child, care about her well-being, and want to find a positive way to help her manage behavior and relate to others. The ideal team is comprised of mental health professionals, such as the counselor, psychologist, nurse, and social worker; an administrator; and teachers, though membership may differ per child. The parent of the child may also be invited to join based on the team's recommendation. The goal is to discuss the child engaging in bullying, try to determine what motivates the behavior, and choose the best intervention. Keep in mind, there is no single effective bullying intervention. The most successful interventions are based on what works best for each child. Here are steps to plan those interventions.

> The pivotal piece in reducing bullying is often missed: *replacing* the aggression of the child who bullies with prosocial behavior. Without that piece, the bullying often continues and may become more frequent and intense.

1. **Form the Student Study Team.** The administrator or counselor generally forms the group based on individuals' expertise and knowledge of the child. Once you form the group, set up the date, time, and location of your first meeting.

2. **Review data.** Review all of the child's prior behavioral referrals, school records, and bullying reports. What patterns are you finding?

3. **Discuss the child's strengths and needs.** See "Twenty Student Study Team Questions to Help a Child Who Bullies" on pages 241–242. These will help you start a conversation so you can select the most effective ways to help a child stop bullying.

4. **Determine the best intervention.** See "Evidence-Based Interventions to Reduce and Replace Bullying" on page 229. Choose the best strategy for the child and select the person who should deliver the intervention. More than one intervention (for instance, coping strategies and service learning) is usually required to replace entrenched behaviors. In some cases, expertise outside the school is necessary, and in rare cases, the student may need to be removed from the school and put in a secured facility. When choosing an intervention also keep in mind that kids may change

roles in the bullying dynamics: the bullied kid bullies; the bullying child is bullied.

5. **Determine the most effective consequences.** See "Five Steps to Setting the Right Consequences for Bullying" on page 223. Refer also to R1: Rules for a list of additional consequences you might use.

6. **Decide how you will monitor and track success.** When is your next meeting? Who will be responsible for monitoring the child's behavior? Who will deliver the next intervention? How will you measure success? And don't overlook this crucial element: How will you form a partnership with the child's parents and help them reinforce the same skills?

Evidence-Based Interventions to Reduce and Replace Bullying

The most promising interventions and replacer behaviors for children who bully are provided in this section. Be sure to teach a child only *one* new replacer behavior at a time. Behavior change needs practice, reinforcement, and time, so it's best to focus on one change at a time to increase the child's chances for success. After the new behavior is mastered you can add the next. The optimum goal of bullying intervention is to create *lasting* behavior change for a child. (*Note:* R1: Rules listed specific tiered consequences for bullying. This section offers interventions—new skills or behaviors—to use to *replace* the bullying behavior. Consequences and interventions are separate elements in bullying prevention.)

Tips for TEACHERS

Mastering a replacer behavior and no longer needing adult reminders or coaxing takes time and practice. Here are ways educators have helped kids adopt a positive new behavior to replace bullying:

• A Minnesota school had students demonstrate to other staff members (a secretary, custodian, or counselor, for example) in private their "new replacer behavior." The kids benefited from the practice, and the staff could gently remind the kids to "keep at it" and encourage their efforts.

• A counselor made a thirty-second video of the student practicing his replacer behavior for controlling anger (or whatever new prosocial skill) and emailed the link to his parents so the parents and child could practice at home.

- A Flint, Michigan, teacher had her student take a "selfie" (a photo of herself) while practicing her new skill of keeping gossip inside of her head. She printed the photo for the girl to keep in her backpack as a reminder. The girl also downloaded the photo as her cell phone screen saver.

- A P.E. coach had a student make a poster that depicted his replacer skill: "Four Ways to Be Kind to Friends," and hang it in his gym locker as a reminder every time he opened it.

AGGRESSION REPLACEMENT AND ANGER MANAGEMENT

Distinctive traits of many children who bully are their use of aggression and their positive attitude toward violence. Craving power and dominance, they use aggressive reactions to control others. They are often quick to fly off the handle, can lack impulse control, and perceive that others are out to get them. These kids can benefit from anger management intervention and learning to replace their aggression with more positive habits, such as yoga, meditation, mindfulness, or other relaxation and emotion regulation techniques. Anger *can* be managed and aggression *can* be replaced, but sustained adult efforts and guidance are required. A successful intervention is based on proven behavioral practices and taught by certified mental health professionals such as school counselors, social workers, nurses, and psychologists. Training other staff members (teachers, aides, secretaries, or cafeteria workers, for example) in the approach can help maximize gains by reinforcing the child's efforts and monitoring behavior whenever possible. It helps to educate the child's parents about the intervention so they can model and reinforce the behavior at home.

Here are some anger management interventions from educators: One middle school set up a "color card" system to help kids manage strong feelings. Students signaled to a teacher by putting a colored chip or index card on their desk if they needed a time-out to calm down. Red: "Ready to explode." Orange: "Near the boiling point." Yellow: "Having trouble staying in control." Green: "All is well." Some teachers arranged a spot in their rooms where the child could calm down. A counselor set up her room as a "Color Zone" where teachers could send kids if they were in red or orange zones. The counselor helped the child calm down until they were back to green. A counselor in Dublin, Ohio, set up a "Homework Log," a monthly calendar with the skill "Managing My Anger" listed on the top, for the student to mark each time he practiced the skill. A Bay Area special education teacher has her students email photos of themselves practicing the skill at home each night. Find ways for your staff to support children who need help managing anger.

Tip for COUNSELORS

A crucial part of anger management is to help the child identify the physiological signs that materialize whenever a person is under stress and has a "fight or flight response." Help the child identify her unique stress signs—such as rapid breathing, pounding heart, light-headedness, sweaty palms, and grinding teeth—*before* she loses her temper. Explain: "We all have our own body signs that warn us we're getting angry, and we should listen to them because they can help us stay out of trouble. Your hands are in a fist. Do you feel yourself getting angry?" *Important:* It may take some time before children can identify their signs. Younger children will need to rely on you to point out the signs. Pass on those warning signs to other adults (staff and parents) who can also *quietly and with dignity* point them out to the child until she can identify those body signals on her own.

SEL SKILL: 2 + 2 + 4

Show the child how to inhale slowly to a count of two, pause for two counts, and then slowly breathe out to a count of four: 2 + 2 + 4. Repeating the sequence creates maximum relaxation, puts the brakes on impulses, and reduces stress that can turn into anger. An adult needs to model: "Take a slow, deep breath from your tummy. Then slowly let your breath out." Ideally, the child should exhale *twice* as long as inhaling to maximize the effect. You might put a card that says 2 + 2 + 4 in the child's pocket, pinned on his backpack, and inside his agenda. It takes frequent, repeated practice for this strategy to be effective so the child can use it *without* adult guidance.

PROBLEM-SOLVING SKILLS

The American Psychological Association published an analysis of 153 bullying studies over thirty years that found that children—especially boys—who demonstrate difficulties solving problems are more at risk of becoming bullying perpetrators, targets, or both. The research found that teaching kids how to solve problems helps prevent bullying and even reduces kids' chances of being targeted.[9] Use caution not to miss kids who may need to replace aggression with learning how to resolve problems peacefully. (See Part I, page 36, for specific strategies.)

COUNSELING AND COGNITIVE BEHAVIOR THERAPY

Sometimes a child who bullies requires a counselor's guidance or individual support. Individual counseling by a trained counselor can help decipher the motivation of a child using bullying behavior and yield intervention recommendations. Cognitive behavioral therapy (CBT), a method intended to change kids' maladaptive thinking patterns and behaviors, is one approach to consider. Multisystemic therapy (MST), in which parents, schools, and communities develop programs to reinforce prosocial behaviors, is another possibility.

Don't overlook depression as a trigger for bullying. Research by Susan Swearer, a professor of educational psychology at the University of Nebraska–Lincoln, found that some children who bully experience high levels of depression and anxiety. Swearer suggests that treating depression may stop kids' need to feel better by making someone else feel worse.[10] If you suspect that a child's mental health or behavior issues necessitate more intense intervention, enlist the help of the mental health providers and psychological services department in your district or county office of education. Share your concerns with the parents and provide a list of possible signs of depression (see the list on page 212).

Also identify "safety nets" (places where the child can go if he's having a hard day). For instance, he could go to the school nurse, counselor, or quiet room with an adult. The ultimate goal is to help the child learn to identify his anger triggers and manage destructive emotions *before* he uses bullying or aggressive behavior.

REDIRECT NEGATIVE ENERGY IN POSITIVE WAYS

The most typical adult response to bullying is punishment, but there are different ways to redirect a child's energy and reap better results. Kids from the Cherry Creek School in Colorado told staff that a fifth grader was "terrorizing" kindergartners and first graders. The school counselor decided to try a different approach and told the fifth-grade boy that she needed his support: "The kindergartners are worried about school and need someone to protect them," she said. "Could you help?" And that's how the child who bullied became the

9. Cook et al., 2010.
10. Bazelon, 2013.

younger children's bodyguard. It turned out that the fifth grader craved attention. Accolades were so rare that he actually looked forward to the punitive sanctions he received (quite regularly) for bullying. The counselor discovered his motive and found a way to replace his bullying with a rare opportunity for positive reinforcement, and it worked! The kids saw him as a knight in shining armor, the boy finally got positive affirmation, and the bullying subsided.

> The goal is to find positive ways for bullying students to feel powerful and for other children to view them in a more positive light.

If you determine that a child is resorting to bullying behaviors to gain attention or status, look for opportunities for the child to see herself in a more positive light. While kids should never be let off the hook for aggression, effective intervention needs to include positive encouragement and earned praise. Pass along your findings to other staff members who have contact with the child. Ideas include:

- If the child is outgoing: Make him the "School Welcomer" to greet visitors and give them a school tour, or hand out pamphlets to parents on open-house night.
- If the child enjoys sports: Pair her with a coach to teach younger kids soccer, basketball, or other sports.
- If the child is musical: He could help the music teacher teach an instrument to beginners.
- If the child is artistic: She could help design posters showing social-emotional skills that the school (or she) is focusing on and hang them in hallways.

The goal is to find positive ways for bullying students to feel powerful and for other children to view them in a more positive light. It is also helpful to pair these students with a staff member who can serve as a positive role model and form caring, respectful relationships with them.

PRAISE GOOD BEHAVIOR

Praise can do wonders to reinforce positive behaviors—especially for kids who may be discouraged. In fact, studies find that kids who bully often receive punitive reinforcement or physical punishment, which only perpetuates their negative, aggressive behaviors. Dan Olweus cites praise and friendly attention as an important means of influencing student behavior. He states that "aggressive students and students who are easily influenced by others should also receive *appreciation for not reacting aggressively* under conditions which normally provoke them, and for not participating in bullying."[11] So look for ways to praise kids' earned efforts to help them realize that change is possible and the staff is taking notice. Effective praise has four traits:

- **Deserved.** Make sure the praise is earned. "That was kind of you to help Kara tape her torn drawing. You made her tears go away."

- **Immediate.** The best time to praise, especially for aggressive kids, is the instant you observe the effort.

- **Specific.** Tell the child exactly what he did so he's more likely to repeat the behavior. "Good job! You stayed calm when Josh made that sound you hate."

- **Sincere.** Kids detect "false flattery" and it can backfire.

Five Simple Ways to Reinforce Positive Behaviors

1. **Use a "Good News Report."** Send a report home to parents describing the child's specific behavior that deserves acknowledgment.

2. **Try a "Sunshine Call."** For younger students, keep a toy phone handy and the moment the child's behavior warrants praise, place the phone on his desk. It means: "Your mom and dad are going to get a 'Sunshine Call' tonight about your good behavior." For older students, substitute a cell phone: I watched one middle school principal pull out his cell phone in the hallways to call the parents to tell them that their child was having a great day. The effect on the student was priceless!

3. **Write a comment on the bottom of a test or paper.** Such as "Nice job today! I saw how you included Kevin in your group by asking his opinions."

4. **Pass along what you overheard.** Such as: "The yard duty aide was saying what a great job you did at recess today controlling your temper. Good job!" Make sure you tell other staff members which behaviors to reinforce.

5. **Give an office pass.** For a change of pace, send the child to the principal (or secretary, counselor, or custodian) for being *good*. Let staff members hear about their positive behavior so they can offer encouragement as well.

---

11. Olweus, 1993, p. 85–86.

SERVICE LEARNING AND EMPATHY BUILDING

Many children who bully exhibit diminished empathy and compassion. SuEllen Fried (coauthor of *Bullies, Targets, and Witnesses*) calls this breed of bullying "elitist" because the perpetrators have such a strong "I'm better than you" attitude that fuels their need of one-upmanship by putting down others. One way to remedy elitist bullying is by requiring kids to do something to help others so they begin to consider others' feelings and needs. Make sure the experience is meaningful for the child and helps him see the world through a lens that doesn't just focus on himself. Keep in mind that more than a one-time service experience is usually required to elevate empathy. *Ideally, the project should match the child's interests, strengths, and abilities, and involve personal, face-to-face contact.* For example:

- Find meaningful community projects such as helping in an animal shelter or a food bank (under adult monitoring).

- Enlist the child as a cross-age tutor in an area that matches her interests. Examples: Reading—help a struggling younger reader. Art—help younger kids design "Be Kind" posters for the school.

- Find a positive adult role model in the school or community with whom the child can form a respectful relationship and observe an example of caring and kindness firsthand.

See also "Possible Consequences and Disciplinary Actions for Bullying Behavior" on page 89, which lists service learning as one of the consequences for bullying.

Tip for COUNSELORS

Roots of Empathy is an evidence-based classroom program that builds empathy in a unique way: a neighborhood parent and her infant visit the classroom every three weeks over the school year. A trained Roots of Empathy instructor coaches the students to observe the baby's development and label the baby's feelings, and then talks to students before and after each family visit to prepare and reinforce the teachings with a specialized lesson plan. The curriculum is divided into nine themes to enhance students' social and emotional learning, with three classroom visits per theme, for a total of twenty-seven visits. The program addresses schoolchildren from kindergarten through eighth grade. The research results from nine independent evaluations and two reviews of the program indicate significant reductions in aggression and increases in prosocial behavior. For more information, see *Roots of Empathy* by Mary Gordon, *Teaching Children Empathy, The Social Emotion* by Tonia Caselman, and rootsofempathy.org.

Using Books to Help Children Replace Aggression

The right book can be a powerful tool to help reform a child who bullies, enhancing empathy and perspective taking. Trudy Ludwig, author of *Confessions of a Former Bully,* told me she has had several of her young readers tell her: "Reading your book made me want to stop bullying." CNN's Anderson Cooper asked a child who had been bullying why he decided to stop. "I read a book about a bullied kid," the boy said. "It made me realize what it was like to be on the receiving end. I couldn't do it anymore." Here are some suggested titles.

Lower Elementary:

• *Billy Bully* by Ana Galan and Alvaro Galan

• *Marlene, Marlene, Queen of Mean* by Jane Lynch, with Lara Embry and A. E. Mikesell

• *My Mouth Is a Volcano!* by Julia Cook

• *One* by Kathryn Otoshi

• *The Recess Queen* by Alexis O'Neill

• *Tough!* by Erin Frankel

Upper Elementary:

• *Confessions of a Former Bully* by Trudy Ludwig

• *Twerp* by Mark Goldblatt

Middle School:

• *Crash* by Jerry Spinelli

• *Dear Bully: 70 Authors Tell Their Stories* edited by Megan Kelley Hall and Carrie Jones

• *Bullying Under Attack* by Stephanie Meyer

Ways to Involve Parents

Educating parents in effective behavior management is crucial. Behavior interventions are more likely to be successful if the home and school use the same approach. Studies show that parents of students who bully often do not set clear limits on aggressive behaviors and may use physical punishment, which increases aggression.[12] Here are ways to build a home-school partnership to replace bullying behaviors:

Be invitational. Try to form positive relationships with parents early on. Keep in mind that parents of children who bully are often discouraged and may not know more effective parenting strategies. Convey that you want to work together to reduce their child's bullying.

Establish regular communication. Decide together how often you should touch base (weekly, biweekly, daily) and your preferred communication method (a quick email, note, call, text) to keep parents in the loop about their child's behavior.

Send positive messages. Find ways to let parents know when their child exhibits positive behavior, such as sending an email or text, so they reinforce efforts at home. (See "Five Simple Ways to Reinforce Positive Behaviors" on page 234.)

Distribute a list of bullying behaviors. Give parents a copy of "Warning Signs of Bullying" (see page 211) at parent-teacher conferences. Post the form on your school website, in the school handbook, and in other visible spaces (school library, office, bulletin boards) to educate parents and prompt them to seek the school's help if they recognize the signs in their child.

Create a home-school lending library. Provide a lending library of resources, books, and films about bullying. Books for parents might include: *Little Girls Can Be Mean* by Michelle Anthony and Reyna Lindert; *The Bully, the Bullied, and the Not-So-Innocent Bystander* by Barbara Coloroso; *Your Child: Bully or Victim?* by Peter Sheras; *Bullied* by Carrie Goldman; and *Girl Wars* by Cheryl Dellasega and Charisse Nixon. Consider initiating a parent book club about bullying.

Hold a parent-student-teacher conference. Involve the student in a parent-teacher conference in which the child describes the social-emotional skill she is working on and enlists her parents' help to reinforce her efforts (see page 177 for details).

---

12. Olweus, 1993.

Create a parent notification system for bullying. Ask the parents how they prefer to be contacted (phone, text, email) about bullying incidents. Then utilize the system. (See page 224 for specific strategies.)

Offer positive behavior intervention strategies. Research shows that many parents of kids who bully use harsh discipline that increases their child's aggression. Offer parents positive behavior management options via the psychologist or counselor, an online behavior course, book clubs, or evening workshops.

Convey: "You make a difference." Parents need to recognize that they can influence the likelihood that their child will engage in bullying—online or off. Remind parents that children who believe that adults in their lives will reprimand them for bullying online are less likely to engage in the behavior.[13]

KEY BULLYING PREVENTION POINTS IN R6: REPLACE

- There is no one profile of a child who bullies, so look for patterns of aggression, and then chart all findings in staff reports to help uncover bullying motivators.

- All adults should be trained in ways to respond safely and effectively during and after a serious bullying incident.

- Inconsistent staff responses to bullying *increase* the chances of bullying and aggression.

- When students know they are being watched they are less likely to bully, so create a system to monitor students and pass it on to all staff members.

- Successful bullying interventions always match the child's needs, are evidence-based, are implemented by trained professionals, and are practiced frequently.

- Some bullying children experience high levels of depression and anxiety. Treating these ailments may curb a child's need to feel better by making someone else feel worse.

- Stress positive discipline approaches—*not* zero tolerance—that aim to help students who engage in bullying replace aggression with more acceptable behaviors.

---

13. Hinduja and Patchin, 2013.

FOUR STEPS TO STOP MILD BULLYING

Step 1: STOP it. Interrupt the students on the spot with a calm, firm statement such as: "Excuse me, stop!" "We don't do that here." Be loud enough so that other students hear you.

Step 2: NAME it. Call out what you saw or heard. Keep the focus on the inappropriate behavior, *not* on the child. Examples: "I heard name-calling." "That's leaving someone out!" "I see you shoving to get your way." (Use the term *bullying* very cautiously.)

Step 3: DESCRIBE it. Give a clear reason why the behavior is inappropriate, against the rules, and harmful. Examples: "Leaving people out is not what we do in this school." "At this school we do not put down others." "I am offended by that language and I'm sure other people at this school are, too."

Step 4: ALTER it. Deliver a short, firm reminder that explains the behavior you expect. Examples: "I expect you to be kind at all times." "You have a choice with your words. I'll be listening for respect." "What will you do next time?"

Decide whether to **REPORT** the behavior. Finally, **MONITOR** the children involved over the next several days.

HOW TO RESPOND TO SERIOUS BULLYING

During the Incident

- **Intervene immediately.**

- **Stay calm.**

- **Use a de-escalating statement.** "Everybody okay?" "Let's take a deep breath." "Do you need some help?"

- **Separate those involved.**

- **Ensure safety.** Call immediately for the school security guard, police, or medical attention if needed. In an imminent threat, pull the fire alarm.

- **Describe what you see.** "I see behavior here that is against school rules."

- **Use the four A's: Assess** the target's well-being. **Acknowledge** her or his discomfort. **Assure** all students involved that adults will help them be safe. **Assist** any student who needs help.

- **Don't label.** Avoid using the terms *bully, victim,* or *bystander.*

- **Don't make students apologize or require conflict resolution.**

After the Incident

- **Encourage active bystanders.**

- **Continue gathering pertinent information.** Do *not* interview students in front of one another; separate them.

- **Notify pertinent stakeholders.** Include parents of both the target and the child bullying.

- **Complete and file a bullying report.**

- **Be vigilant.** Let students involved know you are monitoring their behavior.

TWENTY STUDENT STUDY TEAM QUESTIONS TO HELP A CHILD WHO BULLIES

These questions are designed to help your team choose the best ways to help a student stop bullying behavior. Answering them requires pooling information and data so you can develop positive strategies to help this child.

1. What **concerns** us about this child?

2. Do we know **when the bullying behavior began** and how long it has been a problem?

3. How can we best **summarize the child's emotional, behavioral, cognitive, moral, and physical development?** How are these factors impacting the child's bullying?

4. What is the evidence that the child is bullying? Is there a **bullying pattern**? Where and when is the behavior most likely to occur? Who is usually involved? What type of bullying is used most frequently?

5. Under **what conditions** is the child *more* likely and *less* likely to use bullying behaviors? Can we change these conditions?

6. Which **specific behaviors** does the child demonstrate that should be replaced? What behaviors does the child need to learn to replace inappropriate behaviors?

7. What are the child's **positive strengths, interests, learning styles, and abilities**? How can we tap into these to help our intervention efforts?

8. Which adults and peers are **supports** for this child? Can we enlist them to be positive role models for the child and reinforce his or her behavior change?

9. Are there peers who are **negative influences** on the child's behavior and may encourage or reinforce the aggression? What can be done to curtail or remedy these unhealthy relationships? How can we help this child form healthier peer relationships?

10. Which **behavior management strategies** have proved effective with this child? Why do those strategies appear to work for this child?

11. What strategies have **not been helpful** or may backfire if used with this child?

12. What **interventions** (if any) have been tried? Were any successful? Why or why not?

13. What **resources** (people and programs) does the school have that could help this child?

14. Who is the **best person(s)** to conduct the intervention and why?

15. What is the intervention **timeline:** When should the intervention start? Who should be notified?

16. What **procedures, policies, or programs** need to be in place prior to the intervention?

17. How will intervention **success** be measured?

18. How will the **staff and parents be notified** so they can support the child?

19. What is the **first thing we can do** to help this child and replace this behavior?

20. What is our **hope** for this child?

A Final Word

We've all had "I'll never forget" moments. Mine was April 20, 1999, watching the Columbine High School massacre on TV. As part of my work, I'd spoken to parents in Littleton before the tragedy. I'd come home and told my husband that's where we should raise our three sons. At the moment the reports began broadcasting, I knew there was a seismic shift happening in our children's culture—and in ours.

Over the next several years, I put my energy into researching youth violence and bullying. I combed through hundreds of studies. One line is etched in my mind: *Violence and bullying are learned.* That fact convinced me that educators could, in fact, reduce peer cruelty. I spent the following two decades uncovering the most effective practices for doing so and I wrote a bill on how to prevent bullying and school shootings that utilized those practices.

I'd just delivered my recommendations to an assembly when I had my second "I'll never forget" moment. A teen boy walked up to me and exclaimed, "Great speech, lady!" What could this kid *possibly* like about my (relatively staid and formal) speech? "All that stuff you said about making schools respectful and teaching kids to care," he told me. "That's what we need, you know: respect and caring. It would have kept my brother out of jail."

He was so right. Preventing school violence and bullying is always about creating safe, respectful learning climates with caring adults at the helm. Implementing the strategies in this book will help you and your staff create the kinds of schools this boy and his brother and *all* children deserve: secure, considerate places where they feel cared about and connected. There is simply no better formula for stopping bullying and producing a generation of young people with strong minds and open hearts. And it's nothing short of a moral imperative that we do so.

Resources

The following contains suggested bullying resources for educators, parents, and students.

EDUCATOR RESOURCES

Bullying

The Bully, the Bullied, and the Not-So-Innocent Bystander by Barbara Coloroso (New York: HarperCollins, 2015).

Bullying and Harassment: A Legal Guide for Educators by Kathleen Conn (Alexandria, VA: ASCD, 2004).

Bullying at School: What We Know and What We Can Do by Dan Olweus (Hoboken, NJ: Wiley-Blackwell, 1993).

Bullying in North American Schools: A Socio-Ecological Perspective on Prevention and Intervention edited by Dorothy Espelage and Susan Swearer (New York: Routledge, 2011).

Bullying in Schools by Ken Rigby (New Delhi, India: ACER Press, 2007).

Bullying in Schools: How Successful Can Interventions Be? edited by Peter K. Smith, Debra Pepler, and Ken Rigby (Cambridge, UK: Cambridge University Press, 2004).

Bullying Prevention & Intervention: Realistic Strategies for Schools by Susan Swearer, Dorothy Espelage, and Scott Napolitano (New York: The Guildford Press, 2009).

Childhood Bullying, Teasing, and Violence: What School Personnel, Other Professionals and Parents Can Do by Dorothea M. Ross (Alexandria, VA: American Counseling Association, 2003).

Columbine by Dave Cullen (New York: Twelve-Hachette Book Group, 2009).

Sticks and Stones: Defeating the Culture of Bullying and Rediscovering the Power of Character and Empathy by Emily Bazelon (New York: Random House, 2013).

Cyberbullying

Bullying Beyond the Schoolyard: Prevention and Responding to Cyberbullying by Sameer Hinduja and Justin W. Patchin (Thousand Oaks, CA: Corwin Press, 2015).

Confronting Cyber-Bullying: What Schools Need to Know to Control Misconduct and Avoid Legal Consequences by Shaheen Shariff (Cambridge, UK: Cambridge University Press, 2009).

Cyberbullying: Bullying in the Digital Age by Robin Kowalski, Susan Limber, and Patricia Agatston (Hoboken, NJ: Wiley-Blackwell, 2012).

Cyberbullying and Cyberthreats: Responding to the Challenge of Online Social Aggression, Threats, and Distress by Nancy Willard (Champaign, IL: Research Press, 2007).

Cyberbullying Prevention and Response: Expert Perspectives by Justin W. Patchin and Sameer Hinduja (New York: Routledge, 2012).

Relational Aggression

Girl Wars: 12 Strategies That Will End Female Bullying by Cheryl Dellasega and Charisse Nixon (New York: Fireside, 2003).

Little Girls Can Be Mean: Four Steps to Bully-Proof Girls in the Early Grades by Michelle Anthony and Reyna Lindert (New York: St. Martin's Griffin, 2010).

Odd Girl Out: The Hidden Culture of Aggression in Girls by Rachel Simmons (New York: Mariner Books, 2011).

Queen Bees and Wannabes: *Helping Your Daughter Survive Cliques, Gossip, Boyfriends, and the New Realities of Girl World* by Rosalind Wiseman (New York: Crown Publishers, 2009).

Understanding Girl Bullying and What to Do About It: Strategies to Help Heal the Divide by Julaine E. Field, Jered B. Kolbert, Laura M. Crothers, and Tammy L. Hughes (Thousand Oaks, CA: Corwin Press, 2009).

School-Wide and Classroom Bullying Prevention

The ABC's of Bullying Prevention: A Comprehensive Schoolwide Approach by Kenneth Shore (Chester, NY: National Professional Resources, Inc./Dude Publishing, 2011).

Blueprints for Violence Prevention #9: Bullying Prevention Program by Dan Olweus and Susan Limber (Denver, CO: C & M Press, 1999).

Breaking the Culture of Bullying and Disrespect, Grades K–8: Best Practices and Successful Strategies by Marie-Nathalie Beaudoin and Maureen Taylor (Thousand Oaks, CA: Corwin Press, 2004).

Bully: An Action Plan for Teachers, Parents and Communities to Combat the Bullying Crisis edited by Lee Hirsch and Cynthia Lowen (New York: Weinstein Books, 2012).

Bullying Hurts: Teaching Kindness Through Read Alouds and Guided Conversations by Lester L. Laminack and Reba Wadsworth (Portsmouth, NH: Heinemann, 2012). Gr K–4

Bullying Prevention: Tips and Strategies for School Leaders and Classroom Teachers by Elizabeth A. Barton (Thousand Oaks, CA: Corwin Press, 2006).

Bullying Prevention for Schools: A Step-by-Step Guide to Implementing a Successful Anti-Bullying Program by Allan L. Beane (San Francisco: Jossey-Bass, 2009).

Bullying Prevention Handbook: A Guide for Principals, Teachers and Counselors by John Hoover and Ronald Oliver (Bloomington, IN: Solution Tree, 2008).

Olweus Bullying Prevention Program: Teacher Guide by Dan Olweus and Sue Limber (Center City, MN: Hazelden, 2007).

Peer Harassment in School edited by Jaana Juvonen and Sandra Graham (New York: Guilford Press, 2001).

Roots of Empathy: Changing the World Child by Child by Mary Gordon (New York: The Experiment, 2009).

Safe, Supportive, and Successful Schools: Step by Step by David Osher, Kevin Dwyer, and Stephanie Jackson (Longmont, CO: Sopris West, 2003).

School Climate: Building Safe, Supportive, and Engaging Classrooms and Schools by Jonathan Cohen and Maurice Elias (Port Chester, NY: Dude Publishing, 2011).

Schools Where Everyone Belongs: Practical Strategies for Reducing Bullying by Stan Davis (Champaign, IL: Research Press, 2007).

Teachers' Guide to Inclusive Practices: Behavioral Support by Rachel Janney and Martha Snell (Touson, MD: Brookes Publishing, 2003).

You Can't Say You Can't Play by Vivian Gussin Paley (Cambridge, MA: Harvard University Press, 1992).

Aggression, Anger Management, and Behavior

Aggression Replacement Training: A Comprehensive Intervention for Aggressive Youth by Barry Glick and John C. Gibbs (Champaign, IL: Research Press, 2010).

Antisocial Behavior in Schools: Evidence-Based Practices by Hill M. Walker, Elizabeth Ramsey, and Frank M. Greshman (Belmont, CA: Wadsworth, 2004).

Behavioral Intervention Planning: Completing a Functional Behavioral Assessment and Developing a Behavioral Intervention Plan by Kathleen McConnell Fad, James R. Patton, and Edward Polloway (Austin, TX: Pro-Ed, Inc., 1999).

Elementary Teacher's Discipline Problem Solver by Kenneth Shore (San Francisco: Jossey-Bass, 2003).

High Risk: Children Without a Conscience by Ken Magid and Carole A. McKelvey (New York: Bantam, 1998).

Savage Spawn: Reflections on Violent Children by Jonathan Kellerman (New York: Ballantine, 2003).

Special Kids Problem Solver: Ready-to-Use Interventions for Helping All Students with Academic, Behavioral, and Physical Problems by Kenneth Shore (San Francisco: Jossey-Bass, 1998).

The Tough Kid Book: Practical Classroom Management Strategies by Ginger Rhode, William R. Jenson, and H. Kenton Reavis (Longmont, CO: Sopris West, 1992).

Character Education and Moral Development

The Anti-Defamation League's Hate Hurts: How Children Learn and Unlearn Prejudice by Caryl Stern-LaRosa and Ellen Hofheimer Bettmann (New York: Scholastic, 2001).

Building Moral Intelligence by Michele Borba (San Francisco: Jossey-Bass, 2006).

The Challenge to Care in Schools by Nel Noddings (New York: Teachers College Press, 2005).

Character Matters: In Classrooms, At School, At Home by Edward DeRoche (Port Chester, NY: Dude Publishing, 2008).

Training Peer Helpers: Coaching Youth to Communicate, Solve Problems, and Make Decisions by Barbara B. Varenhorst (Minneapolis: Search Institute Press, 2010).

Conflict Resolution and Restorative Justice

Creating the Peaceable School: A Comprehensive Program for Teaching Conflict Resolution by Richard J. Bodine, Donna K. Crawford, and Fred Schrumpf (Champaign, IL: Research Press, 2004).

Conflict Resolution in the Schools: A Manual for Educators by Kathryn Girard and Susan Koch (San Francisco: Jossey-Bass, 1996).

Learning the Skills of Peacemaking by Naomi Drew (Rolling Hills Estates, CA: Jalmar Press, 1999).

Social-Emotional Learning, Social Skills, and Friendship-Making

Asperger Syndrome and Bullying: Prevention Strategies and Solutions by Nick Dubin (London: Jessica Kingsley Publishers, 2007).

Best Friends, Worst Enemies: Understanding the Social Lives of Children by Michael Thompson, Catherine O'Neill Grace, and Lawrence Cohen (New York: Ballantine, 2002).

Cool, Calm, and Confident: A Workbook to Help Kids Learn Assertiveness Skills by Lisa M. Schab (Oakland, CA: Instant Help, 2009).

Let's Be Friends: A Workbook to Help Kids Learn Social Skills & Make Great Friends by Lawrence E. Shapiro and Julia Holmes (Oakland, CA: Instant Help, 2008).

No Kidding About Bullying by Naomi Drew (Minneapolis: Free Spirit Publishing, 2010).

Unselfie: Why Empathetic Kids Succeed in Our All-About-Me World by Michele Borba (New York: Touchstone, 2016).

PARENT RESOURCES

Bullied: What Every Parent, Teacher, and Kid Needs to Know About Ending the Cycle of Fear by Carrie Goldman (San Francisco: HarperOne, 2012).

Bullies & Victims: Helping Your Child Survive the Schoolyard Battlefield by SuEllen Fried and Paula Fried (New York: M. Evans & Co, 1996).

Easing the Teasing: Helping Your Child Cope with Name-Calling, Ridicule, and Verbal Bullying by Judy S. Freedman (New York: McGraw-Hill, 2002).

Facing the Schoolyard Bully: How to Raise an Assertive Child in an Aggressive World by Kim Zarzour (New York: Firefly Books, 2000).

Good Friends Are Hard to Find: Helping Your Child Find, Make, and Keep Friends by Fred Frankel (Los Angeles: Perspective Publishing, 1996).

The Parent's Guide to Protecting Your Children in Cyberspace by Parry Aftab (New York: McGraw-Hill, 2000).

Sticks and Stones: Seven Ways Your Child Can Deal with Teasing, Conflict, and Other Hard Times by Scott Cooper (New York: Harmony, 2000).

Talking Back to Facebook: The Common Sense Guide to Raising Kids in the Digital Age by James P. Steyer (New York: Scribner, 2012).

Teaching Your Child the Language of Social Success by Marshall P. Duke, Stephen Nowicki, and Elizabeth Martin (Atlanta, GA: Peachtree, 1996).

Your Child: Bully or Victim? Understanding and Ending Schoolyard Tyranny by Peter Sheras and Sherill Tippins (New York: Simon & Schuster, 2002).

STUDENT RESOURCES

Fiction: Primary Ages

A. Lincoln and Me by Louise W. Borden and Ted Lewin (New York: Scholastic, 2001). A tall, skinny, awkward boy learns that Abe Lincoln was often called "Gorilla" and "backward hick" by peers, but obviously endured. Gr K–3

The Berenstain Bears and the Bully by Stan Berenstain and Jan Berenstain (New York: Random House, 2012). Sister Bear is beaten up by the new cub in town and Brother huffs off to set the bully straight, but is in for a surprise: the bully is a girl! Gr K–3

Bullies Never Win by Margery Cuyler (New York: Simon & Schuster Children's Publishing, 2009). Jessica wants the bullying to stop, but how? Gr K–3

Bully B.E.A.N.S. by Julia Cook (Chattanooga, TN: National Center for Youth Issues, 2009). Kids learn to be proactive when it comes to bullying and speak up. Gr K–3

The Bully Blockers Club by Teresa Bateman (Park Ridge, IL: Albert Whitman & Company). Kids form the Bully Blockers Club. When Grant tries to bully someone, they speak up, which gets an adult's attention, and the bullying stops. Gr K–3

Chrysanthemum by Kevin Henkes (New York: Greenwillow Books, 2011). Chrysanthemum loves her name, until kids tease that she's named after a flower. Gr K–3

Don't Laugh at Me by Steve Seskin and Allen Shamblin (New York: Tricycle Press, 2002). Pictures accompany a powerful anti-bullying song (CD included). Gr K–3

Enemy Pie by Derek Munson (San Francisco: Chronicle Books, 2000). One little boy learns an effective recipe for turning your best enemy into your best friend. Gr K–3

Fat, Fat Rose Marie by Lisa Passen (New York: Henry Holt, 2015). Overweight Rose Marie is taunted by a peer, but finds a friend, and they stand up for each other. Gr 1–3

Hey, Little Ant by Phillip M. Hoose (New York: Tricycle Press, 1998). This parable about mercy and empathy asks readers to look at life from an insect's point of view and leads to great potential for discussions concerning bullying and protection of all species. Gr K–2

Hooway for Wodney Wat by Helen Lester (New York: Houghton Mifflin Harcourt, 2003). Rodney Rat can't pronounce Rs and is teased mercilessly, but he saves the class from bullying and surprises even himself. Gr K–2

Howard B. Wigglebottom Learns About Bullies by Howard Binkow (Sarasota, FL: Thunderbolt Publishing, 2008). Howard tries to avoid a bullying kid by himself but fails and finally tells the teacher (who helps!). Gr K–3

The Juice Box Bully: Empowering Kids to Stand Up for Others by Bob Sornson and Maria Dismondy (Northville, MI: Ferne Press, 2010). Instead of being bystanders when it comes to bullying, kids get involved and use "The Promise" to help each other. Gr K–3

King of the Playground by Phyllis Reynolds Naylor (New York: Atheneum, 1991). Sammy is the self-proclaimed "King of the Playground" and won't let Kevin play. But Kevin's father suggests how to beat Sammy with words, not fists. Gr K–3

Loudmouth George and the Sixth-Grade Bully by Nancy Carlson (Minneapolis: Carolrhoda Books, 2003). George is bullied and too afraid to tell until his friend Harriet steps in to help. Gr K–3

My Princess Boy by Cheryl Kilodavis (New York: Aladdin, 2010). Deals with social acceptance and a call to end bullying and judgments. Gr K–3

Nobody! A Story About Overcoming Bullying in Schools (Minneapolis: Free Spirit Publishing, 2015.) Thomas is bullied by his classmate Kyle and learns how to feel more confident while Kyle learns about kindness. Gr K–3

Oliver Button Is a Sissy by Tomie dePaola (Boston: Harcourt Brace Jovanovich, 1979). A little boy is ostracized because he'd rather read, paint, and tap-dance than participate in sports. Gr K–2

The Rat and the Tiger by Keiko Kasza (New York: G.P. Putnam, 2007). Rat stands up for himself and refuses to be Tiger's friend until he learns to stop teasing. Gr K–3

The Recess Queen by Alexis O'Neill (New York: Scholastic Press, 2002). Mean Jean is the reigning Recess Queen, pushing and smooshing anyone who crosses her. But Katie Sue is not the least bit intimidated and uses kindness to tame her. K–3

Simon's Hook: A Story About Teases and Put-Downs by Karen Gedig Burnett (Waverly, IA: GR Publishing, 2000). Simon learns how to handle teases and put-downs. Gr K–4

Spaghetti in a Hot Dog Bun: Having the Courage to Be Who You Are by Maria Dismondy (Northville, MI: Making Spirits Bright, 2008). It's hard to show respect to someone mistreating you, but enter Lucy, the kind child, who teaches all! Gr K–3

Stand Tall, Molly Lou Melon by Patty Lovell (New York: G.P. Putnam's Sons 2001). Bullied Molly Lou is determined not to let anyone shake her belief in herself. Gr K–3

Stinky Stern Forever by Michelle Edwards (Boston: HMH Books for Young Readers, 2007). The second-grader who bullied everyone is hit by a car and killed, and students must deal with the death of someone nobody really liked. Gr 1–3

The Weird Series by Erin Frankel (Minneapolis: Free Spirit Publishing, 2013). A three-part series told from the perspectives of the bullied *(Weird!),* a bystander *(Dare!),* and the child who's bullying *(Tough!).* Gr K–3

William's Doll by Charlotte Zolotow (New York: Harper & Row, 1985). William wants a doll and is taunted for his wish. Then one day someone really understands. Gr K–3

Fiction: Elementary Ages

Attack of the Killer Fishsticks by Paul Zindel (New York: Skylark, 1993). Fun-loving group of fifth graders confronts the Nasty Blobs, two of the meanest kids in school and they help a new kid run for class office. Gr 4–7

Blue Cheese Breath and Stinky Feet: How to Deal with Bullies by Catherine DePino (Washington, DC: Magination Press, 2004). A student favorite, the book provides eleven practical tips to discourage and cope with kids who bully. Gr 1–5

Bully by Patricia Polacco (New York: G.P. Putnam, 2012). New student Lyla deals with online abuse intensified from the cruelty of schoolyard bullying. Gr 4–7

The Bully of Barkham Street by Mary Stolz (New York: HarperCollins, 1985). Told from the view of the kid bullying who sometimes gets into fights but doesn't mean to. Gr 3–7

Bully on the Bus by Carl W. Bosch (Seattle: Parenting Press, 1988). Jack is bullied on the school bus. Should he ignore the kid, fight back, or get help? Gr 2–6

Confessions of a Former Bully by Trudy Ludwig (New York: Tricycle Press, 2011). Told from the view of the kid bullying, tools are given to identify and stop relational aggression. Gr 3–7

Felita by Nicholasa Mohr (New York: Scholastic, 1979). Felita faces verbal and physical bullying from her neighbors for her Puerto Rican heritage. Gr 3–5

The Hundred Dresses by Eleanor Estes (Boston: HMH Books for Young Readers, 2014). A poor Polish girl wears the same dress and claims to have a hundred others. Girls in her class know she doesn't and bully her mercilessly. Gr 3–6

The Invisible Boy by Trudy Ludwig (New York: Random House, 2013). Nobody seems to notice or think to include Brian, until a new kid comes to class. Gr 1–4

Joshua T. Bates in Trouble Again by Susan Shreve (New York: Knopf, 2000). Joshua repeated third grade and struggles to fit in as a fourth grader. But problems increase as a couple of bullying kids get him in trouble. Gr 3–7

Just Kidding by Trudy Ludwig (New York: Tricycle Press, 2006). Vince has a habit of teasing his friend, and then saying "Just kidding." But it doesn't make things okay. A rare look at emotional bullying among boys. Gr 1–4

Mr. Lincoln's Way by Patricia Polacco (New York: Philomel, 2001). The kid who bullies is taught to hate those who are different, but the principal finds a unique way to help. Gr 1–4

Mr. Peabody's Apples by Madonna (New York: Callaway, 2003). A beloved teacher is ostracized by rumors but offers a lesson on choosing our words carefully. Gr 1–4

My Secret Bully by Trudy Ludwig (New York: Tricycle Press, 2006). Monica's "friends" use name-calling and manipulation to humiliate and exclude. Gr 2–6

The Night the Bells Rang by Natalie Kinsey-Warnock (New York: Puffin, 2000). It's World War I, but Mason's biggest problem is an older, larger kid who bullies. Gr 3–6

Nobody Knew What to Do: A Story About Bullying by Becky McCain (Park Ridge, IL: Albert Whitman, 2002). One child finds courage to tell a teacher about Ray, who was bullied by other kids in school. Gr 1–4

Nothing's Fair in Fifth Grade by Barthe DeClements (New York: Puffin, 2008). A fifth-grade class, repelled by the overweight new student who has serious home problems, finally learns to accept her. Gr 3–7

Say Something by Peggy Moss (Thomaston, ME: Tilbury House, 2013). A girl learns that being a silent bystander isn't enough when it comes to watching kids bully. Gr 1–5

The 6th Grade Nickname Game by Gordon Korman (New York: Disney-Hyperion Press, 2004). Two friends are notorious for awarding nicknames to people in their school, but this time their nickname game turns to name-calling and trouble. Gr 3–7

The Sneetches and Other Stories by Theodor Geissel (New York: Random House, 1961). Dr. Seuss shows how pointless prejudice—and bullying—can be costly. Gr 1–5

Trouble Talk by Trudy Ludwig. (New York: Tricycle Press, 2008). The damaging consequences of talking about someone else's troubles to gain attention. Gr 1–4

Fiction: Middle School Ages or More Proficient Readers

Blubber by Judy Blume (New York: Atheneum Books for Young Readers, 2014). What happens when fifth-grade torment of a classmate goes too far. Gr 3–7

Buddha Boy by Kathe Koja (New York: Farrar, Straus and Giroux, 2003). A new kid is ostracized for his cultural differences, but Justin discovers his talent and a friendship emerges. Gr 7 up

Chicken by Alan Gibbons (London: Orion Children's Books, 2010). Davy's too chicken to stand up to kids who bully, but his little sisters help with a secret. Gr 4–6

The Chocolate War by Robert Cormier (New York: Knopf, 2013). Chilling portrait of an all-boys prep school and the pitfalls of conformity, cruelty, and corruption. Gr 7 up

Coram Boy by Jamila Gavin (London: Nick Hern Books, 2006). Tale of an African slave ship on its way to a great estate; examples of racism and incipient bullying. Gr 6 up

Crash by Jerry Spinelli (New York: Yearling, 1997). Told from the point of view of a kid who bullies (a superjock) and how he questions his tormenting treatment of a "dweeby" classmate. Gr 5–8

Fat Boy Swim by Catherine Forde (London: Egmont UK, 2012). Grossly obese Jimmy is bullied mercilessly at school, and he learns he has to take control of his own life. Gr 6 up

Feather Boy by Nicky Singer (New York: Delacorte Books, 2002). More than just about bullying but finding your voice, refusing to back down, and helping a friend. Gr 5–7

Hate List by Jennifer Brown (New York: Little Brown and Company, 2010). A "hate list" created to ease the pain of bullying is used to target victims in a shooting spree. Gr 8 up

Indigo's Star by Hilary McKay (New York: Hachette, 2011). Indigo is different and the perfect target for bullying abuse by a group of mean-spirited boys. Gr 5–8

Inventing Elliot by Graham Garner (New York: Dial, 2004). Elliot starts a new school and is determined not to stand out and be bullied like before, but his plan backfires. Gr 7 up

Lord of the Flies by William Golding (New York: Penguin, 1999). Schoolboys crash on a desert island and their behavior starts to take on savage bullying. Gr 6 up

Real Friends vs. the Other Kind by Annie Fox (Minneapolis: Free Spirit Publishing, 2009). Six kids deal with tough social scenes like gossip, exclusion, and cyberbullying. Gr 6 up

The Revealers by Doug Wilhelm (New York: Square Fish, 2011). Bullied students start an email forum to enlist kids' help, but revenge by the kids bullying threatens their efforts. Gr 5–8

Run, Zan, Run by Cathy MacPhail (New York: Bloomsbury, 2012). No one believes Katie is being bullied, but a unique girl who rises to her defense has more to lose. Gr 4–7

The Skin I'm In by Sharon Flake (New York: Disney-Hyperion, 2011). Maleeka suffers from taunts about her dark black skin, homemade clothes, and good grades. Gr 7 up

Stargirl by Jerry Spinelli (New York: Alfred A. Knopf, 2002). The impact of peer pressure and bullying on Stargirl, the new (and different) girl in high school. Gr 7 up

Thirteen Reasons Why by Jay Asher (New York: Penguin, 2007). Clay finds recordings explaining why a classmate ended her life two weeks earlier. Gr 7 up

Twerp by Mark Goldblatt (New York: Random House, 2013). Julian isn't a bully, but is suspended for a big mistake and journals about the incident. Gr 4–7

Wonder by R.J. Palacio (New York: Knopf Books for Young Readers, 2012). Auggie wants to fit in, but because of his facial deformity, he is bullied and has a difficult time. Gr 4–7

Nonfiction

The Bully Blockers: Standing Up for Classmates with Autism by Celeste Shally (Centerton, AZ: Awaken Specialty Press, 2009). A tool to help children understand classmates on the spectrum and stick up for them. Gr K–4

Bullying Is a Pain in the Brain by Trevor Romain (Minneapolis: Free Spirit Publishing, 2016). Suggestions for kids to cope with bullying told in a humorous way. Gr 3–5

Cliques, Phonies & Other Baloney by Trevor Romain (Minneapolis: Free Spirit Publishing, 1998). Tips to help kids deal with exclusion, cliques, and rejection. Gr 2–5

Don't Pick on Me: Help for Kids to Stand Up and Deal with Bullies by Susan Eikov Green (Oakland, CA: Instant Help, 2010). Tips to help students with bullying. Gr 4–7

Hot Issues, Cool Choices: Facing Bullies, Peer Pressure, Popularity, and Put-Downs by Sandra McLeon Humphrey (Amherst, NY: Prometheus Books, 2007). These stories help kids deal with peer pressure and bullying. Gr 4–7

How to Handle Bullies, Teasers, and Other Meanies: A Book That Takes the Nuisance Out of Name-Calling and Other Nonsense by Kate Cohen-Posey (Highland City, FL: Rainbow Books, 1995). Provides useful tips on dealing with bullying. Gr 3–6

Letters to a Bullied Girl: Messages of Healing and Hope by Olivia Gardner, Emily Buder, and Sarah Buder (New York: William Morrow, 2009). Two sisters initiate a letter-writing campaign to help a cyberbullied teen. Gr 7 up

No More Victims: An Underdog Who Came Out on Top Challenges You to Put a Stop to Bullying in Your School by Frank Peretti (W. Publishing Group, Thomas Nelson Publishers, 2001). Short, but powerful read about bullying. Gr 6–8

Please Stop Laughing At Me! One Woman's Inspirational Story by Jodie Blanco (Avon, MA: Adams Media Corp, 2010). An unforgettable memoir about how one child was shunned and bullied from elementary through high school. Gr 8 up

The Skinny on Bullying by Mike Cassidy (Westport, CO: Rand Media Co., 2010). Helps kids understand what bullying is and how to deal with bullying. Gr 4–7

Speak Up and Get Along! Learn the Mighty Might, Thought Chop, and More Tools to Make Friends, Stop Teasing, and Feel Good About Yourself by Scott Cooper (Minneapolis: Free Spirit Publishing, 2005). Twenty-one strategies to halt bullying and beat unhappy feelings. Gr 3–6

Stand Up for Yourself and Your Friends: Dealing with Bullies and Bossiness and Finding a Better Way by Patti Kelley Criswell (Middleton, WI: American Girl, 2009). Teaches girls how to spot bullying and speak out against it. Gr 3–6

Stand Up to Bullying! (Upstanders to the Rescue!) by Phyllis Kaufman Goodstein and Elizabeth Verdick (Minneapolis: Free Spirit Publishing, 2014). Teaches kids how to safely take a stand against bullying, support kids who are targeted, and spread the word that bullying is not cool—it's cruel. Gr 3–7

Stick Up for Yourself! Every Kid's Guide to Personal Power and Positive Self-Esteem by Gershen Kaufman, Lev Raphael, and Pamela Espeland (Minneapolis: Free Spirit Publishing, 1999). Ways to help kids build self-esteem and assertiveness skills. Gr 3–7

Taking the Bully by the Horns by Kathy Noll and Jay Carter (Greensboro, NC: Unicorn Press, 1998). Tips for kids to handle those who bully without becoming one of them. Gr 4–8

Words Are Not for Hurting by Elizabeth Verdick (Minneapolis: Free Spirit Publishing, 2004). This book teaches kids to think before they speak and learn positive ways to respond when others say mean, unkind words to them. Gr K–2

References

Aftab, Parry. "The StopCyberbullying Toolkit Guide for Parents," wiredsafety.org, 2008.

American Psychological Association Zero Tolerance Task Force. "Are Zero Tolerance Policies Effective in the Schools?" *American Psychologist, 63(9)* (2008).

Arseneault, L., et al. "Childhood Trauma and Children's Emerging Psychotic Symptoms: A Genetically Sensitive Longitudinal Cohort Study." *American Journal of Psychiatry, 168(1)* (2011): 65–72.

Barker, E. D., et al. "Predictive Validity and Early Predictors of Peer-Victimization Trajectories in Preschool." *Archives of General Psychiatry, 65(10)* (2008).

Bazelon, Emily. *Sticks and Stones.* New York: Random House, 2013.

Beane, Allan L. *Bullying Prevention for Schools.* San Francisco: Jossey-Bass, 2009.

Bleeker, M., et al. "Findings from a Randomized Experiment of Playworks: Selected Results from Cohort 1." *Mathematica Policy Research,* April 2012.

Bogart, L. M., et al. "Peer Victimization in Fifth Grade and Health in Tenth Grade." *Pediatrics, 133(3)* (2014): 440–447.

Bolton, José, and Stan Graeve (eds.). *No Room for Bullies: From the Classroom to Cyberspace.* Boys Town, NE: Boys Town Press, 2005.

Boulton, M. J. "Teachers' Views on Bullying: Definitions, Attitudes, and Ability to Cope." *Journal of Educational Psychology, 67* (1997): 223–233.

Bradshaw, C. P., et al. "Bullying and Peer Victimization at School: Perceptual Differences Between Students and School Staff." *School Psychology Review, 36(3)* (2007): 361–382.

Bradshaw, C. P., et al. "Findings from the National Education Association's Nationwide Study of Bullying: Teachers' and Education Support Professionals' Perspectives." National Education Association, 2011.

Brown, E. C., et al. "Outcomes from a School-Randomized Controlled Trial of Steps to Respect: A Bullying Prevention Program." *School Psychology Review, 40(3)* (2011): 423–443.

Browning, C. M., et al. "Help for the Bully/Peer Abuse Problem: Is Bully Busters In-Service Training Effective?" In *VISTAS: Compelling Perspectives on Counseling* edited by G. Walz and R. Yep. Alexandria, VA: American Counseling Association, 2005.

The Canadian Press/Times Colonist. "Children Taught Small Ways of Acting Kindly May Reduce Bullying: U.B.C. Study." Retrieved from timescolinist.com, December 2012.

Casella, R. "Zero Tolerance Policy in Schools: Rationale, Consequences, and Alternatives." *Teachers College Record, 105(5)* (2003): 872–892.

Chen, Cynthia. "New Data Show Children with Autism Bullied Three Times More Frequently Than Their Unaffected Siblings." Kennedy Krieger Institute, 2012.

Cohen, J., and Ann Freiberg. "School Climate and Bullying Prevention." National School Climate Center (NSCC), February 2013.

Coloroso, B. *The Bully, the Bullied, and the Not-So-Innocent Bystander.* New York: HarperCollins, 2015.

Cook, Clayton R., et al. "Predictors of Bullying and Victimization in Childhood and Adolescence: A Meta-Analytic Investigation." *School Psychology Quarterly, 25(2)* (2010).

Craig, W. M., et al. "Observations of Bullying in the Playground and in the Classroom." *School Psychology International, 21(1)* (2000): 22–36.

Darley, J. M., and B. Latané. "Bystander Intervention in Emergencies: Diffusion of Responsibility." *Journal of Personality and Social Psychology, 8(4)* (1968): 377–383.

Davis, S., and C. Nixon. "Preliminary Results from the Youth Voice Research Project: Victimization and Strategies." Youth Voice Project, March 2010.

Denny, Simon, et al. "Bystander Intervention, Bullying, and Victimization: A Multilevel Analysis of New Zealand High Schools." *Journal of School Violence 14(3)* (2015): 245–272.

DeVoe, J. F., and L. Bauer. *Student Victimization in U.S. Schools: Results from the 2009 School Crime Supplement to the National Crime Victimization Survey (NCES 2012-314).* Washington, DC: National Center for Education Statistics, 2011.

DiPasquale, G. "Is Bullying Just Kid Stuff?" *Orbit, 34(2)* (2004): 6.

Duke, M. P., et al. *Teaching Your Child the Language of Social Success.* Atlanta, GA: Peachtree, 1996.

Englander, Elizabeth Kandel. *Bullying and Cyberbullying: What Every Educator Needs to Know.* Cambridge, MA: Harvard Education Press, 2013.

Espelage, D. L., et al. "Examination of Peer-Group Contextual Effects on Aggression During Early Adolescence." *Child Development, 74(1)* (2003): 205–220.

Espelage, D. L., and S. M. Swearer (eds.). *Bullying in American Schools: A Social-Ecological Perspective on Prevention and Intervention.* New York: Routledge, 2003.

Fanger, Suzanne Marie, et al. "Peer Exclusion in Preschool Children's Play: Naturalistic Observations in a Playground Setting." *Merrill-Palmer Quarterly, 58(2)* (2012).

Farrington, David P., and Maria M. Ttofi, "School-Based Programs to Reduce Bullying and Victimization." Cambridge, UK: The Campbell Collaboration, 2009.

Fix School Discipline. "Restorative Justice or Restorative Practices." Retrieved from fixschooldiscipline.org/educator-toolkit, 2016.

Fox, M. "Teens Take Bullying to the Internet, Study Finds." *Reuters,* November 28, 2007.

Fried, SuEllen, and Paula Fried. *Bullies, Targets & Witnesses: Helping Children Break the Pain Chain.* New York: M. Evans and Company, Inc., 2003.

Harris, S., and G. Petrie. "A Study of Bullying in the Middle School." *NASSP Bulletin, 86(633)* (2002).

Harris, S., and W. Willoughby. "Teacher Perceptions of Student Bullying Behaviors." *ERS Spectrum, 21(3)* (2003): 11–18.

Hawkins, D. Lynn, et al. "Naturalistic Observations of Peer Interventions in Bullying." *Social Development, 10(4)* (2001).

Hinduja, S., and J. W. Patchin. "Social Influences on Cyberbullying Behaviors Among Middle and High School Students." *Journal of Youth and Adolescence, 42(5)* (2013): 711–722.

Hirsch, Lee, and Cynthia Lowen (eds.). *Bully: An Action Plan for Teachers, Parents, and Communities to Combat the Bullying Crisis.* New York: Weinstein Books, 2012.

Howard, N., et al. "Self-Efficacy in a New Training Model for the Prevention of Bullying in Schools." In *Bullying Behavior: Current Issues, Research, and Interventions* edited by R. Geffner, M. Loring, and C. Young. New York: Haworth Press, 2001.

Janson, G. R., and R. J. Hazler. "Trauma Reactions of Bystanders and Victims to Repetitive Abuse Experiences." *Violence and Victims, 19(2)* (2004): 239–255.

Kanter, Rosabeth Moss. *The Change Masters.* New York: Free Press, 1985.

Kärnä, A., et al. "A Large-Scale Evaluation of the KiVa Antibullying Program: Grades 4–6." *Child Development, 82(1)* (2011): 311–330

Kasen, S., et al. "The Effects of School Climate on Changes in Aggressive and Other Behaviors Related to Bullying." In *Bullying in American Schools: A Social-Ecological Perspective on Prevention and Intervention* edited by D. L. Espelage and S. M. Swearer. New York: Routledge, 2004.

Keizer, K., et al. "The Spreading of Disorder." *Science, 322(5908)* (2008): 1681–1685.

Keltner, D., and Jason Marsh. "We Are All Bystanders." In *The Compassionate Instinct* edited by Keltner, D., et al. New York: W.W. Norton & Company, 2010.

Kosciw, J. G., et al. *The 2013 National School Climate Survey: The Experiences of Lesbian, Gay, Bisexual and Transgender Youth in Our Nation's Schools.* New York: GLSEN, 2014.

Leadbeater, B. J., and W. L. Woglund. "The Effects of Peer Victimization and Physical Aggression on Changes in Internalizing From First to Third Grade." *Child Development, 80(3)* (2009).

Li, Q. "New Bottle But Old Wine: A Research of Cyberbullying in Schools." *Computers in Human Behavior, 23(4)* (2007): 1777–1791.

Lumpkins, D., and M. Marshall. "Suspensions at Richmond High Plummet." *New America Media,* February 28, 2012.

Menesini, E., et al. "Attribution of Meanings to Terms Related to Bullying: A Comparison Between Teacher's and Pupil's Perspectives in Italy." *European Journal of Psychology of Education, 17(4)* (2002): 393–406.

Mynard, H., et al. "Peer Victimisation and Posttraumatic Stress in Adolescents." *Personality and Individual Differences, 29(5)* (2000): 815–821.

National Education Association. "NEA Calls on States and School Districts to Step Up Anti-Bullying Efforts." Retrieved from nea.org/home/49019.htm, October 2011.

Oden, Sherri, and Steven R. Asher. "Coaching Children in Social Skills for Friendship Making." *Child Development, 48(2)* (1977): 495–506.

Olweus, D. "Bully/Victim Problems Among Schoolchildren: Basic Facts and Effects of a School-Based Intervention Program." In *The Development and Treatment of Childhood Aggression* edited by D. Pepler and K. Rubin. Hillsdale, NJ: Lawrence Erlbaum Associates, 1991.

Olweus, D. "Bully/Victim Problems in School: Facts and Intervention." *European Journal of Psychology of Education, 12(4)* (1997): 495–510.

Olweus, D. *Bullying at School.* Cambridge: Blackwell, 1993.

Olweus, D., and S. P. Limber. "Bullying in School: Evaluation and Dissemination of the Olweus Bullying Prevention Program. *American Journal of Orthopsychiatry, 80(1)* (2010): 124–134.

Orecklin, M., "Beware of the In Crowd." *Time, 156(8)* (2000): 69.

Orpinas, P., et al. "School Bullying: Changing the Problem by Changing the School." *School Psychology Review, 32(3)* (2003): 431–444.

Padgett, Sharon, and Charles E. Notar. "Bystanders Are the Key to Stopping Bullying." *Universal Journal of Educational Research, 1(2)* (2013): 33–41.

Paul, Pamela. "The Playground Gets Even Tougher." *The New York Times,* October 8, 2010.

Pierce, S. (doctoral dissertation) "The Behavioral Attributes of Victimized Children." As quoted by B. Coloroso in *The Bully, the Bullied, and the Bystander.* New York: HarperCollins, 2008: 138.

Polanin, Joshua R., et al. "A Meta-Analysis of School-Based Bullying Prevention Programs' Effects on Bystander Intervention Behavior." *School Psychology Review, 41(1)* (2012): 47–65.

Rivers, I., et al. "Observing Bullying at School: The Mental Health Implications of Witness Status." *School Psychology Quarterly*, *24(4)* (2009).

Robers, S., et al. *Indicators of School Crime and Safety: 2012 (NCES 2013-036/NCJ 241446).* Washington, D.C.: National Center for Education Statistics, U.S. Department of Education, and Bureau of Justice Statistics, Office of Justice Programs, U.S. Department of Justice, 2013.

Rodkin, P.C., et al. "Heterogeneity of Popular Boys: Antisocial and Prosocial Configurations." *Developmental Psychology, 36(1)* (2008).

Roou, Dave. "Fighting the Lunchroom Bully." *Principal Leadership, 4(5)* (2004): 27–29.

Saint Louis, Catherine. "In Bullies' Hands, Nuts or Milk May Be a Weapon." *The New York Times,* June 17, 2013.

Salmivalli, C. "Bullying and the Peer Group: A Review." *Aggression and Violent Behavior, 15(2)* (2010): 112–120.

Salmivalli, C., and M. Voeten. "Connections Between Attitudes, Group Norms, and Behaviors in Bullying Situations." *International Journal of Behavioral Development, 28(3)* (2004): 246–258.

Sanders, J. B. P., et al. "All About Cyberbullies: Who They Are and What They Do." Retrieved from education.com, March 2011.

Shemesh, E., et al. "Child and Parental Reports of Bullying in a Consecutive Sample of Children With Food Allergy." *Pediatrics, 131(1)* (2013).

Shore, Kenneth. *The ABC's of Bullying Prevention.* New York: Dude Publishing, 2005.

Skiba, Russell J., and Kimberly Knesting. "Zero Tolerance, Zero Evidence: An Analysis of School Disciplinary Practices." *Policy Research Report #SRS2,* Indiana Education Policy Center, August 2000.

Smith, P. K., and S. Shu. "What Good Schools Can Do About Bullying: Findings from a Survey in English Schools After a Decade of Research and Action." *Childhood: A Global Journal of Child Research, 7(2)* (2001): 193–212.

Smokowski, P. R., and K. H. Kopasz, "Bullying in School: An Overview of Types, Effects, Family Characteristics, and Intervention Strategies." *Children & Schools, 27(2)* (2005): 101–110.

Snell, J. L., et al. "Bullying Prevention in Elementary Schools: The Importance of Adult Leadership, Peer Group Support, and Student Social-Emotional Skills." In *Interventions for Academic and Behavior Problems: Preventive and Remedial Approaches* edited by M. R. Shinn, et al. Bethesda, MD: National Association of School Psychologists, 2002.

Sojourner, Russ, and Mark Hyatt. "Combating the Bullying Epidemic." *Principal Leadership, 14(4)* (2013): 42–46.

Staub, Ervin, et al. "Passive and Active Bystandership Across Grades in Response to Students Bullying Other Students." In *The Psychology of Good and Evil: Why Children, Adults, and Groups Help and Harm Others* edited by Ervin Staub. New York: Cambridge University Press, 2003: 240–245.

Stueve, A., et al. "Rethinking the Bystander Role in School Violence Prevention." *Health Promotion Practice, 7(1)* (2006): 121.

Sumner, Michael D., et al. "School-Based Restorative Justice as an Alterative to Zero-Tolerance Policies: Lessons from West Oakland." Thelton E. Henderson Center for Social Justice, University of California, Berkeley, School of Law, 2010.

Swearer, Susan M., et al. *Bullying Prevention and Intervention.* New York: The Guilford Press, 2009.

Totura, C. M. Wienke, et al. "Bullying and Victimization Among Boys and Girls in Middle School: The Influence of Perceived Family and School Contexts." *Journal of Early Adolescence, 29(4)* (2009): 571–609.

Ttofi, M. M., and D. P. Farrington. "Effectiveness of School-Based Programs to Reduce Bullying: A Systematic and Meta-Analytic Review. *Journal of Experimental Criminology, 7(1)* (2011): 27–56.

Twyman, K., et al. "Comparing Children and Adolescents Engaged in Cyberbullying to Matched Peers." *CyberPsychology, Behavior, and Social Networking, 13(2)* (2010): 195–199.

Unnever, James D., and Dewey G. Cornell. "Middle School Victims of Bullying: Who Reports Being Bullied?" *Aggressive Behavior, 30(5)* (2004): 373–388.

U.S. Department of Justice, Bureau of Justice Statistics, "School Crime Supplement (SCS) to the National Crime Victimization Survey (NCVS)," 2013.

Veenstra, Rene, et al. "The Complex Relation Between Bullying, Victimization, Acceptance, and Rejection: Giving Special Attention to Status, Affection, and Sex Differences." *Child Development, 81(2)* (2010): 480–486.

Vlachou, Maria, et al. "Assessing Bully/Victim Problems in Preschool Children: A Multimethod Approach." *Journal of Criminology, 2013* (2013).

Vodafone. YouGov survey. Newbury, England: Vodafone Group, September 2015.

Vossekuil, Bryan, et al. "The Final Report and Findings of the *Safe School Initiative:* Implications for the Prevention of School Attacks in the United States." Washington, DC: United States Secret Service and United States Department of Education, July 2004.

Waasdorp, Tracy E., et al. "The Impact of Schoolwide Positive Behavioral Interventions and Supports on Bullying and Peer Rejection." *Archives of Pediatrics and Adolescent Medicine, 166(2)* (2012): 149–156.

Wang, Cixin, et al. "The Critical Role of School Climate in Effective Bullying Prevention. *Theory Into Practice, 52(4)* (2013).

Williams, K., and N. Guerra. "Prevalence and Predictors of Internet Bullying." *Journal of Adolescent Health, 41* (2007): S14–S21.

Ybarra, M., et al. "Defining and Measuring Cyberbullying Within the Larger Context of Bullying Victimization." *Journal of Adolescent Health, 51* (2012): 53–58.

Zarzour, K. *Facing the Schoolyard Bully: How to Raise an Assertive Child in an Aggressive World.* Buffalo, NY: Firefly Books, 2000.

Index

About the Author

Michele Borba, Ed.D., is an internationally renowned educator, award-winning author, and parenting, child, and bullying expert. A sought-after motivational speaker, she has presented workshops and keynote addresses throughout the world and has served as a consultant to hundreds of schools and corporations, including work on U.S. Army bases in Europe and the Asian-Pacific. Her proposal "Ending School Violence and Bullying" (SB1667) was signed into California law in 2002. She offers realistic, research-based advice culled from a career of working with over one million parents and educators worldwide.

Dr. Borba is an NBC contributor who has appeared frequently on the *Today* show and been featured on countless others, including: *Dr. Phil, Dateline, The View, Nightly News with Brian Williams, The Doctors, Anderson Cooper,* MSNBC, *Fox & Friends, Joy Behar, The Daily Buzz, Countdown, Inside Edition,* Fox Headline News, *The Early Show,* CNN Headline News, and *Dr. Drew.* She has been interviewed by numerous publications including *Newsweek, People, U.S. News & World Report, The New York Times, Reader's Digest,* and *The Globe and Mail,* and served as media spokesperson for corporations such as RC2 Learning Curve, Florida OJ, 3M, Ragu, Office Depot, Splenda, Similac, General Mills, All, Galderma, V-Tech, and Cetaphil, and consultant for Wal-Mart, McDonald's, and Johnson & Johnson. She serves on national boards for *Parents,* Character Education Partnerships, CSN (Child Safety Network), Boys & Girls Clubs of America, and McDonald's Global Mom's Panel.

She is the award-winning author of twenty-two books translated into fourteen languages including *Unselfie: Why Empathetic Kids Succeed in Our All-About-Me World; Nobody Likes Me, Everybody Hates Me; No More Misbehavin'; Don't Give Me That Attitude!; 12 Simple Secrets Real Moms Know; Building Moral Intelligence; Parents Do Make a Difference; The Big Book of Parenting Solutions: 101 Answers to Your Everyday Challenges and Wildest Worries;* and *Esteem Builders* (used by 1.5 million students worldwide).

Dr. Borba is a former classroom and college teacher and has a wide range of teaching experience, including work in regular education as well as with